8/04   4.69

Property Rights

OTHER BOOKS IN AMERICA'S FREEDOMS
Donald Grier Stephenson, Jr., Series Editor

Cruel and Unusual Punishment,
Joseph A. Melusky and Keith A. Pesto

Equal Protection of the Laws, Francis Graham Lee

Freedom of Association, Robert J. Bresler

Freedom of Speech, Ken I. Kersch

Religious Freedom, Melvin I. Urofsky

The Right to Bear Arms, Robert J. Spitzer

The Right to Counsel and Privledge against Self-Incrimination,
John B. Taylor

The Right to Privacy, Richard A. Glenn

PROPERTY RIGHTS

Rights and Liberties under the Law

POLLY J. PRICE

ABC☉CLIO

Santa Barbara, California • Denver, Colorado • Oxford, England

Copyright 2003 by Polly J. Price

All rights reserved. No part of this publication may be reproduced, stored in a retrieval system, or transmitted, in any form or by any means, electronic, mechanical, photocopying, recording, or otherwise, except for the inclusion of brief quotations in a review, without prior permission in writing from the publishers.

Library of Congress Cataloging-in-Publication Data
Price, Polly, J.
  Property rights : rights and liberties under the law / Polly J. Price.
    p.   cm. — (On trial)
  Includes bibliographical references and index.
  ISBN 1-57607-768-3 (hardcover : acid-free paper); ebook 1-57607-769-1
  1. Rights of property—United States—Juvenile literature. 2. Economic liberties (U.S. Constitution)—Juvenile literature. I. Title. II. Series.
KF652.P74   2003
346.7304—dc21   2003006519

07 06 05 04 03 02   10 9 8 7 6 5 4 3 2 1

This book is also available on the World Wide Web as an e-book. Visit abc-clio.com for details.

ABC-CLIO, Inc.
130 Cremona Drive, P.O. Box 1911
Santa Barbara, California 93116–1911

This book is printed on acid-free paper.
Manufactured in the United States of America

For my mother and my father

Contents

Series Foreword   xi
Preface and Acknowledgments   xxi

1   Introduction   1

Constitutional Protection of Property, 1
Property as the "Guardian of Every Other Right," 3
Property Rights in International Context, 4
Property Rights (and Responsibilities) in
   the United States, 8
Property Clauses in the U.S. Constitution, 12
Plan of the Book, 15
References and Further Reading, 17

2   Origins and Early Development   19

English Origins, 21
Property Regulation in Colonial America, 25
The American Revolution, 27
State Constitutions and Property Rights, 29
Property Protection in the U.S. Constitution, 35
Property Protection in the Bill of Rights, 42
Property Regulation after the Founding Period, 48
Native American Lands, 54
The Federal Contracts Clause and the Protection of
   Vested Rights, 56
Slaves as Property, 61

VII

Eminent Domain in the State Courts, 65
The Close of the Nineteenth Century: The Fourteenth
  Amendment and Incorporation, 67
Conclusion, 69
References and Further Reading, 71

3 Twentieth-Century Issues and Development   75

The Rise of Substantive Due Process and Liberty of
  Contract, 78
The Progressive Era and Labor Legislation, 81
Federal Legislation during the New Deal, 86
The Constitutional Revolution of 1937, 87
Civil Rights at the Forefront: *Carolene Products*, 89
The Advent of the Regulatory Takings Doctrine, 92
Land-Use Planning by Local Governments, 96
Environmental Legislation, 101
Historic Preservation: *Penn Central*, 103
Constitutional Protection of Private Property:
  Contemporary Applications, 105
Property Rights Legislation, 128
Conclusion, 129
References and Further Reading, 131

4 Into the Twenty-first Century: Issues and Prospects   135

What Is "Property" for Purposes of Constitutional
  Protection? 137
Intellectual Property: Takings Implications, 140
Use of Patented Inventions by the Federal Government, 144
The Inventions Secrecy Act and Federal Export
  Regulations, 147
State Government Immunity for Patent Infringement, 150
Regulatory Takings and Intellectual Property, 152
Property Rights and the Human Body, 155
Presumed-Consent Statutes and Due Process, 158
Stem Cells and Cloning, 162

Redefining Property for Community Rights: Implications for Environmental Law, 166
Water and Air as Common Property, 171
Conclusion, 176
References and Further Reading, 178

5   Key People, Cases, and Events 183

6   Documents 217

The U.S. Constitution: Property Clauses, 217
Federalist No. 10, 218
Fletcher v. Peck (1810), 222
Wynehamer v. The People (1856), 226
Lochner v. New York (1905), 230
Pennsylvania Coal v. Mahon (1922), 235
Village of Euclid v. Ambler Realty Co. (1926), 237
Penn Central Transportation Co. v. New York (1978), 243
PruneYard Shopping Center v. Robins (1980), 249
Hawaii Housing Authority v. Midkiff (1984), 252
Nollan v. California Coastal Commission (1987), 257
Yee v. City of Escondido (1992), 260
Lucas v. South Carolina Coastal Council (1992), 265
Tahoe-Sierra Preservation Council v. Tahoe Regional Planning Agency (2002), 272
Private Property Protection Act of 1995 (Bill Proposed in the U.S. House of Representatives), 280
State Property Rights Legislation, 285

Chronology	293
Table of Cases	299
Bibliography	305
Index	311
About the Author	321

Series Foreword

America's Freedoms promises a series of books that address the origin, development, meaning, and future of the nation's fundamental liberties, as well as the individuals, circumstances, and events that have shaped them. These freedoms are chiefly enshrined explicitly or implicitly in the Bill of Rights and other amendments to the Constitution of the United States and have much to do with the quality of life Americans enjoy. Without them, America would be a far different place in which to live. Oddly enough, however, the Constitution was drafted and signed in Philadelphia in 1787 without a bill of rights. That was an afterthought, emerging only after a debate among the foremost political minds of the day.

At the time, Thomas Jefferson was in France on a diplomatic mission. Upon receiving a copy of the proposed Constitution from his friend James Madison, who had helped write the document, Jefferson let him know as fast as the slow sailing-ship mails of the day allowed that the new plan of government suffered one major defect—it lacked a bill of rights. This, Jefferson argued, "is what the people are entitled to against every government on earth." Madison should not have been surprised at Jefferson's reaction. The Declaration of Independence of 1776 had largely been Jefferson's handiwork, including its core statement of principle:

> We hold these truths to be self-evident, that all men are created equal, that they are endowed by their Creator with certain unalienable Rights, that among these are Life, Liberty, and the pursuit of Happiness. That to secure these rights, Governments are instituted among Men, deriving their just powers from the consent of the governed.

Jefferson rejected the conclusion of many of the framers that the Constitution's design—a system of both separation of powers among the legislative, executive, and judicial branches, and a federal division of powers between national and state governments—would safeguard liberty. Even when combined with elections, he believed strongly that such structural checks would fall short.

Jefferson and other critics of the proposed Constitution ultimately had their way. In one of the first items of business in the First Congress in 1789, Madison, as a member of the House of Representatives from Virginia, introduced amendments to protect liberty. Ten were ratified by 1791 and have become known as the Bill of Rights.

America's Bill of Rights reflects the founding generation's understanding of the necessary link between personal freedom and representative government, as well as their experience with threats to liberty. The First Amendment protects expression—in speech, press, assembly, petition, and religion—and guards against a union of church and state. The Second Amendment secures liberty against national tyranny by affirming the self-defense of the states. Members of state-authorized local militia—citizens primarily, soldiers occasionally—retained a right to bear arms. The ban in the Third Amendment on forcibly quartering troops in houses reflects the emphasis the framers placed on the integrity and sanctity of the home.

Other provisions in the Fourth, Fifth, Sixth, Seventh, and Eighth amendments safeguard freedom by setting forth standards that government must follow in administering the law, especially regarding persons accused of crimes. The framers knew firsthand the dangers that government-as-prosecutor could pose to liberty. Even today, authoritarian regimes in other lands routinely use the tools of law enforcement—arrests, searches, detentions, as well as trials—to squelch peaceful political opposition. Limits in the Bill of Rights on crime-fighting powers thus help maintain democracy by demanding a high level of legal scrutiny of the government's practices.

In addition, one clause in the Fifth Amendment forbids the taking of private property for public use without paying the owner just compensation, and thereby limits the power of eminent domain, the authority to seize a person's property. Along with taxation and conscription, eminent domain is one of the most awesome powers any government can possess.

The Ninth Amendment makes sure that the listing of some rights does not imply that others necessarily have been abandoned. If the Ninth offered reassurances to the people, the Tenth Amendment was designed to reassure the states that they or the people retained those powers not delegated to the national government. Today, the Tenth is a remainder of the integral role states play in the federal plan of union that the Constitution ordained.

Despite this legacy of freedom, however, we Americans today sometimes wonder about the origin, development, meaning, and future of our liberties. This concern is entirely understandable, because liberty is central to the idea of what it means *to be American.* In this way, the United States stands apart from virtually every other nation on earth. Other countries typically define their national identities through a common ethnicity, origin, ancestral bond, religion, or history. But none of these accounts for the American identity. In terms of ethnicity, ancestry, and religion, the United States is the most diverse place on earth. From the beginning, America has been a land of immigrants. Neither is there a single historical experience to which all current citizens can directly relate: someone who arrived a decade ago from, say, southeast Asia and was naturalized as a citizen only last year is just as much an American as someone whose forebears served in General George Washington's army at Valley Forge during the American War of Independence (1776–1783). In religious as in political affairs, the United States has been a beacon to those suffering oppression abroad: "the last, best hope of earth," Abraham Lincoln said. So, the American identity is ideological. It consists of faith in the value and importance of liberty for each individual.

Nonetheless, a longstanding consensus among Americans on the *principle* that individual liberty is essential, highly prized, and widely shared hardly assures agreement about liberty *in practice*. This is because the concept of liberty, as it has developed in the United States, has several dimensions.

First, there is an unavoidable tension between liberty and restraint. Liberty means freedom: we say that a person has a "right" to do this or that. But that *right* is meaningless unless there is a corresponding *duty* on the part of others (such as police officers and elected officials) not to interfere. Thus, protection of the liberty of one person necessarily involves restraints imposed on someone else. This is why we speak of a *civil* right or a *civil* liberty: it is a claim on the behavior of another that is enforceable through the legal process. Moreover, some degree of order (restrictions on the behavior of all) is necessary if everyone's liberties are to be protected. Just as too much order crushes freedom, too little invites social chaos that also threatens freedom. Determining the proper balance between freedom and order, however, is more easily sought than found. "To make a government requires no great prudence," declared English statesman and political philosopher Edmund Burke in 1790. "Settle the seat of power; teach obedience; and the work is done. To give freedom is still more easy. It is not necessary to guide; it only requires to let go the rein. But to form a *free government*;

that is, to temper together these opposite elements of liberty and restraint in one consistent work, requires much thought; deep reflection; a sagacious, powerful, and combining mind."

Second, the Constitution does not define the freedoms that it protects. Chief Justice John Marshall once acknowledged that the Constitution was a document "of enumeration, and not of definition." There are, for example, lists of the powers of Congress in Article I, or the rights of individuals in the Bill of Rights, but those powers and limitations are not explained. What is the "freedom of speech" that the First Amendment guarantees? What are "unreasonable searches and seizures" that are proscribed by the Fourth Amendment? What is the "due process of law" secured by both the Fifth and Fourteenth amendments? Reasonable people, all of whom favor individual liberty, can arrive at very different answers to these questions.

A third dimension—breadth—is closely related to the second. How widely shared is a particular freedom? Consider voting, for example. One could write a political history of the United States by cataloging the efforts to extend the vote or franchise to groups such as women and nonwhites that had been previously excluded. Or, consider the First Amendment's freedom of speech. Does it include the expression of *all* points of view or merely *some*? Does the same amendment's protection of the "free exercise of religion" include all faiths, even obscure ones that may seem weird or even irritating? At different times questions like these have yielded different answers.

Similarly, the historical record contains notorious lapses. Despite all the safeguards that are supposed to shore up freedom's foundations, constitutional protections have sometimes been worth the least when they have been desperately needed. In our history the most frequent and often the most serious threats to freedom have come not from people intent on throwing the Bill of Rights away outright, but from well-meaning people who find the Bill of Rights a temporary bother, standing in the way of some objective they want to reach.

There is also a question that dates to the very beginning of American government under the Constitution. Does the Constitution protect rights not spelled out in, or fairly implied by, the words of the document? The answer to that question largely depends on what a person concludes about the source of rights. One tradition, reflected in the Declaration of Independence, asserts that rights predate government and that government's chief duty is to protect the rights that everyone naturally possesses. Thus, if the Constitution is read as a document designed, among other things, to protect liberty, then protected liberties are not limited to those in the text of the Constitution but may also be derived from experience, for example, or from one's assessment of the requirements of a free society. This tradition places a lot of discretion in the hands of judges, because in the American political system, it is largely the judiciary that decides what the Constitution means. Partly due to this dynamic, a competing tradition looks to the text of the Constitution, as well as to statutes passed consistent with the Constitution, as a *complete* code of law containing *all* the liberties that Americans possess. Judges, therefore, are not free to go outside the text to "discover" rights that the people, through the process of lawmaking and constitutional amendment, have not declared. Doing so is undemocratic because it bypasses "rule by the people." The tension between these two ways of thinking explains the ongoing debate about a right to privacy, itself nowhere mentioned in the words of the Constitution. "I like my privacy as well as the next one," once admitted Justice Hugo Black, "but I am nevertheless compelled to admit that government has a right to invade it unless prohibited by some specific constitutional provision." Otherwise, he said, judges are forced "to determine what is or is not constitutional on the basis of their own appraisal of what laws are unwise or unnecessary." Black thought that was the job of elected legislators who would answer to the people.

Fifth, it is often forgotten that at the outset, and for many years afterward, the Bill of Rights applied only to the national government, not to the states. Except for a very few restrictions, such as those in section 10 of Article I in the main body of the Constitution, which expressly limited state power, states were restrained only by their individual constitutions and state laws, not by the U.S. Bill of Rights. So, Pennsylvania or any other state, for example, could shut down a newspaper or barricade the doors of a church without violating the First Amendment. For many in the founding generation, the new central government loomed as a colossus that might threaten liberty. Few at that time thought that individual freedom needed *national* protection against *state* invasions of the rights of the people.

The first step in removing this double standard came with ratification of the Fourteenth Amendment after the Civil War in 1868. Section 1 contained majestic, but undefined, checks on states: "*No State* shall make or enforce any law which shall abridge the privileges or immunities of citizens of the United States; nor shall any *State* deprive any person of life, liberty, or property, without due process of law; nor deny to any person with in its jurisdiction the equal protections of the laws" (emphasis added). Such vague language begged for interpretation. In a series of cases mainly between 1920 and 1968, the Supreme Court construed the Fourteenth Amendment to include within its meaning almost every provision of the Bill of Rights. This process of "incorporation" (applying the Bill of Rights to the states by way of the Fourteenth Amendment) was the second step in eliminating the double standard of 1791. State and local governments became bound by the same restrictions that had applied all along to the national government. The consequences of this development scarcely can be exaggerated because most governmental action in the United States is the work of state and local governments. For instance, ordinary citizens are far more likely to encounter a local police officer than an agent of the Federal Bureau of Investigation or the Secret Service.

A sixth dimension reflects an irony. A society premised on individual freedom assumes not only the worth of each person but citizens capable of rational thought, considered judgment, and measured actions. Otherwise democratic government would be futile. Yet, we lodge the most important freedoms in the Constitution precisely because we want to give those freedoms extra protection. "The very purpose of a Bill of Rights was to . . . place [certain subjects] beyond the reach of majorities and officials and to establish them as legal principles to be applied by the courts," explained Justice Robert H. Jackson. "One's right to life, liberty, and property, to free speech, a free press, freedom of worship and assembly, and other fundamental rights may not be submitted to vote; they depend on the outcome of no elections." Jackson referred to a hard lesson learned from experience: basic rights require extra protection because they are fragile. On occasion, people have been willing to violate the freedoms of others. That reality demanded a written constitution.

This irony reflects the changing nature of a bill of rights in history. Americans did not invent the idea of a bill of rights in 1791. Instead it drew from and was inspired by colonial documents such as the Pennsylvania colony's Charter of Liberties (1701) and the English Bill of Rights (1689), Petition of Right (1628), and Magna Carta (1215). However, these early and often unsuccessful attempts to limit government power were devices to protect the many (the people) from the few (the English Crown). With the emergence of democratic political systems in the eighteenth century, however, political power shifted from the few to the many. The right to rule belonged to the person who received the most votes in an election, not necessarily to the firstborn, the wealthiest, or the most physically powerful. So the focus of a bill of rights had to shift too. No longer was it designed to shelter the majority from the minority, but to shelter the minority from the majority. "Wherever the real power in a Government lies, there is the danger of oppression," commented Madison in his exchange of letters with Jefferson in 1788. "In our Government, the real power lies in the majority of the Community, and the invasion of private rights is *chiefly* to be apprehended, not from acts of government contrary to the sense of its constituents, but from acts in which the Government is the mere instrument of the major number of the Constituents."

Americans, however, do deserve credit for having discovered a way to enforce a bill of rights. Without an enforcement mechanism, a bill of rights is no more than a list of aspirations: standards to aim for, but with no redress other than violent protest or revolution. Indeed this had been the experience in England with which the framers were thoroughly familiar. Thanks to judicial review—the authority courts in the United States possess to invalidate actions taken by the other branches of government which, in the judges' view, conflict with the Constitution—the provisions in the Bill of Rights and other constitutionally protected liberties became judicially enforceable.

Judicial review was a tradition that was beginning to emerge in the states on a small scale in the 1780s and 1790s and that would blossom in the U.S. Supreme Court in the nineteenth and twentieth centuries. "In the arguments in favor of a declaration of rights," Jefferson presciently told Madison in the late winter of 1789 after the Constitution had been ratified, "you omit one which has great weight with me, the legal check which it puts into the hands of the judiciary." This is the reason why each of the volumes in this series focuses extensively on judicial decisions. Liberties have largely been defined by judges in the context of deciding cases in situations where individuals thought the power of government extended too far.

Designed to help democracy protect itself, the Constitution ultimately needs the support of those—the majority—who endure its restraints. Without sufficient support among the people, its freedoms rest on a weak foundation. The earnest hope of *America's Freedoms* is that this series will offer Americans a renewed appreciation and understanding of their heritage of liberty.

Yet there would be no series on America's Freedoms without the interest and support of Alicia Merritt at ABC-CLIO. The series was her idea. She approached me originally about the series and was very adept at overcoming my initial hesitations as series editor. She not only helped me shape the particular topics that the series would include, but guided me toward prospective authors. As a result, the topic of each book has been matched with the most appropriate person as author. The goal in each instance has been to pair topics with authors who are recognized teachers and scholars in their field. The results have been gratifying. A series editor could hardly wish for authors who have been more cooperative, helpful, and accommodating.

Donald Grier Stephenson, Jr.

Preface and Acknowledgments

The title of this book, *Property Rights*, is misleading in one sense. The U.S. Constitution is silent about the distribution of property in society at any given moment. The constitutional structure tolerates, and even envisions, that there may be vast disparities in property ownership among U.S. citizens. The Constitution confers no right to property in the sense that those without property are entitled to have some property. The "right" of property is, instead, a right to acquire property, if one has the means, and a subsequent right to have that property protected from interference by the government. The Constitution does protect the liberty to pursue property based on individual effort. However, because "the Constitution protects rather than creates property interests" (*Phillips* 164), as the U.S. Supreme Court said in *Phillips v. Washington Legal Foundation* (1998), the Constitution's property rights provisions are neutral with respect to who owns property and how much.

Contemporary debates over the extent to which the U.S. Constitution protects private property are complicated and fiercely fought. This book does not claim that these issues are easy to resolve. The purpose is to emphasize that these modern disagreements have always been with us: The question of the legitimate role of government with respect to private property has defied easy resolution throughout U.S. history. If there is any agreement, it is that a government cannot exercise its power of *eminent domain*—the taking of private property for public use—without compensation to the property owner. Eminent domain is a striking governmental power. The death penalty, imprisonment, or fines imposed by a government are at least cast as retribution for criminal or otherwise wrongful conduct. Eminent domain, by contrast, requires law-abiding citizens to give up their property, in return for money, even if that particular piece of property is desperately important to them. Although the basic proposition that government takings of private property must be compensated was settled at the founding of the United States, no historical consensus has ever been reached on the extent to which compensation is required for other government actions, short of outright appropriations under eminent domain, that affect private property.

In an undertaking of this nature, in which the primary goal is to provide a general audience with a succinct overview of the major historical points of debate concerning the constitutional status of property rights, it is inevitable that the book will omit some topics and avoid extended discussion of others. This book, for example, addresses the property protections to be found in the U.S. Constitution. Property is also protected by state constitutions and their courts, and in recent years many property rights advocates have concentrated their efforts and criticisms on state law, a topic mentioned only briefly in this book. To compensate for the necessarily abbreviated nature of what is offered, a Further Reading section is provided at the end of each chapter. The listed works provide longer and fuller discussions of issues presented in this book for readers who wish to pursue them. In addition, Chapter 6 provides extensive excerpts of important cases and other documents relevant to the constitutional protection of property. Readers can examine for themselves the analyses of particular issues addressed there.

The cases and other documents provided in Chapter 6 have been edited to remove footnotes and extraneous citations in order to present more of the primary texts. An additional note about citation format: Cases referred to in this book are from the U.S. Supreme Court unless otherwise indicated. A table of cases, with the full citation to each case, is provided at the end of the book.

Work on this book was largely completed while I served as visiting professor at Vanderbilt Law School. I am grateful for that opportunity. I am indebted to my colleague there, James W. Ely Jr., for his critical comments on parts of this book, and for the opportunity to observe his course, "Constitutional Protection of Property Rights." I also benefited from the able research assistance of Margaret Clemens, Nicholas A. Goodling, Ashley A. Palermo, and Leticia Soto, students at Vanderbilt Law School. At Emory Law School, I thank professors Margo Bagley and David Bederman for their comments on Chapters 3 and 4; students Ryan Compton, Amanda "Brooke" Lewis, and Joan Tomlinson for their research assistance; and Will Haines of Emory's MacMillan Law Library for providing suggestions for the book's cover. Christopher Curtis (Ph.D., Emory, 2002) graciously shared his research on the Virginia abolition debate discussed in Chapter 2. Chet Tisdale, an environmental lawyer at King & Spalding (where I worked as an associate prior to becoming a law professor), provided valuable insights for Chapter 4. The series editor, Donald Grier Stephenson Jr., deserves accolades for his overall vision as well as for his encouragement through the sometimes tedious details of the book-writing process.

Polly J. Price
Emory University School of Law

1

Introduction

In the final analysis the Bill of Rights depends upon the existence of private property. Civil liberties must have a basis in property, or bills of rights will not preserve them.
—Charles A. Reich, "New Property" (1964, 771)

Constitutional Protection of Property

In 2002, the U.S. Supreme Court considered a claim brought by more than 400 California and Nevada property owners who, for a period of nearly three years, were prevented from constructing homes on undeveloped lots they had purchased near Lake Tahoe. The moratorium on construction had been imposed by a government agency due to fears that runoff from the hillsides would adversely affect the lake. The property owners argued that the delay deprived them of all "economically viable use" of their land for that period and that they should be compensated for the deprivation.

In *Tahoe-Sierra Preservation Council v. Tahoe Regional Planning Agency* (2002), a closely divided Supreme Court disagreed.

Writing for the majority, Justice John Paul Stevens affirmed the "fundamental distinction" (*Tahoe* 1480) between a government seizure of private property and a regulation that limits an owner's desired use of land. "Land-use regulations are ubiquitous and most of them impact property values in some tangential way—often in completely unanticipated ways. Treating them all as *per se* takings would transform government regulation into a luxury few governments could afford" (*Tahoe* 1479). For this reason, Justice Stevens wrote,

> A rule that required compensation for every delay in the use of property would render routine government processes prohibitively expensive or encourage hasty decision making. . . . In our view the answer to the abstract question whether a temporary moratorium effects a taking is neither "yes, always" nor "no, never": the answer depends on the particular circumstances of the case. (*Tahoe* 1478, 1475)

Property rights issues such as this have captured public attention and appear on the front pages of newspapers. In but one example, the front-page headline "JUSTICES WEAKEN MOVEMENT BACKING PROPERTY RIGHTS" appeared in the *New York Times* following the announcement of the *Tahoe-Sierra* decision (Greenhouse 2002, A1). As that headline indicated, the Supreme Court's decision in the case was a disappointment to property rights advocates. Supporting the property owners around Lake Tahoe, a number of property rights groups had urged the Court to recognize that a land-use restriction that even temporarily deprives property owners of the use of their land is a "taking" requiring compensation under the U.S. Constitution. An equally large number of government, planning, and environmental groups opposed that claim. The intense media interest surrounding this case followed a series of earlier Supreme Court decisions probing the boundaries of the constitutional protection of property. Those boundaries are the subject of this book.

Property as the "Guardian of Every Other Right"

The U.S. Constitution protects private property rights. But property rights are not absolute, and the extent to which privately owned property is constitutionally protected is a complicated and controversial issue. Because in the United States the judicial branch is the ultimate authority on the interpretation of constitutional rights, this book explores how courts have interpreted the various constitutional provisions related to private property. The goal is to provide a historical context for understanding the rights and liberties associated with private ownership of property, including the many changed circumstances that have forced courts, over time, to consider new parameters for such rights. What constitutional protection of private property has meant in the courts has changed since the founding era. The purpose of this book is to explore these changes through the present day.

Why is the protection of private property often considered fundamental to constitutionalism in the United States? The answer has to do with historical antecedents in state constitutions and natural rights philosophy. Following the Revolution and prior to the drafting of the federal Constitution, every state constitution was based on the idea that the purpose of government was to preserve natural rights to "life, liberty, and property." Many of these state constitutions, in fact, explicitly placed "property" on the same level with "liberty" and "life." James Madison, one of the primary authors of the U.S. Constitution, wrote that "Government is instituted to protect property of every sort.... This being the end of government, that alone is a just government, which impartially secures to every man, whatever is his own" (Madison 1906, 102). Security of private property was linked to liberty and was sometimes said to be the "guardian of every other right" (Ely 1998, 26).

This historic link between property and liberty still drives much of the rhetoric about property rights today. The link between property and liberty acquired additional importance in the early decades following the Revolution because voting rights were often tied to property ownership. Although voting rights are no longer dependent upon the amount of property the voter owns, it is common today to view the protection of private property to be fundamental for the protection of other civil rights. The quotation at the outset of this introduction, taken from an important article by Charles Reich entitled "New Property," underscores the link between civil rights of individuals and the economic basis to assert these rights.

Property Rights in International Context

It is useful to compare constitutional protection of private property in the United States with the experience of some other nations. The twentieth century witnessed several instances of government appropriation and redistribution of private property without compensation to the owners. The formation of the Soviet Union, following the Russian Revolution in the early decades of the twentieth century, was the farthest-reaching example. Government confiscation of privately owned factories and other means of production occurred swiftly. At the First All-Russian Congress of Soviets in 1917, the congress issued the "Peasant's Mandate on Land," article 1 of which stated: "The right of private ownership of land shall be abolished forever; land can neither be sold, bought, leased and mortgaged, nor alienated by any other means. All land shall be alienated without compensation, shall become public property, and shall be used by all the working people on it" (Syrodoev 1975, 9). The subsequent constitution of 1918 incorporated this provision, and the nationalization of private land was one of the most striking features of the Soviet regime for most of the twentieth century.

In Cuba, following the Fidel Castro–led revolution in 1959, uncompensated government confiscations of private property occurred—including the taking of mines, agricultural land, and oil refineries owned by U.S. citizens and companies. Cuba's refusal to compensate the United States for these property confiscations led to decades of punitive legislation from the United States (Morley 1987). In socialist systems generally, possession of property is regarded as contingent upon duties owed to the state. Although Fidel Castro's justifications for appropriating foreign-owned property differed from the Soviet-era declarations that denied the existence of private property, Cuba, like the Soviet Union, also developed the category of "quasi-property," that is, giving individuals the right to exclusive possession of some property for a period of years.

More recently, the African nation of Zimbabwe has been roiled by a government-initiated land-redistribution scheme from white-owned farms to landless blacks, a legacy of Zimbabwe's colonial past. In 2000, the country's supreme court ruled that occupations of the white-owned farms were illegal and ordered militants to cease occupying private property. President Robert Mugabe criticized the Supreme Court for its protection of British colonial land laws that placed most of the country's farm land in the possession of a small white minority. Hundreds of government-backed demonstrators stormed the supreme court building and threatened to remove the judges by force unless they resigned or reversed their rulings (Swarns 2001, A3). Several justices resigned. Other African nations with a similar colonial legacy also face the problem of illegal occupations of white-owned private property, as those governments push for a more equitable land-distribution scheme.

Protection of private property as a matter of international law did not receive prominence until the mid-twentieth century. As a reaction to the Soviet example, in 1948 the United Nations (UN) Universal Declaration of Human Rights included protection of private property. Article 17, section 1, states that "everyone has the right to own property alone as well as in association with others." Section 2 adds that "no one shall be arbitrarily deprived of his property." In recent years, the UN Commission on Human Rights has reaffirmed these values when governments have engaged in uncompensated land expropriation.

It is more common than not for modern nations to protect private property rights. Upon the reunification of Germany, for example, the new government set in place procedures to compensate those who had lost property under the prior regime. The Unification Treaty mandated the return of property in East Germany to its former owners who fled to West Germany. When the return of property was not possible—either because it was occupied by new residents or was converted to public use by the government of East Germany—the treaty required the government to compensate the former owners (Gartin 1995, 776). Numerous investment treaties between nations also include a prohibition on appropriation of private property. The 1992 North American Free Trade Agreement (NAFTA), for example, contains a "just compensation" provision. NAFTA prohibits signatory countries from nationalizing or expropriating investment property owned by citizens of other member countries, except for a "public purpose" and only with payment of compensation based upon the fair market value of the property.

The prospect of uncompensated government confiscations or redistribution of privately owned land would have horrified James Madison. In *Federalist No. 10,* Madison wrote that "an equal division of property" is both an "improper . . . [and] wicked project" of government. The U.S. Constitution, since the addition of the Bill of Rights in 1791, specifically prohibits government confiscations of private property without just compensation. The Fifth Amendment to the U.S. Constitution provides: "Nor shall any person be deprived of life, liberty, or property, without due process of law; nor shall private property be taken for public use without just compensation." The Constitution's specific prohibition on arbitrary deprivations of private property, as well as the requirement that just compensation accompany any government taking of private property, predate the UN Declaration of Human Rights by more than 150 years.

Protecting life, liberty, and property from government interference was not a new idea, however; it was considered by the American colonists to be among their fundamental rights as subjects of England. The concept of *due process* for property rights first appeared in the Magna Carta (1215). Political thought during the revolutionary period in the colonies drew from this tradition in addition to the natural rights philosophy known to the Founders through the writings of John Locke. Locke maintained that the principle purpose of government was to protect natural rights. This belief system posited that natural rights included the right to acquire and protect private property. In turn, the security of private property brought with it security of life and liberty. Americans did not create the idea that property should be protected from specific forms of government interference. Instead, the founding generation's innovation was to protect this received tradition by formalizing property rights in written constitutions. A number of state constitutions in the founding period affirmed the natural right of "acquiring, possessing, and protecting property."

Recognizing this as a fundamental right, the United States can thus claim a long tradition of protecting private property from government redistribution. Compared to the twentieth-century examples of the Soviet Union, Cuba, and Zimbabwe, courts in the United States exhibit a greater ability to protect this right. Even if the U.S. Constitution did not provide for just compensation of government takings of private property, long-standing political traditions—together with the structure and relative stability of government—make radical events such as those in the former Soviet Union, Cuba, and Zimbabwe unlikely to occur in the United States. The Framers of our federal Constitution believed that the structure of the government they created—with its divided sovereignty and checks and balances among three branches—

provided the most important protections for preserving property rights, more so than the specific property clauses later to appear in the Bill of Rights.

Property Rights (and Responsibilities) in the United States

In the United States today, eminent domain, or the government's power of condemnation, is the most visible and intrusive exercise of governmental power over individual property owners. When a federal, state, or local government or agency desires to build a road or convert private land to some other public use, it can do so against the property owner's wishes if just compensation is given in return. The government can force the involuntary purchase of the owner's property through its power of eminent domain as long as it pays fair market value for the property.

But what if a particular regulation or use restriction (as opposed to a formal condemnation proceeding requiring the government to purchase the owner's land at fair market value) leaves a landowner with a less economically beneficial use of property? What if an airport is located near a residential area? Must the government compensate nearby homeowners for the resulting noise and vibration? Although the exercise of eminent domain power clearly requires compensation from the government, the question of who must be compensated for other government actions that adversely affect property is less clear.

Also problematic is the question of what constitutes just compensation. Is it simply a matter of assessing the fair market value of the property on the basis of what others are willing to pay for similar property? Or should other valuation mechanisms factor into the determination of just compensation? Interpretation of these issues has been difficult for courts because the federal Constitution does not provide much guidance beyond the directive that compensation must be just.

The Constitution does not explicitly confer eminent domain power on Congress; instead, as is the case for most state governments, eminent domain is assumed to be an inherent power of sovereignty. In other words, because the Fifth Amendment prohibits government takings of property without adequate compensation, it is assumed Congress has this power, even though eminent domain is not one of the specifically enumerated powers of the federal government.

The theory that the government is the original owner of land within its territory has from the beginning justified the government's power to appropriate property for public use. The importance of the assumption that private property originates from the government is that private property remains subject to the capacity of the government to reclaim the property for a public purpose, a view that derives from English law. The basic doctrine of English feudal law was a tenure-based land system with the English monarch at its head. English "subjects" who owed allegiance to the king were permitted certain land rights in return. In the event of treason, or in a few other circumstances, landholding rights could be revoked, and the land reverted to royal control.

U.S. governmental practices after the Revolution substituted three key components in this English tradition: "subject" became "citizen"; allegiance was owed to the state, not to the king; and tenure rights of landholding became allodial (i.e., outright ownership of land, or ownership in "fee simple," rather than "holding" of land ultimately owned by the English monarch). In the United States, the new state governments became the substitute for the English monarch as successor-in-interest to all property rights held by the crown. The most striking example of this succession is the early endorsement by the Supreme Court, under Chief Justice John Marshall, of the notion that the United States had succeeded to all British land rights with respect to Native American lands. The federal and state governments also quickly assumed the power to distribute land to individuals. These early distribution practices, in which unoccupied land was practically given away with few explicit reservations of government rights, accelerated the westward expansion of the United States and the further displacement of Native Americans. These government actions set basic expectations of the rights that accompany private property in the United States.

But the right of private property in the United States is not now, and never has been, absolute. All privately owned property—whether real estate, intellectual property, automobiles, or other personal property—is subject to a number of limitations that may be imposed by the government without compensation from public funds (government tax dollars) for restrictions on the use of the property.

The range of permissible government action with respect to one's property is broad. The most obvious example is the power of taxation. Failure to pay property taxes, for example, can result in a forced sale of the property to satisfy a delinquent tax bill. As the percentage rate of a tax increases, the line between a "taking" and a "tax" is not easy to draw. Under Franklin Roosevelt's administration, for example, top marginal tax rates on individual income reached 90 percent during World War II. As another example, historically, inheritance tax rates have meant that above a certain estate value the government is entitled to a very large percentage of property upon the owner's death. The power to tax is not a taking, although use of the tax power to engage in redistribution of wealth seriously concerned Justice Stephen Field in *Pollock v. Farmer's Loan & Trust Co.* (1895).

Under a state's police power—defined as the authority to protect the health and welfare of its citizens—a state government may determine that some types of property may not be owned or may not be used in certain specified ways. During the prohibition era, the U.S. Supreme Court upheld state and federal laws prohibiting the possession and sale of alcohol. To some extent, a state's police power also may be exercised to determine which persons may own certain types of property. For example, convicted felons are routinely barred from owning firearms. A person's citizenship status may determine whether that person can own or inherit real estate located in the United States (Price 1999, 152–153).

Other examples of government control over property abound. Most states specify that a married person may not disinherit a spouse by executing a will that leaves that spouse without any part of the estate. Furthermore, a person's property holdings at death can become the property of the state if that person dies with no known living relative and has not designated by will that some other person or group should receive the property. Federal, state, and local governments may also require licensing, inspection, insurance coverage, and other controls upon uses of personal property, such as automobiles. The purchase of an automobile does not of itself give the owner the right to drive it on streets. And landowners may not impose on their neighbors noxious odors, noise, or other property use that constitutes a "nuisance."

Moreover, the federal and state governments have taken an increasingly aggressive stance on property forfeiture by those who are convicted of crimes. The most notable instance has included drug forfeitures: Private homes, automobiles, and other property of persons involved in illicit drug trafficking have been converted to government property as a forfeiture for violation of criminal law. Sometimes these forfeitures affect the private property of innocent co-owners. Several federal statutes permit the government to seize property of accused wrongdoers prior to conviction, including assets that the defendant has pledged for bail or that the defendant proposes to use to pay attorney's fees for his or her defense.

All of these instances of governmental regulation or outright appropriation of private property are not considered to conflict with the fundamental rights of property found in the U.S. Constitution. However, if regulation of private property goes too far—which is a case-by-case judgment—the use regulation will be recognized as a taking. Local governments have long imposed restrictive zoning ordinances that significantly limit what a property owner may do with his or her property, and governmental authority in this area is considerable. Local governments may restrict the use of real estate by, for example, prohibiting operation of a business in a residential zoning area, or restricting in some way the type of structure that may be built on the property. In addition, federal and state environmental laws sometimes prevent development of privately owned land. Environmental laws may require that a portion of private land be temporarily or permanently set aside from development to protect wetlands or endangered species. Restrictions of these types on private property are among the most pressing questions concerning the scope of constitutional protection of property rights.

Property Clauses in the U.S. Constitution

Although the focus of this book is on the Contracts, Due Process, and Takings Clauses of the federal Constitution, to some extent protection of private property as a constitutional matter is always informed by the protection accorded private homes through the Fourth Amendment, as well as other clauses applicable to property scattered throughout the federal Constitution. The Fourth Amendment's prohibition of unreasonable search and seizure recognizes the "right of the people to be secure in their persons, houses, papers, and effects." Many important U.S. Supreme Court cases regarding criminal procedure have addressed the constitutional restrictions on police searches of private homes, and most recently attention has focused upon the appropriate parameters of electronic surveillance.

The Supreme Court has said that the sanctity of the home from unauthorized government intrusion extends even to nonphysical invasions. Government investigators, for example, may not survey a home's contents with a thermal imaging device without first obtaining a warrant with probable cause, according to *Kyllo v. United States* (2001). In that case, which involved a police attempt, without a warrant, to scan for heat emissions to detect lights used for growing marijuana, the Supreme Court noted the potential erosion of homeowners' reasonable expectations of privacy from government intrusion by advancing technology. The Court wrote: "At the very core of the Fourth Amendment stands the right of a man to retreat into his home and there be free" (*Kyllo* 31). The Fourth Amendment thus envisions a realm of protection for private "living spaces" against unwarranted government intrusion.

In addition, the Third Amendment provides that "no Soldier shall, in time of peace be quartered in any house, without the consent of the Owner, nor in time of war, but in a manner to be prescribed by law." This amendment came from the immediate experience of British colonial practices and the recent Revolutionary War. The Third Amendment is probably the least-known among the Bill of Rights because courts have not been presented with situations requiring that it be enforced. Nonetheless, the Third Amendment stands alongside other constitutional provisions as evidence of the importance placed on private property by the founding generation.

The civil jury trial guarantee in the Seventh Amendment also addresses concerns about protection of private property. Two leading anti-Federalists—Richard Henry Lee and the anonymous essays of "Brutus"—criticized the original federal Constitution for its failure to include a guarantee of juries for civil matters, particularly for private property disputes (Rakove 1998, 118, 130). These writers, like many of their contemporaries, believed that juries, as representatives of the citizenry of a local community, were an important safeguard for property rights even in disputes that did not involve the government—a clear imputation that judges, as representatives of the government, were not necessarily neutral arbiters in private disputes.

In addition to the property-related clauses in the Bill of Rights, several clauses in the main text of the U.S. Constitution also concern property rights. The most important of these are found in Article I, section 10: States may not "coin Money; emit Bills of Credit, make any Thing but gold and silver Coin a Tender in Payment of Debts; pass any Bill of Attainder, ex post facto Law, or Law impairing the Obligation of Contracts." Although these clauses are primarily directed to federalism—the division of power between states and the federal government—the Contracts Clause of this section is an individual property right. The Contracts Clause was the primary source of federal court intervention in state legislative activity in the nineteenth century. The Contracts Clause gradually declined in importance after 1900, but throughout the nineteenth century contractual rights were regarded as a vested right of property subject to constitutional protection.

Constitutional scholars point to all of these clauses—in addition to the Takings Clause—to conclude that the founding generation was particularly concerned with the security of private property. The founding generation believed that written constitutions preserved property rights, even if the exact nature of those rights remained vague. The concern that state legislatures would violate settled property expectations was borne out in several noteworthy instances in the early nineteenth century, leading to intervention by the U.S. Supreme Court in cases such as *Fletcher v. Peck* (1810) and *Dartmouth College v. Woodward* (1819), under the authority of the Contracts Clause. These cases, described in more detail in Chapter 2, made it clear that the U.S. Supreme Court would provide strong protection against interference with property rights represented by contracts.

Later generations also were concerned with constitutional protection of private property. The Fourteenth Amendment to the U.S. Constitution, ratified after the Civil War, provides, "Nor shall any State deprive any person of life, liberty, or property, without due process of law." Prior to the Civil War and Reconstruction, the Fifth Amendment's Takings Clause did not apply specifically to state governments. Unless a state constitution prohibited uncompensated government takings, the Takings Clause did not provide a barrier to state property confiscations because it prohibited only uncompensated takings by the *federal* government. In 1897, the U.S. Supreme Court interpreted the Fourteenth Amendment to have "incorporated" the Fifth Amendment's just compensation principle to apply to states as well. As a result, today the Fifth Amendment's requirement that takings of private property be accompanied by just compensation restricts state and local governments as well as the federal government.

Plan of the Book

This book will examine constitutional protection of property primarily through the decisions of the U.S. Supreme Court, which by necessity must interpret phrases in the federal constitution that are vague and open-ended. The clauses themselves lack definition and content. What does it mean to say that compensation must be "just" or that property may only be taken by the government for a "public use"? The meanings ascribed to these phrases have varied throughout history as much as the context of property has changed, a recognition that historical definitions may not be appropriate for contemporary conditions. Property in the form of "persons," via the institution of slavery, was once protected in the United States as a fundamental right. Although property in persons was prohibited by the Thirteenth Amendment, other forms of property in living things—or at least in cell lines derived or cloned from human embryos—is at present a perplexing problem to courts and legislatures.

This book will focus primarily on the property rights of private persons and corporations. Corporations can own property (particularly important today is intellectual property), and their rights with respect to private property are equal with those of persons. This focus excludes property disputes between states, between the states and the federal government, and between the United States and other nations, although some attention is given to international law for comparative purposes.

This book is organized to present a chronology of developments in the constitutional protection recognized for property. Chapter 2, "Origins and Early Development," provides a summary of property rights from the colonial period through the end of the nineteenth century. This chapter will explain the significance of the appearance in written constitutions of just compensation clauses for government takings of private property. Important court decisions in the nineteenth century interpreted these just compensation clauses as well as other constitutional provisions, including the Contracts Clause of the federal Constitution, to determine the boundaries of government action with respect to private property.

Chapter 3, "Twentieth Century Issues and Development," considers economic liberty as a component of the constitutional protection of property. Some use the broader term "economic liberty" to categorize the property interests protected collectively by the Due Process, Contracts, and Takings Clauses. In the twentieth century, the Contracts Clause was relatively unimportant, but new understandings of constitutional economic liberty emerged to replace it. At the beginning of the twentieth century, substantive due process (a concept explained in Chapter 3) was the most prominent constitutional tool to further a particular view of economic liberty. The dominant story of twentieth-century property law, however, is the rise of the regulatory takings doctrine—an interpretation of the Takings Clause that extends the compensation requirement beyond the actual exercise of eminent domain by a government. The claim that a regulation governing the use of property constitutes a regulatory taking has become the central issue of constitutional property rights in U.S. courts.

Chapter 4, "Into the Twenty-first Century: Issues and Prospects," discusses three areas that present unresolved issues for constitutional property rights: intellectual property, biotechnology, and the environment. New forms of property have constantly emerged throughout U.S. history. One purpose of this chapter is to describe the new contexts in which property rights have been the subject of important court decisions. Ownership of biological property, such as human organs, DNA sequences, cell lines, and the like, will present difficult issues in coming years. This chapter concludes with a consideration of competing theories of property rights in environmental law.

Chapter 5 (Key People, Cases, and Events) and Chapter 6 (Documents) provide more general information on the topics discussed throughout this book. They are intended to direct readers to more specific sources or to familiarize them with related texts.

The range of topics in this book is broad because constitutional protection of property is not neatly confined to one place in the Constitution, and property itself is not limited to a house or land. Historically, the degree of permissible governmental regulation of private property has been consistently a topic without consensus among legislators and judges. Because private property has constitutional status, courts play a central role in defining and protecting private property rights in the United States, as this book will relate.

References and Further Reading

Cohen, F. S. 1954. "Dialogue on Private Property." *Rutgers Law Review* 9:357–387.

Coyle, D. J. 1993. *Property Rights and the Constitution.* Albany: State University of New York Press.

Ely, J. W. 1998. *The Guardian of Every Other Right.* 2d ed. New York: Oxford University Press.

Epstein, R. 1985. *Takings: Private Property and the Power of Eminent Domain.* Cambridge, MA: Harvard University Press.

Gartin, T. L. 1995. "Parity and the Litigation of Private Property Rights in the United States and Germany." *Northern Illinois University Law Review* 15:747–781.

Greenhouse, L. 2002. "Justices Weaken Movement Backing Property Rights." *New York Times,* April 24, p. A1.

Levy, L. W. 1996. *A License to Steal: The Forfeiture of Property.* Chapel Hill: University of North Carolina Press.

Madison, J. 1906 (G. Hunt, ed.). *The Writings of James Madison, volume 6: 1790–1802.* New York: G. P. Putnam's Sons.

Morley, M. H. 1987. *Imperial State and Revolution: The United States and Cuba, 1952–1986.* Cambridge, UK: Cambridge University Press.

Nedelsky, J. 1990. *Private Property and the Limits of American Constitutionalism.* Chicago: University of Chicago Press.

Price, P. 1999. "Alien Land Restrictions in the American Common Law." *American Journal of Legal History* 43:152–208.

Rakove, J. N. 1998. *Declaring Rights.* Boston: Bedford Books.

Reich, C.A. 1964. "The New Property." *Yale Law Journal* 73:733–787.

Rose, C. 1996. "Property as the Keystone Right?" *Notre Dame Law Review* 71:329.

Siegan, B. H. 1997. *Property and Freedom.* New Brunswick, NJ: Transaction Publishers.

Swarns, R. L. 2001. "Zimbabwe's Judges Are Feeling Mugabe's Wrath." *New York Times,* February 4, p. 3.

Syrodoev, N. A. 1975. *Soviet Land Legislation.* Moscow: Progress Publishers.

2

ORIGINS AND EARLY DEVELOPMENT

The third absolute right, inherent in every Englishman, is that of property, which consists in the free use, enjoyment, and disposal of all his acquisitions, without any control or diminution, save only by the law of the land.

—WILLIAM BLACKSTONE, 1765

The concept that government should protect and preserve the private property of its citizens was not an innovation of the revolutionary period or of the U.S. Constitution. The Fifth Amendment's Due Process and Takings Clauses were modeled upon similar clauses in some of the first state constitutions, enacted as those states declared independence from the rule of Great Britain. These state constitutions, in turn, drew from a lengthy English tradition that viewed the protection of private property to be a fundamental obligation of government. The American colonists, like most English subjects, believed that individual liberty depended to a large degree upon the protection and security of private property.

The authors of the U.S. Constitution shared the view that private property provided an essential basis for political freedom. In particular, they believed that property could best be protected through a strong federal government. Yet the U.S. Constitution does not define the word "property" or describe the scope of protection for private property that the Framers may have had in mind. The Framers worked within an English tradition that exalted property rights as a form of individual liberty. William Blackstone, the author of an influential treatise on English common law that was widely available in late-eighteenth-century America, wrote: "There is nothing which so generally strikes the imagination, and engages the affections of mankind, as the right of property; or that sole and despotic dominion which one man claims and exercises over the external things of the world, in total exclusion of the right of any other individual in the universe" (Blackstone 1765, 2). Blackstone was careful to note, however, that this "absolute right" of property could be properly limited by "the law of the land." From the outset, the concept of private property as a limitation on governmental power exhibited a tension between individual property rights and government-imposed limitations on property for the protection of community values.

This chapter considers the historical tradition of constitutional protection of property rights in the United States from the late colonial era through the end of the nineteenth century. The historical record in the United States is consistent with Blackstone's model of private property rights. Private property has always received special protection in both state and federal courts, but it has never been absolute. State and local governments routinely set the terms for property acquisition, the uses to which that property might be put, and the terms by which property might be disposed of after the death of the owner. Economic regulation, including property forfeiture for noncompliance with state and local laws concerning that property, was a prominent feature of the early landscape in the United States. Courts rarely interfered with these government activities. Although after ratification of the federal Constitution the U.S. Supreme Court fiercely defended notions of vested property rights from state government interference, at other times it upheld laws that seriously diminished the value of some private property.

Modern constitutional debates on the protection of property rights focus almost exclusively on the Fifth Amendment's Takings Clause. This emphasis in contemporary law contrasts sharply with the history of property rights in the 1800s. As was true for many other individual rights listed in the Bill of Rights, the Takings Clause had little application in the first century of the United States because it restricted the activities of only the federal government, not state governments. The power to regulate and control property was located in the states. State and local laws regulating property (and protecting citizens from uncompensated takings by their own state governments) thus provide important background from which to judge the contemporary legal status of private property under the Constitution.

English Origins

The tradition of government protection of private property in the United States has its roots in Great Britain. The American colonists drew from a lengthy tradition of legal protection of private property rights in England, including centuries of respect for the sanctity of homes from unlawful entry and from takings of property by government officials. The revered and ancient Magna Carta, the great charter between King John and English nobles in 1215, set forth the concept of due process of law: "No free man shall be taken, imprisoned or disseised [dispossessed of property], outlawed, banished, or in any way destroyed, nor will We proceed against or prosecute him, except by the lawful judgment of his peers and by the law of the land" (Rakove 1998, 8). The 1628 Petition of Right guaranteed additional rights, including a prohibition against requiring English subjects to quarter soldiers in their private homes. The Declaration of Rights, approved by both houses of Parliament in 1689, included a list of 13 "undoubted Rights and Liberties" of the English people, including parliamentary approval prior to any taxation, freedom from excessive fines or bail, and the right to a jury trial before forfeiture of property (Rakove 1998, 28, 43).

The colonists considered these and other traditional rights to be their own by virtue of their English heritage. Many colonial charters, including that of Virginia in 1606, guaranteed colonists the "rights" of Englishmen: The colonists were to "have and enjoy all Liberties, Franchises, and Immunities . . . to all Intents and Purposes, as if they had been abiding and born, within this our Realm of England" (Schwartz 1971, 54). Thus, it is not surprising that these specifically British notions of property rights appear with some frequency in colonial and revolutionary-era documents.

The English philosopher John Locke, whose theories were extraordinarily influential in the colonies and in the early years of the republic, grounded his theory of government on the right of property, which included a right of individuals to protect their property against a tyrannical government (Rakove 1998, 20). Locke contended that government was a social compact between citizens and the government. Government legitimately existed to take the necessary steps to preserve life, liberty, and property as the most fundamental interests of those it governed. Locke maintained that all landed property was originally available to mankind in common but could be appropriated to individual ownership by a person's labor. Property could be acquired by individuals for their own use, and in turn an individual's claim to specific property deserved government protection.

Locke recognized a significant limitation on the acquisition of private property. There must be "enough, and as good left in common for others," meaning that individuals should not acquire more land than needed for a livelihood. Locke believed that everyone enjoyed an "equal right" or "a right in common ... [to] provide for their subsistence," a natural right that at least as an initial distributional matter "gives every man a title to so much out of another's plenty, as will keep him from extreme want, where he has not the means to subsist otherwise."

Locke speculated, however, that conditions might be different in the colonies:

> There Men will not be apt to enlarge their Possessions of Land, were it never so rich, never so free for them to take.... In the middle of the in-land parts of *America,* where he had no hopes of Commerce with other Parts of the World ... we should see him give up again to the wild Common of Nature whatever was more than would supply the Conveniences of Life to be had there for him and his family. (Katz 1976, 467)

The amount of land in England was limited. Locke saw vast land in America. Regardless, Locke recognized that a common societal interest in the acquisition of individual property required government to protect property necessary for the common good.

Similar to Locke, Blackstone viewed the protection of property as necessary for freedom and therefore a principle aim of government. Unlike Locke, however, Blackstone did not view the rights associated with property ownership to be determined by natural law. Although the origin of private property was "probably founded in nature," Blackstone wrote, "certainly the modifications under which we at present find it, the method of conserving it in the present owner, and of transmitting it from man to man, are entirely derived from society" (Blackstone 1765, 1:138, 299). Property ownership in England, according to Blackstone, was governed by customary usage and could be limited by "the laws of the land," which included numerous common law restrictions.

Common law rules related to property were far more developed in England than in the colonies. But particularly in the early years of the new republic, jurists often considered these common law rules to be controlling. The most readily accessible list of property rules came from Blackstone's treatise, *Commentaries on the Laws of England* (1765). Rules prescribing the use and transfer of property, according to Blackstone, were properly determined by a society's laws and traditions. Existing common law rules in England, Blackstone recognized, stood in some contradiction to claims that private ownership of property carried with it "absolute" dominion.

Several differing ideas about private property thus influenced the early experience in the United States, including Locke's natural law philosophy and the inherited English common law, which imposed accepted limits on the use and possession of private property. Writings available to the colonists were contradictory on the legal status of private property as "absolute," just as they were contradictory in England.

The inherited property rights from the English tradition were specific. These included the notions that property should not be forfeited as a punishment for crime without a proper trial; that private persons should not have to house soldiers on demand; that a person's home and possessions should not be subject to government search and seizure without a specific warrant; that government should not take private property for public use without compensation; that government cannot tax its citizens without their consent; and that the government (primarily through its courts) should protect private property against incursion by other citizens. The fact that the colonists viewed these and other English rights to have been violated does not contradict the tension between ownership of land as an absolute privilege and specific limitations on property ownership imposed by "the law of the land." The same contradictions would emerge in the early national period in the United States.

Property Regulation in Colonial America

Two points are noteworthy from the colonial period. First, there was widespread acceptance of the notion that an inherent power of sovereign government included the right to take land for public use, a power later commonly referred to as "eminent domain." Both the English common law and natural law doctrines espoused by European jurists supported the notion that government takings of privately owned property required compensation (Ely 1992, 16). Blackstone, for example, wrote:

> If a new road were to be made through the grounds of a private person . . ., the law permits no man, or set of men, to do this without the consent of the owner of the land. . . . In this, and similar cases the legislature alone can, and indeed frequently does, interpose, and compel the individual to acquiesce. But how does it interpose and compel? Not by absolutely stripping the subject of his property in an arbitrary manner; but by giving him a full indemnification and equivalent for the injury thereby sustained. (Blackstone 1765, 134–35).

Locke also believed that eminent domain was an appropriate power of government under a "consent" theory of representative government: "The essence of representative government is that the citizen delegates to his legislative representatives a power to act for him on his behalf. Because of this delegated power, the legislators may consent on the citizen's behalf that his property shall be given up" (Locke 1970, 378–80).

Historians disagree about the extent to which colonial and early state governments honored the compensation principle (Treanor 1985, 694). But there is no doubt that both before and after the American Revolution governments exercised powers of eminent domain with some frequency, with only the question of valuation, at times, being contentious (Ely 1992, 15). As one legal scholar has summarized, "Early recognition of *eminent domain,* among other forms of property regulation in America, signaled that property rights were not absolute and were subject to numerous legislative controls" (Schultz 1992, 23).

The second noteworthy point from the colonial period is the apparently widespread acquiescence in the power of local government to regulate for the public health, safety, and welfare, later known as the "police power." In general, there was diversity across the laws of the colonies, especially with respect to property. The legal system of each colony consisted of a slow accretion of legislation, selected elements of English common law, and local custom—all leading to divergence among the colonial legal systems. These exercises of self-government resulted in a wide array of property regulation.

In Virginia and Massachusetts, examples included price regulation for commodities such as tobacco, the regulation of bread sold by bakers, the services provided by and the locations of inns, as well as laws governing debt collections. In the Pennsylvania colony, taverns were regulated with respect to location and prices that could be charged for alcohol, meals, lodging, and stable accommodations; and prices for wood products, meat, and grain were approved by the colonial assembly. Inspectors charged inspection fees, and at one time the colony forbade the sale of leather that had not been stamped by an inspector. Any leather sold without inspection could be confiscated. Persons could not construct or operate ferries, bridges, or toll roads without government approval; neither could they charge more than the government-established rate. Prior to the Revolution, Pennsylvania regulated fishing in the Schuylkill River (Hayes 1936, 163, 174). Price controls, commodity regulation, and government control of the right to enter certain occupations continued well after these states established independent governments.

The current justification for applying the Takings Clause broadly to modern land-use regulation relies to some extent upon the historical premise that colonial governments, and the state governments that followed them, regulated land use only minimally. John Hart, among others, suggests that government in the colonial period, contrary to the conventional image of minimal land-use regulation, often exerted extensive authority over private land for many government purposes (Hart 1996, 1252). The Maryland Ironworks Act of 1719, fisheries preservation legislation, and business regulation in colonies such as Pennsylvania provide examples of prerevolutionary property regulation by local governments. Colonial governments also exercised powers of eminent domain to further economic development. Colonial mill acts in several colonies, for example, required owners of property to give up their land, often for minimal payment, to other private citizens who would promise to build a mill.

THE AMERICAN REVOLUTION

In the years leading up to the American Revolution, increasing discontent with British government policies in the colonies focused to a large extent on violations of what the colonists considered to be their property rights. The Quartering Act of 1765, enacted by the British Parliament, forced colonists to house British soldiers upon demand. Writs of assistance gave British government officials a wide-ranging power to search and seize colonists' property. Various customs duties and other taxes imposed on the colonists were mandated by the Parliament, in which the colonists were not represented, and therefore were imposed without consent. The American colonists cited many such instances of abuse of their customary rights in written remonstrations against British government policies. The most well known of these—the Declaration of Independence, of which Thomas Jefferson was the principal author—listed many specific grievances, as though the document itself were a legal brief to prove that the colonists' rights as British subjects had been violated by their government in England. According to this document, the English king had violated his subjects' natural rights, including the right to jury trials before forfeiture of property for a crime and the right to representation in Parliament before being subject to taxation.

Revolution was necessary, according to Jefferson in the Declaration of Independence, to preserve the private property and other rights already granted and protected by English common law. Jefferson drew upon John Locke's philosophy that the protection of property and other natural rights forms the basis for citizens to consent to governmental authority. When a government fails to protect these natural rights, citizens may change their form of government. The colonists declared independence in order to form a new government that would protect their property from government takings in the way that the English common law recognized.

Not all persons shared equally in the emerging concepts of property rights in the colonial period, an inequality that would remain legally sanctioned for a lengthy period in the United States. The Massachusetts Body of Liberties (1641), for example, guaranteed the right to own property, but only to free men. (It also made it illegal for government to take their property away without fair compensation.) In Massachusetts, Jesuits and other groups were excluded from owning property in the colony. In Virginia, property in persons was clearly evident in a 1705 act ("An Act Declaring the Negro Mulatto, and Indian Slaves Within This Dominion, to Be Real Estate") recognizing the status of a person to be a slave if the person's mother was a slave. Slavery as a form of property had existed for more than a century in the American colonies at the time of the Revolution. In addition, under English common law, married women experienced a number of legal disabilities that restricted their ability to own property in their own names. They also encountered numerous restrictions on their business activities, a situation that began to be remedied only with the passage of the Married Women's Property Acts in the middle of the nineteenth century (Salmon 1986, xvi, 97). American independence would have little effect on the legal status and property rights of these persons.

STATE CONSTITUTIONS AND PROPERTY RIGHTS

At the time of the Revolution, the colonists lacked written guarantees of individual rights to which they might turn as a defense to abuses of governmental authority. The emphasis on written guarantees of individual rights in constitutions was a direct result of the revolutionary period. The colonists consistently used the rhetoric of natural rights, and especially property rights, to justify independence and the establishment of new state governments. The constitutions that they enacted following independence from Britain were in operation well before the federal Constitution and the Bill of Rights. It is instructive, therefore, to consider whether the practices of the new state governments—after the establishment of written constitutions—were consistent with the rhetoric of individual property rights advocated by the colonists during the Revolution. Statements regarding the justifications for independence—particularly the necessity to protect individual property rights against British usurpation—sometimes clashed with state governments' regulation of property, and government exercises of authority often prevailed.

Every state constitution was considered higher law and was based on the Lockean idea that the purpose of government as a social compact was to preserve natural rights to life, liberty, and property. The 1776 Declaration of Independence substituted the word "happiness" for "property" in the traditional Lockean trilogy of natural rights, but the "life, liberty, and property" formula was used in many state constitutions. Of the specific rights declared in these early state constitutions, a major emphasis was criminal procedure and the right to a jury trial to guard against the tyranny of the executive power. Although no state had a comprehensive list of rights that were to be protected by government, all states included procedural guarantees of due process and protection from illegal search and seizure of property, in accordance with the rights the colonists viewed themselves as already possessing by virtue of their English heritage.

Preambles of the early state constitutions were full of rhetoric on the protection of natural rights to property. Some examples:

- The Pennsylvania Declaration of Rights of 1776 maintained: "That all men are born equally free and independent, and have certain natural and inherent and inalienable rights, amongst which are the enjoying and defending life and liberty, acquiring, possessing and protecting property, and pursuing and obtaining happiness and safety."
- Similarly, the Virginia Bill of Rights (1776) stated: "That all men are by nature equally free and independent, and have certain inherent rights, of which, when they enter into a state of society, they cannot by any compact deprive or divest their posterity; namely the enjoyment of life and liberty, with the means of acquiring and possessing property, and pursuing and obtaining happiness and safety."
- As another example, the Massachusetts Declaration of Rights of 1780 stated in Article I: "All men are born free and equal, and have certain natural, essential, and unalienable rights; among which may be reckoned the right of enjoying and defending their lives and liberties; that of acquiring, possessing, and protecting property; in fine, that of seeking and obtaining their safety and happiness." Furthermore, Article X stated: "Each individual of the society has a right to be protected by it in the enjoyment of his life, liberty and property, according to standing laws."

The most common language with respect to property rights in the first state constitutions was merely a restatement of Magna

Carta's principle of due process: No free man may be "deprived of his life, liberty, or property, but by the judgment of his peers, or by the law of the land" (Stoebuck 1972, 591). Blackstone recognized that the law of the land provided the rules for usage and ownership of private property. When the new state constitutions invoked similar language, it is unclear precisely what their framers had in mind. At a minimum, any due process clause included the right to jury trials before imprisonment, fines, or deprivation of property as a sanction by the state. Due process also appeared to require equal and neutral enforcement of existing laws, whether common law property rights or duly enacted legislation. Scholars disagree whether the law of the land clause—later to be expressed as due process of law—included substantive limitations on the kinds of laws a legislature might enact, or whether it merely reflected the notion that no one should be deprived of property except under a duly enacted, generally applicable legislative command (Siegan 1989, 116; Letwin 1989, 122).

Interestingly, only a few states included a specific just compensation clause in their constitutions. The Massachusetts Declaration of Rights, for example, stated:

> No part of the property of any individual can, with justice, be taken from him, or applied to public uses, without his own consent, or that of the representative body of the people.... And whenever the public exigencies require that the property of any individual should be appropriated to public uses, he shall receive a reasonable compensation therefor.

The Massachusetts reasonable compensation clause was something of a rarity among the early state constitutions. Only three other state constitutions contained provisions concerned with takings, and none featured a just compensation requirement. The Virginia Declaration of Rights is typical, providing that "no part of a man's property can be taken from him, or applied to public uses, without his own consent, or that of his legal representatives." Government takings of property in these early state documents commonly required "consent" of the owner through the legislature or action by "the representative body of the people." The Vermont constitution stated that "private property ought to be subservient to public uses, when necessity requires it."

The absence of specific compensation clauses in many of the first state constitutions does not mean that those states failed to protect private property from uncompensated government takings. Many state courts held that compensation for government takings was required by the common law. By the 1820s, one author has noted, the principle of just compensation was generally accepted, and courts in five states without a constitutional takings clause nonetheless respected the compensation requirement as a natural right (Treanor 1985, 714–715). For example, in *Vanhorne's Lessee v. Dorrance* (1795), a case decided by the federal Circuit Court of Pennsylvania, the court interpreted Pennsylvania's Declaration of Rights to require compensation for deprivation of title to land even though that document did not explicitly provide for it:

> Such an act would be a monster in legislation, and shock all mankind. The legislature, therefore, had no authority to make an act devesting one citizen of his freehold, and vesting it in another, without a just compensation. It is inconsistent with the principles of reason, justice, and moral rectitude; it is incompatible with the comfort, peace, and happiness of mankind, it is contrary to the principles of social alliance in every free government; and lastly, it is contrary both to the letter and spirit of the [Pennsylvania] Constitution. (*Vanhorne's Lessee* 310)

The specific controversy in that case involved an attempt by the Pennsylvania legislature to resolve a dispute between private citizens over title to land that was itself claimed by both the states of Pennsylvania and Connecticut. The Pennsylvania act had attempted to settle the matter by awarding the disappointed claimants a stake in land elsewhere.

Without a takings clause in its state constitution, a New York court also found the requirement of government compensation for a taking to be grounded in the concept of due process and natural law. In *Gardner v. Village of Newburgh* (1816), Chancellor James Kent required town officials to pay compensation for diverting a stream (in order to create a public water system) that supplied water to a property owner's brickyard, distillery, and mill. Calling the compensation requirement "a clear principle of natural equity" (*Gardner* 166), Kent stated that it would be "unjust, and contrary to the first principles of government" (*Gardner* 168), to take from the landowner his use and enjoyment of the stream of water on his property without compensation.

Yet state governments sometimes assumed sweeping powers with respect to private property. For example, the new state government of Pennsylvania invested the Council of Safety with authority to seize goods "for the army and for the inhabitants" as part of its vast powers "to promote and provide for the preservation of the Commonwealth" (Friedman 1985, 107). During the revolutionary period and thereafter, state governments routinely confiscated property held by former residents who were alleged to have committed treason by their loyalty to Great Britain rather than to the new state governments. These forfeitures were long a source of difficulty for the new federal government in its relations with Britain.

In addition, states also routinely interfered with specific land uses by granting monopolies to private citizens and preventing others from using their own property to engage in that type of business. State courts also enforced the common law of nuisance, through which one property owner could prohibit specific uses of his neighbor's property, and the doctrine of public nuisance permitted the government to accomplish the same thing.

The most notorious activities of state governments with respect to private property—at least according to those who were instrumental in designing the federal Constitution—were debtor relief legislation and the issuance of paper money. Following the American Revolution, state legislatures responded to the volatile and dire economy by enacting laws delaying or preventing the collection of certain debts, including debts that would require forfeiture of the debtor's land. Often pitting commercial interests against individual landowners, this legislation was viewed with alarm by those who contended that such legislation was an interference with natural property rights—the right to invoke state authority to enforce debt collection for contracts. In addition, states attempted to deal with the economic upheaval following the Revolution by repeatedly issuing paper money and declaring the new currency to be satisfactory for the payment of existing debts, practices that led immediately to the devaluation not only of the currency itself but of the economic value of most assets.

State legislatures also asserted the power to tax property of all kinds. Consistent with Locke's view, a tax was a legitimate power of government over property, and not a taking, unless the tax was imposed without legislative approval: "The supreme power cannot take from any man any part of his property without his own consent . . ., that is, the consent of the majority, given it either by themselves of their representatives chosen by them." The 1689 English Declaration of Rights had contained a provision for no taxes without parliamentary consent. The Stamp Act protests by the colonists prior to the Revolution asserted this fundamental right to representation (Rakove 1998, 48).

These justifications for independence from Great Britain, however, were not an indication that the colonists rejected governmental power to tax property. The Pennsylvania Declaration of Rights of 1776, for example, stated that "every member of society hath a right to be protected in the enjoyment of life, liberty and property, and therefore is bound to contribute his proportion towards the expense of that protection." State authority to tax property of all sorts—including land, horses, carriages, and slaves—

was considered a legitimate legislative power by the framers of the new state governments. If property, particularly landed property, were in fact viewed as an inviolable natural right, a property tax that resulted in forfeiture for nonpayment would have no place as a legitimate governmental power. The fact that the power to tax property was not viewed in this way is one manifestation of the general acceptance of Blackstone's view that property rights were limited by the laws of the land.

PROPERTY PROTECTION IN THE U.S. CONSTITUTION

Following independence, the newly constituted states assumed many of the powers previously exercised by colonial governments—and some additional powers as well. Attempts at a stronger federal union through the Articles of Confederation had proven less than successful. The Federalists, the political party most responsible for enactment of the U.S. Constitution in 1789, began their work in response to apparent shortcomings of confederation, particularly in dealings with foreign powers. For many reasons, the Federalists viewed the Articles of Confederation as an embarrassment in foreign relations. The Federalists viewed the confederation government to be stymied and impotent, and they were concerned about "the fate of an empire in many respects the most interesting in the world" (*Federalist Papers* 1788, 1).

The *Federalist Papers*, the classic series of essays written by John Jay, Alexander Hamilton, and James Madison and published in 1787 and 1788, portrayed five primary aims in an effort to convince citizens to ratify the federal Constitution. A federal union as proposed by the Constitutional Convention was necessary

> as our bulwark against foreign danger, as the conservator of peace among ourselves, as the guardian of our commerce and other common interests, as the only substitute for those military establishments

which have subverted the liberties of the Old World, and as the proper antidote for the diseases of faction, which have proved fatal to other popular governments, and of which alarming symptoms have been betrayed by our own. (*Federalist Papers* 1788, 79)

The economic situation in the states led to pessimistic views about the new country's prospects for prosperity and strength under the Articles of Confederation. Alexander Hamilton wrote in *Federalist No. 6*, for example, of "the extreme depression to which our national dignity and credit have sunk" (*Federalist Papers* 1788, 33). The confederation could not compete with European nations in trade, for example, because of conflicting state policies. Many states repudiated foreign obligations and refused to apportion funds toward the debts incurred during the Revolutionary War. Defense from foreign invasion presented yet another difficulty. Federalists viewed with alarm competing proposals to abolish the Articles of Confederation in favor of smaller confederations of states by region, because, along with Hamilton, they firmly believed that "the prosperity of America depended on its Union" (*Federalist Papers* 1788, 12).

Federalists in the 1780s had also become increasingly concerned about the security of individual property rights against the incursions of state legislatures, particularly in light of the number of states that issued paper money and enacted debtor-relief laws. A stronger federal government, they believed, should govern commerce from a national vantage point and prevent such state actions. Because the differing commercial interests of states inevitably led to contention and unwise fiscal policy, the federal government should become the guardian of commerce. In addition, as Hamilton wrote in *Federalist No. 7*,

> Laws in violation of private contracts, as they amount to aggressions on the rights of those States whose citizens are injured by them, may be considered as another probable source of hostility. We are not au-

thorized to expect that a more liberal or more equitable spirit would preside over the legislation of the individual States hereafter, if unrestrained by any additional checks, than we have heretofore seen in too many instances disgracing their several codes. (*Federalist Papers* 1788, 40)

Jennifer Nedelsky has argued that "the original structure of [federal] constitutionalism rested on an effort to prevent democratic control of property. The great focus of the framers was the security of basic rights, property in particular" (Nedelsky 1990, 3, 92). James Madison, the primary author of the federal Constitution, believed that "the two cardinal objects of Government" were "the rights of persons, and the rights of property." Madison, among others, was concerned that factions of citizens in state legislatures would endanger property rights. Madison believed that the function of a constitution should be to protect property, and he favored a federal constitution that would balance rights of individuals and of property (Katz 1976, 479–88). Madison feared tyranny of the majority because of the reality of unequal property distribution. The majority, Madison wrote, would have a natural interest to redistribute larger property accumulations of a smaller percentage of the population (Rakove 1998, 151). "The diversity in the faculties of men, from which the rights of property originate, is not less an insuperable obstacle to an uniformity of interests. The protection of these faculties is the first object of government.... The most common and durable source of factions has been the various and unequal distribution of property" (*Federalist Papers* 1788, 55–56).

John Adams, another important public figure of the postrevolutionary period, agreed:

Power always follows property.... The balance of power in a society, accompanies the balance of property in land. The only possible way, then of preserving the balance of power on the side of equal liberty and virtue, is to make the acquisition of land easy to every member of society, to make a division of land into small quantities, so that the multitude may be possessed of landed estates. If the multitude is possessed of the balance of real estate, the multitude will have the balance of power, and in that case the multitude will take care of the liberty, virtue and interest of the multitude, in all acts of government. (Taylor 1979, 210)

In other words, Adams believed the danger of redistribution of private property was real but could be mitigated by making property ownership a possibility for a larger percentage of the population.

The Founders believed that only property ownership conferred sufficient independence for political participation, and accordingly most states (at least initially) provided that only landowners, or "freeholders," were qualified to vote. Americans frequently cited Blackstone to justify the requirement that voters be property owners. Blackstone wrote:

> The true reason of requiring any qualification, with regard to property, in voters, is to exclude such persons as are in so mean a situation that they are esteemed to have no will of their own. If these persons had votes, they would be tempted to dispose of them under some undue influence or other. This would give a great, an artful, or a wealthy man, a larger share in elections than is consistent with general liberty. (Blackstone 1765, 171)

As late as 1829, Virginia still required that voters own freehold land. Many of the Federalists also supported a landownership requirement for the right to vote as another mechanism to protect private property. Property owners would be more likely to elect representatives who would pursue their interests, and accordingly property would receive a greater measure of protection in legislatures than it might otherwise receive.

Federalists greatly feared any redistributional impulses deriving from the poorer elements in society should they gain majorities in state and local representative bodies. Majority factions in local governments, they thought, were particularly prone to endanger individual property rights. The preventive measure, according to Madison in *Federalist No. 10,* was a larger republic as proposed in the federal Constitution: "A rage for paper money, for an abolition of debts, for an equal division of property, or for any other improper or wicked project, will be less apt to pervade the whole body of the Union than a particular member of it; in the same proportion as such a malady is more likely to taint a particular county or district, than an entire State" (*Federalist Papers* 1788, 61).

Prior to the addition of the Bill of Rights, the federal Constitution protected private property in several key ways. The most important was the Contracts Clause, contained in Article I, section 10. This clause prohibits the states from passing any laws that would "impair the obligation of contracts," a phrase that came to have great significance in the early decades of the nineteenth century as the federal judiciary asserted the authority of judicial review to invalidate state laws that it believed to be prohibited by this clause. The Contracts Clause, about which very little was said at the Constitutional Convention, prohibited state governments from passing laws that prevented enforcement of existing contracts, equating a contractual expectation to a form of property. The primary example of such state legislation had been state debtor relief laws promulgated by virtually every state legislature. The Contracts Clause meant, among other things, that a state legislature could not pass a law releasing people from the responsibility to pay their debts. James Madison and Alexander Hamilton justified the clause as a "constitutional bulwark in favor of personal security and private rights," as well as a "precaution against . . . those practices of State governments, which have undermined the formation of property and credit." Concerning the new federal Constitution generally, Hamilton praised "the additional security which its adoption will afford to the preservation of that species of government, to liberty, and to property" (*Federalist Papers* 1788, 6).

The Constitution contained a number of other restrictions on state legislative power. States could not, for example, pass ex post facto laws, which was understood to prohibit the enactment of criminal laws that operated retroactively (e.g., to punish a person for conduct that had already occurred and was not specifically prohibited at the time). The states also were prohibited from issuing currency or bills of credit, and they could not require anything other than gold or silver coin for payment of debts.

The federal government was given the power to tax as well as exclusive authority to enact uniform bankruptcy laws, to coin money, and to regulate commerce with foreign nations and among the states. Congress was also given authority to "promote the Progress of Science and useful Arts, by securing for limited Times to Authors and Inventors the exclusive Right to their respective Writings and Discoveries," that is, to create rights in intellectual property. Like states, Congress was prohibited from passing ex post facto laws. Congress was also prohibited from passing bills of attainder and imposing a direct tax on state inhabitants.

The primary goal of these property clauses—the limitations on the states as well as the enumerated rights of the federal government—was to protect national commerce and credit. The Federalists viewed the authority to regulate commerce among the states to be critical for national prosperity. The years following independence had proven that each state would pursue a system of commercial policy favorable to itself and would attempt to secure benefits to its own citizens at the expense of the citizens of other states.

In addition to the specific clauses preventing state government interference with private contracts, debts, and the ability to issue currency, Madison's plan to protect private property relied upon the structure of government itself, an institutional design that he hoped would prove sufficient as a method to protect property rights.

Madison argued that the federal legislature, because it was divided into two bodies drawn from a vast geographic area and from large electoral districts, would diffuse the tendency of factions to pass unwise legislation benefiting themselves at the expense of minorities. The enactment process for bills in Congress was purposefully lengthy, and should an unwise measure survive this process, the president possessed the power to veto it. The additional checks and balances among the executive, the legislature, and the judiciary, according to Madison, provided a structural design that would better respect property rights than was the case in state legislatures.

Madison's vision of the central role of property can be seen in his statement that "government is instituted to protect property of every sort.... This being the end of government, that alone is a *just* government, which *impartially* secures to every man, whatever is his *own*" (Madison 1907, 102). Madison himself did not deem it necessary to specifically list individual rights in the federal Constitution in order to accomplish his central purpose of promoting the stability of private property rights. Madison was the most prominent spokesman for many like-minded Federalists who feared that representative governments might not be inclined to protect rights of private property, particularly where the majority owned significantly less property than the minority of wealthy landowners. The result, as had been seen recently in state governments, would be a tendency for the majority to enact economic measures detrimental to the development of individual wealth. In short, they feared that redistribution of wealth would inevitably result from the natural inequalities of property holdings that would exist in any society. Madison believed that it was in the interest of all—both poor and rich—to respect property rights, because only if previously acquired property and contracts were secure would the nation develop a strong economy, a necessary prerequisite for poor citizens to better their lot in life through individual effort. Although the views of those who opposed the federal Constitution are not explored here, it is fair to portray anti-Federalists, in general, as more willing to trust economic matters to state legislative control.

The Framers of the Constitution all seemed to emphasize to some degree the idea that private property should provide a boundary to the scope of legitimate government action. But we have few details of how they expected this to occur or the extent to which state property laws (other than those discharging debts) were violations of private property rights. James Wilson, for example, an important member of the Constitutional Convention, believed that government could legitimately, through the consent of the governed, make whatever property arrangements it saw fit (Nedelsky 1990, 105). Even for Madison, who wrote more about property rights than perhaps any other leading politician of the period, it is unclear what sort of legislative modifications to existing property rules he thought should be prevented.

In sum, contemporary scholars agree that Federalists—the prime movers behind the formation of the federal Constitution and its ratification—believed that a society that safeguarded private property would grow in wealth, and they saw redistribution of property as a central threat. The core group, however, feared majority tyranny as an inherent problem of republican government, with the threat to property "as the paradigmatic instance of majority tyranny" (Nedelsky 1990, 187). If the federal government, not the unreliable states, maintained rules of property and contract, then personal wealth could be better secured. But apart from the potentially expansive goals of the Contracts Clause, it is fair to conclude that the original U.S. Constitution provided no specific protection of private property from the myriad state laws that governed how one might use it.

Property Protection in the Bill of Rights

The U.S. Constitution was not completed with its ratification in 1789. In response to significant anti-Federalist opposition, the first Congress that was elected under the new Constitution proposed the Bill of Rights, a specific list of individual rights to mirror the state constitutions already in existence. Several clauses in the Bill of Rights address property concerns. The most important, the Fifth Amendment, contains in one phrase two clauses with direct reference to property, the Due Process clause and the Takings Clause: "Nor shall any person be deprived of life, liberty, or property, without due process of law; nor shall private property be taken for public use without just compensation."

The Due Process Clause mirrored the standard language of similar clauses in state constitutions and drew from formulations dating back to Magna Carta ("nor shall any person... be deprived of life, liberty, or property, without due process of law"). This standard formulation represented the concept that property forfeitures or other kinds of monetary exactions of individual citizens must be according to generally applicable, duly enacted legislation. As noted previously, the concept of a due process limitation on government action may include a substantive limitation as well, an issue of significant importance in contemporary law.

There are no recorded debates regarding the Takings Clause, and it was not specifically proposed by any state. The Takings Clause appears to be entirely the work of James Madison. Madison introduced the just compensation principle as part of his original draft of the Bill of Rights in Congress on June 8, 1789. The language of this proposal stated: "No person shall be obliged to relinquish his property; where it may be necessary for public use, without a just compensation." The final result preserved Madison's proposal that government takings of private property must receive "just compensation" if "taken for public use."

Madison's proposal as well as the revised final version were modeled upon a clause contained in the Northwest Ordinance, the congressional legislation enacted under the Articles of Confederation to govern the vast area of western lands not yet constituted into state governments. The compensation provision of the Northwest Ordinance stated: "Should the public exigencies make it necessary, for the common preservation, to take any person's property, or to demand his particular services, full compensation shall be made for the same." Earlier, the first Continental Congress, in 1774, listed as the first "right" of the colonists "that they are entitled to life, liberty, [and] property, and they have never ceded to any sovereign power whatever, a right to dispose of either without their consent" (Rakove 1998, 65). Consistent with some of the early state declarations, the Continental Congress apparently would require consent for government takings of private property, but this form of consent, under the Lockean view, could be attributed to a democratic legislature, not an individual right to object to a government's taking of private property for public use. The Fifth Amendment's Takings Clause, deliberately or not, does not invoke consent in either of its possible meanings. Instead, the Takings Clause permits government takings over the objection of property owners as long as just compensation is paid.

The lack of recorded debate about the Takings Clause is not surprising given the relatively lengthy experience in the states with the principle of just compensation. But it is surprising that no state included a just compensation clause among the suggestions submitted for inclusion in the Bill of Rights. The introduction of just compensation in the Fifth Amendment appears to be purely James Madison's idea. Perhaps state citizens were not concerned about takings of private property because the federal government seemed to pose little threat in this regard—as a government of enumerated powers, it was unlikely to be involved in extensive land development plans like state governments. Or perhaps those who considered the subject at all viewed just compensation to be a natural law requirement of sovereign government, exemplified by the due process or law-of-the-land clauses that existed in all state constitutions, which the states had specifically included in proposals for the federal Bill of Rights. Because the concept of compensation for government takings of private property for public use was so thoroughly ingrained in the received English common law, it might not have occurred to the anti-Federalists to specifically propose a compensation clause.

Madison had no illusions about the efficacy of what he termed the mere "parchment barriers" of the Bill of Rights. He also firmly believed that the greatest threat to property rights existed in the states, where factions might gain control and redistribute property for their own benefit. In his speech to the House of Representatives introducing his proposed Bill of Rights, Madison said:

> But I confess that I do conceive, that in a government modified like this of the United States, the great danger lies rather in the abuse of the community than in the legislative body. The prescriptions in favor of liberty, ought to be leveled against that quarter where the greatest danger lies, namely, that which possess the highest prerogative of power: But this is not found in either the executive or legislative departments of government, but in the body of the people, operating by the majority against the minority. (Rakove 1998, 177)

Madison merely repeated what he had previously written in many of his *Federalist* essays, most notably in *Federalist No. 10:* The greatest danger to private property came from state and local legislation, not the national government.

Interestingly, although the federal Constitution was understood to confer upon Congress only those powers enumerated, the Takings Clause assumes a power in the federal government to appropriate land for public use that is not elsewhere specified as an enumerated right. An early federal court decision, *Vanhorne's Lessee v. Dorrance* (1795), treated eminent domain as an inherent power of government. Explaining the origin of this power not only in the federal government but also in the states, the U.S. Supreme Court later wrote in *Kohl v. United States* (1875):

> Such an authority is essential to the [federal government's] independent existence and perpetuity. These cannot be preserved if the obstinacy of a private person, or if any other authority, can prevent the acquisition of the means or instruments by which alone governmental functions can be performed.... No one doubts the existence in the State governments of the right of *eminent domain*—a right distinct from and paramount to the right of ultimate ownership. It grows out of the necessities of their being, not out of the tenure by which lands are held. The right is the offspring of political necessity; and it is inseparable from sovereignty, unless denied to it by its fundamental law. (*Kohl* 371–372)

In addition to the Due Process and Takings Clauses of the Fifth Amendment, the Seventh Amendment was also understood to protect private property. The Seventh Amendment guarantees the right to jury trials in civil cases arising under the common law. The amendment reflects the commonly held view that juries were essential to the protection of private property rights. The Virginia Declaration of Rights in 1776, for example, included "That in controversies respecting property, and in suits between man and man, the ancient trial by jury is preferable to any other, and ought to be held sacred" (Rakove 1998, 84). The Pennsylvania Declaration of Rights of that same year copied this language, substituting "the parties have a right to trial by jury" for the phrase "ancient trial by jury is preferable to any other" (Rakove 1998, 86). The commonwealth of Massachusetts, in its 1780 Declaration of Rights, included a modified version of the same sentiment: "In all controversies concerning property; and in all suits between two or more persons . . ., the parties have a right to trial by jury; and this method of procedure shall be held sacred" (Rakove 1998, 92). State constitutions routinely included the right to jury trials in civil as well as criminal cases, specifically to include the resolution of property disputes.

In an essay opposing ratification of the federal Constitution, one writer again linked the protection of private property to the availability of jury trials:

These provisions are as necessary under the general government as under that of the individual states; for the power of the former is as complete to the purpose of requiring bail, imposing fines, inflicting punishments, granting search warrants, and seizing persons, papers, or property, in certain cases, as the other. For the purpose of securing the property of the citizens, it is declared by all the states, "that in all controversies at law, respecting property, the ancient mode of trial by jury is one of the best securities of the rights of the people, and ought to remain sacred and inviolable." Does not the same necessity exist of reserving this right, under this national compact, as in that of this state? (Rakove 1998, 130)

In the states, juries also were viewed to be the proper body to decide what constituted just compensation for government takings of private property for public use. In *Vanhorne's Lessee v. Dorrance* (1795, 315), Justice William Patterson wrote that "the interposition of a jury is . . . a constitutional guard upon property, and a necessary check to legislative authority. . . . As long as it is preserved, the rights of private property will be in no danger of violation, except in cases of absolute necessity, or great public danger." In that case, the Pennsylvania legislature had provided for the amount of compensation to be determined by a board of property, not a jury, one of the reasons that the court invalidated the act under the Pennsylvania constitution.

The U.S. Constitution's Bill of Rights, however, had little effect on private property rights, one way or another, for the first century following the establishment of the United States. The implicit understanding at the time was that amendments two through eight restricted only the national government, not state governments. In *Barron v. Baltimore* (1833), the U.S. Supreme Court confirmed that the Takings Clause applied only to the federal government. The city of Baltimore made harbor improvements that caused a privately owned wharf to no longer accommodate ships. The owner of the wharf sued the city under the Fifth Amendment for just compensation for the city's actions. The Supreme Court rejected the claim because the Takings Clause applied only to the federal government; it did not restrict state or local governments, the primary authorities over the private property of most U.S. citizens. The fact that the Takings Clause would apply to the states at the close of the nineteenth century is itself the story of a remarkable constitutional transformation.

Property Regulation after the Founding Period

The tradition in which the U.S. Constitution was created recognized that regulation of private property was primarily, if not exclusively, a state and local government responsibility. In *Gibbons v. Ogden* (1824), Chief Justice John Marshall recognized that "the right to use all property, must be subject to modification by municipal law. . . . It belongs exclusively to the local state legislatures, to determine how a man may use his own, without injuring his neighbor" (*Gibbons* 53–54). The federal government's enhanced supervisory role with respect to contracts and commerce did not displace the broad range of state and local authority over private property.

State common law rules governing the use of private property were extremely important in this period. Among other limitations recognized by state courts, a property owner whose use of his property constituted a nuisance could be prevented from that use as a result of a lawsuit brought by affected neighbors. Particular uses of property that might constitute a nuisance never received precise description but were said generally to be any unreasonable interference with the use or enjoyment, or convenience and comfort, of an adjacent landowner. A nuisance might be the diversion of water from a mill, interference with a market, smoke from a foundry, noxious gases or unpleasant odors (such as keeping pigs in an urban area), the pollution of a stream, unsightly premises, or a pond harboring mosquitoes. The common law of nuisance reflected relative property rights: Whether a particular use of property constituted a nuisance with respect to neighbors depended upon whether that use was deemed appropriate for the location. Particularly when juries determined whether a particular use constituted a nuisance, the outcome can be said to have reflected community values with respect to the appropriate uses of property.

State and local governments might also prosecute an individual landowner for activity on his land that constituted a public nuisance. A public nuisance was defined as an interference with the rights of the community and could be remedied by either a criminal prosecution by local authorities or the abatement of the nuisance by an injunctive decree or court order. English common law defined a public nuisance to be anything that "obstructs or causes inconvenience or damage to the public in the exercise of rights common to all Her Majesty's subjects," a definition readily adopted by U.S. courts. Public gaming houses, houses of prostitution, keeping a vicious dog, or even "the collection of an inconvenient crowd" were some of the activities held by state courts to constitute a public nuisance.

The related doctrine of public necessity recognized that property might be destroyed or damaged, without compensation to the owner, to prevent a threatened injury or danger to a community or group of persons. In the nineteenth century, examples included the destruction of a building to prevent the spread of a fire, shooting a dangerous dog in the street, burning clothing thought to be infected with smallpox, destruction of alcohol to prevent misuse, and, during wartime, the destruction of property to prevent its use by the enemy. The owner's loss of property in these circumstances did not require compensation.

A number of common law doctrines also adjusted rights between individual property owners. For a time, U.S. courts recognized the English common law doctrine of ancient lights, by which a landowner could be prohibited from building a structure that would block the sunlight flowing to an adjacent owner. Other common law rights for property owners included the right of downstream owners to water flow and the right of lateral support for adjacent preexisting structures. State courts also readily enforced servitudes, easements, and other contracts restricting the use of land.

The common law (and statutory law in some states) recognized some limitations upon the disposition of property by an owner. Married women had the right of widow's dower in property owned by their husbands (typically one-third life interest in land owned by the husband at death). This doctrine sometimes resulted in the forfeiture of property innocently purchased if the sale made by the husband would have the effect of disinheriting his wife from her right of dower. Furthermore, a property owner might lose ownership of his land through the common law doctrine of adverse possession. Under this doctrine, a trespasser might gain ownership rights in land by living on it, or through some other substantial and open use for a period of years set by the legislature, if the original owner did not enforce his rights to evict the trespasser. Adverse possession favored active over passive use of property. In these instances, community values reflected in the common law restricted an owner's perceived absolute dominion over his property.

State governments in the decades following ratification of the federal Constitution also enacted legislation that significantly restricted the uses of private property and sometimes, in so doing, imposed severe economic burdens without compensation (Novak 1996; Hart 2000). Town planning was a prime example of property regulation for a larger community benefit. State legislatures in New York, Georgia, Virginia, Connecticut, and Massachusetts authorized local governments to appoint surveyors and create rules for buildings in urban areas, including setbacks, minimum size, and other aesthetic and safety regulations. In New Haven, Connecticut, for example, the city required landowners to obtain permission from the town prior to erecting a building in order that "a regular and beautiful arrangement of the buildings be preserved" (Hart 2000, 1109–1111).

Other state legislation required landowners to erect fences, construct dikes or ditches, and drain land and compelled suitable private lands to be used for mining and metal production (although with compensation if the owner chose not to develop a mine or metal production on his land). Some states also enacted laws designed to ensure productive use of land, most notably the threat of forfeiture for property owners who did not occupy or improve their land (Hart 2000, 1130–1131). William Novak has argued that private property was heavily regulated in the antebellum era, and there was no clear separation of the market from government (Novak 1996).

State legislatures also changed inheritance laws with some frequency. Thomas Jefferson, in particular, advocated abolition of primogeniture and entail, English laws that tended to concentrate lands in family dynasties and prohibited sales of parts of large estates. States enacted laws providing a statutory share of an estate for spouses and, in the absence of a will, providing equal distribution to children. One author has noted that reform of inheritance laws

> manifested a philosophical reorientation with respect to the concept of property rights. The remaining presupposition—that the power of testamentary disposition, like other capacities to use and transfer property, is a 'natural right' upon which the state cannot rightly infringe—was permanently displaced by the doctrine that an individual's rights in property subsist by grace of society. Under this view, the state justifiably limits property rights where their exercise would contravene higher social values. (Katz 1977, 25)

That state governments retained considerable control over the regulation of uses of private property seems consistent with Federalist views of the arrangement of power under the new Constitution. Hamilton wrote in *Federalist No. 17* that one "transcendent advantage belonging to the province of State governments"—the ordinary administration of criminal and civil justice—"being the immediate and visible guarding of life and property . . . regulating all those personal interests and familiar concerns to which the sensibility of individuals is more immediately awake, contributes, more than any other circumstance, to impressing upon the minds of the people, affection, esteem, and reverence towards the government" (Hamilton 1788, 102). Madison added that

> The powers delegated by the proposed Constitution to the federal government are few and defined. Those which are to remain in the State governments are numerous and indefinite. . . . The powers reserved to the several States will extend to all the objects which, in the ordinary course of affairs; concern the lives, liberties, and properties of the people, and the internal order, improvement, and prosperity of the State. (Madison 1788, 298)

And *Federalist No. 54* noted that in "several of the States, and particularly in the State of New York, one branch of the government is intended more especially to be the guardian of property, and is accordingly elected by that part of the society which is most interested in this object of government" (Madison 1788, 351–352). Even in the states, then, legislatures also played a role as the guardian of property.

Although states exerted significant control over the acquisition and uses of private property, at the same time the states were equally committed, along with the Federalists, to the security of private property. The authors of both the federal and the various state constitutions would have viewed a primary government obligation to be the protection of private property from the forceful deprivation of others as well as the government. State courts and law enforcement personnel aggressively enforced state laws protecting private property from trespass and theft by others. State constitutions frequently contained explicit protection of private homes from government intrusion, as did the Massachusetts Declaration of Rights of 1780: "Every subject has a right to be secure from all unreasonable searches, and seizures of his person, his houses, his papers, and all his possessions." Due process and jury trial guarantees were designed to ensure, among other things, that no property was confiscated as a penalty for a crime without a proper trial.

States as well as the federal government clearly possessed the authority to take property as a penalty for violation of a law. Americans accepted Blackstone's view that if "a member of any national community violates the fundamental contract of his association, by transgressing the municipal law . . ., the state may very justly resume that portion of property, or any part of it, which the laws have before assigned him" (Blackstone 1765, I: 138, 299).

Where did this state authority over private property originate? Most state governments after independence from Britain simply assumed the same role with respect to private property that the British sovereign had claimed. The primary example was the issuance of land patents, in most colonies solely a prerogative of the crown government. For example, the present-day version of an early statue in Georgia, entitled "Origin of Title to Land," states: "The title to all lands originates in grants from the Government, and since its independence, from the state." Another provision of the Georgia code provides: "All realty in this state is held under the state as the original owner thereof." This statute, too, is the modern version of a statute enacted soon after independence. Valid title to land, after statehood, meant that the owner could trace his or her title back to a land patent issued either from the crown or from the new state government. (Land title to property located in territories that had not yet become states required a land patent issued by the federal government.) Under British law, vacant lands—those not already granted by the crown—were vested in the crown, and the exclusive power to grant them resided there. The principle was fully recognized in this country after the Revolution.

The distribution of public land to private owners was an interesting phenomenon in the early years of the republic. The states as well as the federal government issued land patents to raise government funds. The process was often rife with abuse and confusion. After the Revolutionary War, Governor George Mathews of Georgia signed land grants of significantly greater amounts than the legislature had authorized. He granted 1.5 million acres to a single man and a total of 2.6 million acres to three persons in a county with an area of only 400,000 acres. By the end of his term, outstanding land grants totaled three times the amount of land available in Georgia.

Native American Lands

The question of original landownership proved particularly troublesome with respect to lands occupied by Native Americans. Georgia was not alone in its effort to sell Native American lands to settlers, even those lands explicitly protected by treaties with the U.S. government. A series of cases decided by the Supreme Court in the early 1800s, most importantly *Johnson v. M'Intosh* (1823), established several propositions with respect to Indian lands. The government of the United States, not those of the states, succeeded to the rights of the British crown with respect to Indian land. Under the European doctrine of discovery, the European power that first "discovered" land in America had the exclusive right to appropriate for itself any lands occupied by native inhabitants, either through conquest or purchase. English law, adopted by the Court in *Johnson v. M'Intosh,* treated Native American lands as owned in fee simple by the crown, subject to a vague right of occupancy in the tribes. Thus, if their lands were neither conquered nor purchased, Native Americans retained a right of occupancy only.

In *Worcester v. Georgia* (1832), Chief Justice John Marshall wrote that "the United States succeeded to all the claims of Great Britain, both territorial and political" (*Worcester* 544). Because the U.S. Constitution provided an exclusive right in the federal government to engage in commerce with the Native Americans (the so-called Indian Commerce Clause), states could not grant land occupied by Indians or pass laws regulating property rights or other matters for tribal land. Georgia ignored these Supreme Court rulings and allowed settlers to appropriate gold mines on Cherokee land within the state's boundaries, a situation leading to the forced removal of the Cherokees by the federal government in an episode that became known as the Trail of Tears.

This series of Supreme Court decisions not only centered rights to Native American lands in the federal government; they also nullified any individual claim to land that had been purchased directly from a Native American tribe. Any such purchase was worthless, as it would not be upheld by state or federal courts. Many disappointed purchasers appeared in court proceedings in the decades following independence.

The succession of the federal government to the rights of the British crown with respect to Native American lands is only one manifestation of the more general phenomenon of the transfer of sovereignty after the Revolution. States issuing land patents on occasion did so with an express reservation of right with respect to that land, either for the use to which it might be put, or to the type of buildings that might be placed there, particularly in urban areas. State government practices with respect to land patents were in some tension with the Lockean view that the right to obtain and hold property does not derive from the sovereign but is the common heritage of man.

The theory that the new state and federal governments were the original owners of lands has a number of other manifestations. The power to retake land for public use, in one line of thought, is impliedly reserved when land is patented by the state. The Constitutional Court of South Carolina was evenly divided on this question in *Lindsay v. Commissioners* (1796). The reversion to the state of any property owned by a person who dies without a will or without living heirs is another manifestation. Forfeitures of property for treason or lesser crimes, and limiting property ownership to citizens, also seem to originate here. These beliefs about the origins of private property rights figure in contemporary debates about the extent to which the government, as the original owner, retains property interests in private land as a justification for regulatory restrictions on its use.

The Federal Contracts Clause and the Protection of Vested Rights

The U.S. Supreme Court's enforcement of the Contracts Clause of the federal Constitution was a significant protection for private property for most of the nineteenth century. The federal judiciary, under the lead of Chief Justice John Marshall, used the Contracts Clause and a natural law concept of vested rights in property to nullify state legislation that interfered with property and contract rights. The Contracts Clause prohibited states from enacting any laws that would "impair the obligation of contracts," a phrase that the Marshall Court interpreted to protect economic rights from retroactive impairment by state governments.

Fletcher v. Peck (1810) was the first important decision by the U.S. Supreme Court on the extent to which the federal Constitution would override state legislation affecting property rights. At the close of the eighteenth century, the Georgia legislature sold more than 40 million acres of land, for about a penny an acre, to several land companies, all of whom had bribed members of the legislature. A number of Georgia legislators were major stockholders in the companies. Public outcry following the sale resulted in the election of a new legislature, which promptly rescinded the prior sale.

The state refunded the money paid for the land, but some of the land had already been resold by the companies to other persons, a large number of whom lived in other states. One such purchaser brought suit in federal court, claiming that the Georgia legislature could not rescind the deal with respect to innocent purchasers of the land. Chief Justice Marshall agreed. The Supreme Court struck down the Georgia legislature's attempt to rescind the deal as unconstitutional.

Justice Marshall's opinion extolled the sanctity of vested rights in property and secured a broad meaning to the Contracts Clause:

> The framers of the constitution viewed, with some apprehension, the violent acts which might grow out of the feelings of the moment.... The people of the United States, in adopting that instrument, have manifested a determination to shield themselves and their property from the effects of those sudden and strong passions to which men are exposed. The restrictions on the legislative power of the states are obviously founded in this sentiment. (*Fletcher* 137–138)

In *Fletcher*, Marshall equated a state's grant of land with a contract right. Marshall did not ground the unconstitutionality of the Georgia act solely on the authority of the Contracts Clause. He also cited "certain great principles of justice," "equity," and "those rules of property which are common to all citizens of the United States" (*Fletcher* 133, 134). Justice William Johnson, concurring in the result, did not base his decision on the Contracts Clause at all. Instead, he invoked natural law to invalidate the Georgia legislature's action: "A State does not possess the power of revoking its own grants . . . on a general principle, on the reason and nature of things: a principle which will impose laws even on the Deity" (*Fletcher* 143). However, Johnson noted that state regulations were often "within the most correct limits of legislative powers, and most beneficially exercised" (*Fletcher* 145).

Following *Fletcher v. Peck*, the Supreme Court invoked the Contracts Clause to protect corporate charters (*Dartmouth College v. Woodward* [1819]) and other types of agreements, as well as property in land, from state legislative control. Consistent with views expressed by Madison and others, the federal judiciary interpreted the Contracts Clause to encompass vested rights as expressed in contracts to protect private property against the whims of legislative majorities. The Marshall Court used the concept of vested rights to protect almost anything to which one could claim preexisting ownership against certain kinds of state intrusion. The concept of a vested right in property signified an ownership interest that had become complete, such that depriving a person of the property upset settled expectations. The vested rights doctrine of the nineteenth century was based largely on a natural rights view of property ownership.

The protection of vested rights in property was not only an interest of the federal judiciary; many state courts enforced this doctrine as well, even though state constitutions typically did not contain a contracts clause. In *Wynehamer v. The People* (1856), for example, a New York court held that a state liquor prohibition statute violated the due process clause of the New York constitution to the extent that it forbade the sale of alcoholic beverages owned prior to the enactment of the law. The New York court defined "property" broadly enough to include liquor, deeming it "as much entitled to the protection of the constitution as lands, houses, or chattels of any description" (*Wynehamer* 384). Because alcohol previously had been bought and sold commercially, it qualified as property subject to constitutional protection. "It is certain," the court wrote, "that the legislature cannot totally annihilate commerce in any species of property, and so condemn the property itself to extinction" (*Wynehamer* 399). According to the New York court, "All property is equally sacred in view of the constitution" (*Wynehamer* 385).

The *Wynehamer* court recognized that legislative regulation of property was a necessary and justified exercise of state sovereignty, but those powers had limits: "Between a regulation and destruction there is somewhere, however difficult to define with precision, a line of separation" (*Wynehamer* 399). The court thought this line had been crossed because the New York statute forbade the sale of alcohol already in stock: "We only say that, in all such legislation, the essential right of the citizen to his property must be preserved; a right which includes the power of disposition and sale, to be exercised under such restraints as a just regard both to the public good and private rights may suggest" (*Wynehamer* 405). Throughout the nineteenth century, disagreement centered on where to draw the line between legitimate government regulatory authority and violation of individual private property rights.

The U.S. Supreme Court struggled to find a line of demarcation as well. In *Calder v. Bull* (1798, 388), Justice Samuel Chase wrote: "There are certain vital principles in our free republican governments which will determine and overrule an apparent and flagrant abuse of legislative power." Justice Chase gave as an example "a law that takes property from A, and gives it to B"; such an act, according to Chase, violated natural law: "It is against all reason and justice for a people to intrust a legislature with such powers; and, therefore, it cannot be presumed that they have done it" (*Calder* 388). Nevertheless, Chase recognized that other rules governing private property, short of a legislature's taking property from one person to give to another, were properly determined by society:

> It seems to me, that the *right of property*, in its origin, could only arise from *compact express*, or *implied*, and I think it the better opinion, that the *right*, as well as the *mode*, or *manner*, of acquiring property, and of alienating or transferring, inheriting, or transmitting it, is conferred by society ... and is always subject to the rules prescribed by positive law. (*Calder* 394)

The Supreme Court eventually settled on the view that states might, consistent with the Contracts Clause, enact legislation that affected only future property rights. Even though evidence from the founding period suggests that the Framers intended the Contracts Clause primarily to prevent state debtor relief laws, the U.S. Supreme Court recognized in *Ogden v. Saunders* (1829) that states could enact bankruptcy laws that had prospective effect. That is, a state did not violate the sanctity of an existing contract by prescribing debtor relief rules that operated only on contracts entered in the future and did not affect any preexisting contractual obligations.

Throughout the nineteenth century, the traditional concept of a state's police power was an important determining factor between state legislation that would violate property rights protected by the federal Contracts Clause and legitimate governmental regulation of property. Police powers were said to be those government endeavors that relate to the safety, health, morals, and general welfare of the public. At the close of the U.S. Civil War, an influential law treatise described a state's police power to

> embrace its system of internal regulation, by which it is sought not only to preserve the public order and to prevent offenses against the state, but also to establish for the intercourse of citizen with citizen those rules of good manners and good neighborhood which are calculated to prevent a conflict of rights, and to insure to each the uninterrupted enjoyment of his own, so far as is reasonably consistent with a like enjoyment of rights by others. (Cooley 1868, 572)

Police powers were broad-ranging and were considered an essential component of state sovereignty.

The U.S. Supreme Court recognized that states exercised wide authority to enact laws that affected property rights under the authority of its police power. In *Mugler v. Kansas* (1887), for example, the Court upheld a prohibition law as a valid use of the state police power to protect health and morals. Justice John Harlan noted, however, that there were "limits beyond which legislation cannot rightfully go" (*Mugler* 661), although neither this court opinion, nor others in the nineteenth century, described what those limits might be.

Slaves as Property

One form of property that came to be viewed as a vested right—property in persons—held a peculiar place in the constitutional doctrines of the antebellum United States. The introduction in the colonies of the institution of slavery brought with it a need for the colonists, and subsequently the independent states, to establish rules governing ownership of slaves. Slavery was unknown in English common law—it did not exist in Great Britain, and British law recognized slavery as contrary to the law of nature. This view posited that slavery could not exist in the absence of government laws creating and sanctioning the institution, a view that categorized the existence of slavery as a matter of positive law created by sovereign mandate.

The colonial governments, and later those independent states that retained slavery following the Revolution, slowly developed a body of law governing the institution of slavery. Statutes dictated that the children of a slave mother would also be slaves. Other legislation further defined the classification of slaves as property—including how this property in persons would be treated under the laws of succession (following the death of the owner), as well as mechanisms for taxing the value of the property represented by slaves. Drawing upon ancient Roman law as well as English rules applicable to other forms of property, judges in slave states fashioned a number of common law rules to deal with property disputes over slaves as they arose. Slaves fit uneasily into the received English common law tradition because of their dual status as chattel (personal property) and living persons. But it was clear that for most purposes that mattered to slave owners, slaves were defined as private property and were treated as such under the law.

Although many courts in the United States recognized that slavery did not exist as a matter of natural or common law, this form of property, once created, was due the same degree of protection as any other property. Slave ownership was viewed as a vested right of property. With some noted disagreement from a few abolitionist lawyers and legislators, the standard view was that any government effort to abolish the institution of slavery would require compensation to slave owners for the market value of their slaves. State governments, for example, routinely compensated the owners of slaves executed by the state for rebellion or other crimes. The Kentucky constitution of 1850 unambiguously declared the ownership of slaves to be a constitutionally protected right: "The right of the owner of a slave, to such slave, and its increase, is the same, and as inviolable as the right of the owner of any property whatever."

Debates in the Virginia legislature in 1832, at a time in which Virginia was the largest slave-holding state in the union, provide an interesting example of the view of slavery as a constitutionally protected form of property. Abolitionist legislators in that year proposed a plan for the gradual end of slavery in Virginia. Under this plan, all children born to slaves after 1840 would eventually gain their freedom. The plan did not disturb property rights in slaves currently owned, but it did not provide compensation for the emancipation of slave children born after 1840. The proposal was modeled after similar successful plans for gradual abolition in Northern states, including Pennsylvania.

The proposal was defeated with little effort. In opposition to the plan, James Gholson said that it was a "monstrous and unconstitutional" violation of property rights because it "proposed the appropriation of private property without just compensation." The future progeny of slaves was a vested right, he maintained, equally subject to the requirement of compensation for the government's taking as land would be. Slavery in Virginia had acquired the same constitutional protections as any other property, and thus the proslavery delegates argued that they were defending not merely slavery but the inviolability of all private property from government intrusion.

The sponsors of the proposal disagreed that principles of just compensation would require payment to slave owners for emancipation of children of slaves born in the future. Instead, they had argued, the state's police power justified emancipation of slaves without compensation. They suggested that slavery as a species of property had become so harmful to the public safety and morals that state legislatures could rightfully regulate the property—even abolish it as a form of property—without any compensation to the owners. They maintained that the constitutional guarantee of just compensation for property referred exclusively to the common law definition of property. They argued that property rights in slaves, unknown to the common law or natural law, were created by the legislature. Accordingly, the legislature could declare that slaves were no longer property, without the necessity to provide just compensation. This argument did not succeed in Virginia or anywhere else in the antebellum period. The Virginia abolitionists' arguments about the police power were a distinctly minority view, even though they were similar to the arguments states used to defend their regulatory power against the federal judiciary's interpretations of the Contracts Clause.

Abraham Lincoln also believed that emancipation required compensation, as the plan for emancipation in the District of Columbia required. The Emancipation Proclamation (1863) freed only slaves in states then in rebellion during the Civil War, leaving in bondage all of the slaves remaining in states loyal to the Union. In accordance with the prevalent view, only a constitutional amendment could alter slaves' status as property in states remaining in the Union unless slave owners were compensated. The

Thirteenth Amendment eventually ended slavery everywhere in the United States, but it did so without compensation.

The compensation question was significant. In 1832, in Virginia, one legislator estimated the cost to purchase all of the slaves located in that state to be $115 million. The total value of slaves in the United States in 1860, on the eve of the Civil War, was thought to be approximately $3 billion (Huston 1999, 251). Fulfillment of the obligation to compensate slave owners for emancipation was well beyond the means of the federal or any state government.

Drawing on the rhetoric of the founding period, some Southerners defined their "liberties" as the right to own slaves with no federal governmental interference. These slave owners viewed Congress's attempts to prevent slavery in federal territories as a violation of the federal Constitution. They claimed the right to emigrate to the territories with their property, citing, among other provisions, the Fugitive Slave Clause of the federal constitution as a recognition of slavery as a property right. According to Jefferson Davis, soon to become president of the Confederacy, "As a property recognized by the Constitution, and held in a portion of the States, the Federal Government is bound to admit it into all the Territories, and to give it such protection as other private property receives" (Cooper 2000, 204).

The U.S. Supreme Court in *Dred Scott v. Sandford* (1856) endorsed this Southern view of property rights. In *Dred Scott* Chief Justice Roger Taney wrote that Congress was without authority to ban slavery in federal lands. More importantly, *Dred Scott* essentially recognized slave ownership as a vested right of property and hence subject to constitutional protection. Abraham Lincoln and the Republicans stated their intention to disregard the *Dred Scott* decision, one of the contributing factors leading to secession and the Civil War.

Following secession, the states of the Confederacy enacted a constitution that mirrored almost exactly the federal Constitution, including its Contracts, Due Process, and Takings Clauses, with the addition of a clause explicitly recognizing slaves as property. Interestingly, Jefferson Davis recognized that constitutional protection of slavery required the exercise of a local government's police powers over this form of property. Davis wrote that if the inhabitants of a territory refused to adopt "police regulations" for the protection of slave property, "it would be rendered more or less valueless—the insecurity would be so great that the owner could not ordinarily retain it." The right to own slaves would remain, but "the remedy withheld, it would follow that the owner would be practically debarred by the circumstances of the case, from taking slave property into a territory where the sense of the inhabitants was opposed to its introduction" (Cooper 2000, 328). In slave states, the institution of slavery was highly regulated, and slave codes were often justified as necessary to preserve the property interests of slave owners.

The slavery issue was one of the most prominent areas of debate about property rights in the first half of the nineteenth century. The debates over slavery were central events leading to the Civil War, yet these debates reflected more generally American views of the status of private property in constitutional government. The events leading to the Civil War made clear what had been implicit at the time of the founding: The U.S. Constitution's property guarantees rely upon state definitions and historical tradition to determine what constitutes a vested interest in property. These societal definitions, in turn, could define even persons as property for the purpose of constitutional protection. The *Dred Scott* decision itself may contribute to the modern Supreme Court's tendency to claim that the federal judiciary is not responsible for defining property; it merely enforces what custom or state law has decreed to be property.

Eminent Domain in the State Courts

The compensation principles at issue in the debate over slavery derived from the long experience in the states with exercises of the government's power of eminent domain. Throughout the nineteenth century, state governments engaged in extensive development efforts, including the construction of highways, railroads, and canals, necessitating the condemnation of private land. By comparison, the federal government was rarely involved in such activities.

Many states routinely delegated their power of eminent domain to private companies for construction of public utilities and transportation. These private companies had the power to negotiate with landowners for purchase of their land, including stone and timber on adjacent land to be used for construction projects. Failing agreement on price, state legislatures gave some private companies authority to initiate a condemnation proceeding for the land. The condemnation proceeding required a court's valuation of the land to complete the process of eminent domain.

State courts and legislatures in the nineteenth century developed a number of practices to limit the amount of compensation required to be paid to landowners, thereby aiding state governments' development aims generally and the private companies specifically (Scheiber 1971). The primary example was the judicially created doctrine of offsetting benefits. A property owner whose land was crossed by a railroad track, for example, might receive payment that reflected the supposed benefit he received from having a railroad nearby. Often, the payment due to the landowner for the value of the land taken was offset by this supposed benefit, deducted from what would otherwise be the fair market value of the property (Ely 2001). Some courts believed that the value to the owner of the nearby railroad track, highway, or canal exceeded the value of the condemned portion of the land, resulting in no payment at all for the taking of that property.

State courts also limited the requirement of just compensation to a narrow view of what constituted a government taking. Inadvertent damage to an adjacent structure from construction of a road, for example, was not a taking. Furthermore, a depreciated value of land did not entitle a landowner to compensation because there had been no direct appropriation of the landowner's title (Ely 1998, 77).

Until the 1870s, the federal judiciary had few opportunities to construe the Fifth Amendment's Takings Clause because Congress rarely engaged directly in federal projects that required the exercise of eminent domain. When the Supreme Court did have the opportunity to consider the meaning of the Takings Clause, however, it seemed to construe the clause to require compensation only for direct appropriations of title to land or instances in which the government's actions resulted in a physical invasion of a permanent nature. In the *Legal Tender Cases* (1871, 551), for example, the Supreme Court noted that the federal Takings Clause "has always been understood as referring only to a direct appropriation, and not to consequential injuries resulting from the exercise of lawful power. It has never been supposed to have any bearing upon, or to inhibit laws that indirectly work harm and loss to individuals." In *Pumpelly v. Green Bay Co.* (1871), the Court required compensation to be paid to a property owner whose land was permanently flooded during the construction of a dam. Government actions that indirectly impaired the value of land, without a physical invasion or appropriation of title to the land, did not require compensation.

The Close of the Nineteenth Century: The Fourteenth Amendment and Incorporation

In the latter part of the nineteenth century, the Supreme Court assumed an important role in defining the economic rights of individuals and corporations. The Fourteenth Amendment (1868) prohibited states from denying "due process of law" to any persons within its borders, a prohibition enforceable by the federal government and its courts. Beginning in the mid-1880s, the

Supreme Court interpreted the Fourteenth Amendment's Due Process Clause to impose substantive limits on state laws regulating economic activity, referred to by later jurists as "substantive," or "economic," due process. The Court struck down a number of state laws that it viewed as infringing private property rights. In *Allgeyer v. Louisiana* (1897), for example, the Supreme Court recognized the concept of economic due process as a constitutionally protected liberty interest. The doctrine of substantive due process reached its highest point in the early decades of the twentieth century. (Chapter 3 considers this evolution in greater detail.)

The Contracts Clause, by contrast, declined in importance in the late nineteenth century, and since then the Supreme Court has rarely invalidated state actions on the basis of that clause. Scholars offer several explanations for the decline of the Contracts Clause (Ely 1998, 93, 115–116). The most important factor appears to be the emergence of a new tool for federal court review of state actions alleged to impair private property rights. As explained in Chapter 3, the relative demise of the Contracts Clause coincided with the Supreme Court's new view that the Due Process Clause of the Fourteenth Amendment prevented state governments from interfering with economic rights. Through the Fourteenth Amendment, federal courts could protect the same interests formerly considered to violate the obligation of contracts. The choice of the Fourteenth Amendment, rather than the Contracts Clause, to protect economic interests from state interference may have been the judiciary's response to the changed constitutional priorities following the Civil War.

The ratification of the Fourteenth Amendment in 1868 resulted in another fundamental change in U.S. constitutionalism, although not one that was recognized immediately. In the early decades of the twentieth century, the U.S. Supreme Court determined that the Fourteenth Amendment "incorporated" a number of the provisions in the federal Bill of Rights to apply against state action, reversing a long-established tradition dating back to at least *Barron v. Baltimore* (1833). In *Chicago, B. & Q. R.R. v. City of Chicago* (1897), the Supreme Court concluded that the just compensation principle for takings of private property applied to state and local governments. Because the Court believed that just compensation was an essential element of due process of law, the Fourteenth Amendment effectively abrogated the long-standing tradition that the Takings Clause of the Fifth Amendment applied only to the federal government.

The decision in *City of Chicago* discussed the compensation requirement as one of due process:

> If, as this court has adjudged, a legislative enactment, assuming arbitrarily to take the property of one individual and give it to another individual, would not be due process of law, as enjoined by the fourteenth amendment, it must be that the requirement of due process of law in that amendment is applicable to the direct appropriation by the state to public use, and without compensation of the private property of the citizen. The legislature may prescribe a form of procedure to be observed in the taking of private property for public use, but it is not due process of law if provision be not made for compensation. (*City of Chicago* 236)

It is customary today to attribute to this case the incorporation of the Takings Clause, as a long line of Supreme Court cases has recognized. The application of the federal Takings Clause to state and local government activity, along with the new doctrine of substantive due process examined in Chapter 3, profoundly influenced the course of constitutional property doctrines in the twentieth century.

Conclusion

A more vivid understanding of the property-related clauses in the federal Constitution requires at least a brief inquiry into the prior experience with government and private property. That experience included colonial land practices, the Revolution, independence from Great Britain, and the practices of state governments leading up to the framing of the federal Constitution and Bill of Rights.

The federal Takings Clause did not apply to state governments until the close of the nineteenth century. State courts and legislatures construed their own just compensation provisions in such a way that only a condemnation proceeding to obtain title, or a physical invasion of land directly caused by a government, could be expected to require compensation. Moreover, the doctrine of off-setting benefits reduced the amount of compensation paid to landowners for property taken for transportation projects, in effect subsidizing the cost of infrastructure improvements. In the twentieth century, the Takings Clause assumed a more prominent role.

For these reasons, attempts to understand the contemporary significance of the original meaning of the Takings Clause are fraught with difficulty. Originalism—the view that the federal Constitution should be interpreted and applied today strictly in accordance with the understanding and practice of the founding period—is difficult with respect to the Takings Clause because not much was said about it at the time of its enactment and because it was so rarely the subject of court decisions. Modern court interpretations of the clause have dramatically expanded nineteenth-century understandings. Court interpretations of the just compensation principle in the nineteenth century point to the conclusion that the Takings Clause was understood to apply only to actual dispossessions of property through eminent domain or a physical invasion of some type, not to the broader range of laws restricting particular uses of private property. By contrast, the federal Contracts Clause and the emerging concept of due process provided greater protections for private property in the nineteenth century than did the principle of just compensation.

The view that private property, reduced to possession by an individual, constituted a natural right to be protected inherently conflicted with the accepted understanding that state governments had the power to define the terms of ownership. The Framers recognized that property rights were defined, determined, and regulated by society, at least to some degree. Throughout the nineteenth century, state governments maintained some degree of control over the uses of private property. The common law of the states played a critical role in defining these rights. As one court recently noted,

> In the concrete taking case the court must initially decide if the plaintiff has an actual property interest, if this is a point of dispute. This determination is based upon long and venerable case precedent, developed over two centuries. The Anglo-American case precedent is literally made up of tens of thousands of cases defining property rights over the better part of a millennium. *Hage v. United States* (Fed. Cl. 1996, 151)

Private property rights were very important to the founding generation. Courts then struggled to find a balance between appropriate governmental regulation of property and individual rights. That struggle would continue, as the debates over substantive due process and economic liberty in Chapter 3 suggest.

References and Further Reading

Alexander, G. 1998. "Property as Propriety." *Nebraska Law Review* 77:653.
———. 1997. *Commodity and Propriety.* Chicago: University of Chicago Press.
Blackstone, W. 1765. *Commentaries on the Law of England.* 4 vols. Rpt. 1992. Buffalo, NY: William S. Hein.
Bruchey, S. 1980. "The Impact of Concern for the Security of Property Rights on the Legal System of the Early American Republic." *Wisconsin Law Review* 1980:1135.

Commager, H. S., and Cantor, M. 1988. *Documents of American History, vol. 1.* 10th ed. Englewood Cliffs, NJ: Prentice Hall.

Cooley, T. 1868. *A Treatise on Constitutional Limitations Which Rest upon the Legislative Power of the State of the American Union.* Boston: Little, Brown.

Cooper, W. 2000. *Jefferson Davis, American.* New York: Vintage Books.

Ely, J. W. 2001. *Railroads in American Law.* Lawrence: University Press of Kansas.

———. 2000. "The Marshall Court and Property Rights: A Reappraisal." *John Marshall Law Review* 33:1023.

———. 1999. "The Oxymoron Reconsidered: Myth and Reality in the Origins of Substantive Due Process." *Constitutional Commentary* 16:315.

———. 1998. *The Guardian of Every Other Right.* 2d ed. New York: Oxford University Press.

———. 1992. "The Fifth Amendment and the Origins of the Compensation Principle." *American Journal of Legal History* 36:1–18.

Epstein, R. 1985. *Takings: Private Property and the Power of Eminent Domain.* Cambridge, MA: Harvard University Press.

Friedman, L. 1985. 2d ed. *A History of American Law.* New York: Simon and Schuster.

Hamilton, A., Madison, J., and Jay, J. (R. Scigliano, ed.). 1788. *The Federalist Papers.* Rpt. 2000. New York: Modern Library.

Hart, J. 2000. "Land Use Law in the Early Republic and the Original Meaning of the Takings Clause." *Northwestern University Law Review* 94:1099.

———. 1996. "Colonial Land Use Law and its Significance for Modern Takings Doctrine." *Harvard Law Review* 109:1252.

Hayes, R. E. 1936. "Business Regulation in Early Pennsylvania." *Temple Law Quarterly* 10:155–178.

Hobson, C. F. 1996. *The Great Chief Justice: John Marshall and the Rule of Law.* Lawrence: University Press of Kansas.

Huston, J. L. 1999. "Property Rights in Slavery and the Coming of the Civil War." *Journal of Southern History* 65:249.

Kades, E. 2001. "History and Interpretation of the Great Case of Johnson v. M'Intosh." *Law and History Review* 19:67–116.

Katz, S. 1977. "Republicanism and the Law of Inheritance." *Michigan Law Review* 76:1.

———. 1976. "Thomas Jefferson and the Right to Property in Revolutionary America." *Journal of Law and Economics* 19:467–488.

Letwin, W. 1989. "The Economic Policy of the Constitution." In Ellen Frankel Paul and Howard Dickman, eds., *Liberty, Property, and the Foundations of the American Constitution.* Albany: State University of New York Press.

Locke, J. 1970 (P. Laslett, ed.). *Two Treatises of Government.* Cambridge, UK: Cambridge University Press.

Madison, J. 1907 (G. Hunt, ed.). *The Writings of James Madison, Volume 6: 1790–1802.* New York: G. P. Putnam's Sons.

Nedelsky, J. 1990. *Private Property and the Limits of American Constitutionalism.* Chicago: University of Chicago Press.

Novak, W. J. 1996. *The People's Welfare: Law and Regulation in Nineteenth-Century America.* Chapel Hill: University of North Carolina Press.

Paul, E. F., and Dickman, H., eds. 1989. *Liberty, Property, and the Foundations of the American Constitution.* Albany: State University of New York.

Price, P. 1999. "Alien Land Restrictions in the American Common Law." *American Journal of Legal History* 43:152–208.

Rakove, J. 1998. *Declaring Rights.* Boston: Bedford Books.

Salmon, M. 1986. *Women and the Law of Property in Early America.* Chapel Hill: University of North Carolina Press.

Scheiber, H. 1971. "The Road to *Munn:* Eminent Domain and the Concept of Public Purpose in the State Courts." In D. Fleming and B. Bailyn, eds., *Law in American History.* Boston: Little, Brown.

Schultz, D. 1993. "Political Theory and Legal History: Conflicting Depictions of Property in the American Political Founding." *American Journal of Legal History* 37:464.

———. 1992. *Property, Power, and American Democracy.* New Brunswick, NJ: Transaction Publishers.

Schwartz, B. 1971. *The Bill of Rights: A Documentary History.* New York: Chelsea House Publishers.

Siegan, B. H. 2001. *Property Rights: From Magna Carta to the Fourteenth Amendment.* New Brunswick, NJ: Transaction Publishers.

———. 1989. "One People as to Commercial Objects." In Ellen Frankel Paul and Howard Dickman, eds., *Liberty, Property, and the Foundations of the American Constitution.* Albany: State University of New York Press.

Stoebuck, W. B. 1972. "A General Theory of Eminent Domain." *Washington Law Review* 47:533–608.

Taylor, R., ed. 1979. *The Papers of John Adams, Volume 4: February–August 1776.* Cambridge, MA: Belknap Press.

Treanor, W. 1985. "The Origins and Original Significance of the Just Compensation Clause of the Fifth Amendment." *Yale Law Journal* 94:694.

3

TWENTIETH-CENTURY ISSUES AND DEVELOPMENT

> *Government could hardly go on if to some extent values incident to property could not be diminished without paying for every such change in the general law.... [And] while property may be regulated to a certain extent, if regulation goes too far it will be recognized as a taking.*
> —U.S. SUPREME COURT, *Pennsylvania Coal Co. v. Mahon*
> (1922, 413, 415)

Courts in the United States have long recognized the common law maxim *sic utere tuo ut alienum non laedas* (one should use one's own so as not to injure another) as a starting principle to decide disputes between neighboring landowners. When property disputes between private citizens reach the courts, judges and juries must determine which person has the better claim. If the dispute involves one property owner's objection to what another property owner does on neighboring land—excessive noise or pollution from a factory, for example—courts must balance the demand to use property as one wishes against the competing demand of the other property owner.

Accordingly, government protection of private property has many forms. One is protection of private property against interference by others, even if that means a person's use of property is limited in favor of community norms for acceptable use. As for government intrusion, U.S. courts have always protected private property rights to a greater or lesser extent, but the considerations that must be balanced are different. On the one hand, the individual property owner should expect that the rights she enjoys against neighboring property owners will also be respected by the government. On the other hand, governments have the need and the authority to regulate the conduct and property of individuals to advance goals beneficial to all citizens. The issue ultimately requires a balance between rights of property owners and public goals and interests.

In the twentieth century, constitutional protections regarding property rights changed significantly. In 1900, the federal Takings Clause was still relatively unimportant and applied only to physical invasions and outright appropriation of property via eminent domain. However, by 2000 the Takings Clause had become the primary constitutional provision protecting private property rights. Court interpretations of the Takings Clause expanded significantly in the twentieth century to include so-called regulatory takings, a recognition that excessive governmental regulation of private property may require government compensation.

The ascendance of the regulatory takings doctrine, which is examined in this chapter, followed the decline of the Contracts Clause as a significant protector of property. The regulatory takings doctrine also rose in importance as courts reconsidered their role with respect to business and economic legislation. In the late nineteenth and early twentieth centuries, the U.S. Supreme Court interpreted the Due Process Clauses of both the Fifth and Fourteenth Amendments to allow sweeping, substantive review of economic legislation under the guise of freedom of contract. Invoking what is known as substantive due process, the Court struck down minimum wage laws, child labor acts, maximum workweek hours, and other legislation with the belief that such were not within the legitimate powers of state government. In particular, the case of *Lochner v. New York* (1905) became associated with judicial activism (although some legal scholars now reevaluate this association in light of the many decisions during the same era in which economic legislation was upheld).

When the U.S. Supreme Court used substantive due process and federalism concerns to strike down significant legislative efforts by Congress during the New Deal, President Franklin Roosevelt, among others, charged that the Supreme Court justices were judicial activists who projected their own economic views and preferences into their decisions to thwart democratic government. Roosevelt's court-packing plan—an effort to change the outcome of these cases by increasing the number of justices on the Supreme Court—grew out of the president's frustration with the Court's repeated invalidation of New Deal laws. In the so-called constitutional revolution of 1937, the Court changed its substantive due process approach to economic legislation. The result today, as this chapter will illuminate, is a virtual disappearance of the Supreme Court's sweeping review of business regulations during the *Lochner* era.

However, in many respects today the Takings Clause has replaced substantive due process as an important protection for individual property rights. Contrary to the first 150 years of Takings Clause interpretations, in *Pennsylvania Coal Co. v. Mahon* (1922) the Supreme Court indicated that regulation of property—short of a physical invasion or an outright taking through eminent domain—may require compensation as a taking if the regulation "goes too far" (*Pennsylvania Coal* 415). This relatively recent notion of regulatory takings has become a significant area of litigation, with the Supreme Court frequently engaging in searching reviews of state and federal laws to determine whether they reach so far that compensation is required of the government. On occasion, courts will invalidate the regulations altogether rather than simply awarding compensation for an unconstitutional taking.

The topics examined in this chapter include substantive due process, regulatory takings, and other important developments. The first section considers the U.S. Supreme Court's use of substantive due process in the early decades of the twentieth century as a significant limitation on government activity. The second section explores the expansion of the Takings Clause to include regulatory takings as environmental and land-use planning by government agencies increased. The remainder explains how the Supreme Court currently resolves claims brought by property owners against federal, state, and local governments. As one scholar has characterized, the result is a "bewildering array of rules" (Michelman 1967, 173).

The Rise of Substantive Due Process and Liberty of Contract

In the latter part of the nineteenth century, a new interpretation of the Fourteenth Amendment's Due Process Clause emerged known as substantive due process. Beginning in the mid-1880s, the U.S. Supreme Court (and many state courts) interpreted the Fourteenth Amendment's Due Process Clause to impose substantive limits on state laws regulating economic activity. Blending the new doctrine of substantive due process with the notion of freedom of contract, during the subsequent 50 years the Supreme Court struck down a number of state laws that it viewed to violate private property rights.

By contrast, procedural due process refers to the requirement that governments must provide some form of individual review and an opportunity to be heard prior to confiscation of property or imprisonment. Procedural due process is designed to avoid arbitrary government actions against individuals and includes the idea that all persons are entitled to equal and neutral enforcement of existing laws. Procedural protection is the most obvious interpretation of the Due Process Clauses in founding-era constitutions and in the following language in the Fourteenth Amendment: "Nor shall any State deprive any person of life, liberty, or property, without due process of law."

The new emphasis on substantive due process represented the view that the judiciary should review the content of legislative acts to determine whether they transgressed fundamental property rights of individuals, particularly freedom of contract. Prevalent economic thought in the late nineteenth and early twentieth centuries extolled the virtues of the free market without government intervention. Many judges believed liberty of contract was a fundamental natural right, which is not strictly textual in the Constitution. Liberty of contract, viewed as a fundamental natural right, received protection under a substantive reading of due process of law in the late nineteenth and early twentieth centuries.

Substantive due process is thus a different conception of the prohibition against deprivation of life, liberty, or property without due process of law. It presupposes that the Due Process Clause is not limited to procedural protections prior to deprivation of a property interest; the Due Process Clause also limits the kinds of laws legislatures may enact in the first place—with the judiciary to police the limits of legislative power. Whereas the Contracts Clause protected existing contracts from subsequent legislation that would retroactively impair them, substantive economic due process purported to protect the right of individuals (employers, employees, businesses, and corporations) to enter future economic agreements unrestricted by states. Committed to a view of laissez-faire capitalism that looked sidelong at governmental regulation of business activities, courts invalidated industrial-era legislation that judges viewed as unreasonable interference with the free-market economy.

In the decades following ratification of the Fourteenth Amendment (1868), the Supreme Court had not yet viewed the amendment's Due Process Clause to provide substantive rights with respect to state economic regulation. For example, in the *Slaughterhouse Cases* (1873) the Court refused to invalidate a Louisiana statute that created a monopoly for the butchering of animals in New Orleans. The Court reasoned that legislation of this sort was within the state's police power to promote health and safety; economic rights per se were not intended for federal oversight by the Fourteenth Amendment. The majority were unwilling to attribute to the drafters of the Fourteenth Amendment an intent to give the federal government the power to prevent deprivations of occupational rights (in this instance, the right to engage in the slaughtering business despite the state-created monopoly). The Supreme Court would later decide, in *Allgeyer v. Louisiana* (1897), that the Fourteenth Amendment's Due Process Clause should protect individual economic interests, including the liberty to "pursue any livelihood or avocation, and for that purpose to enter into all contracts which may be proper, necessary and essential to ... carrying out to a successful conclusion the purposes above mentioned" (*Allgeyer* 589).

In *Munn v. Illinois* (1877), decided a few years after the *Slaughterhouse Cases,* the Supreme Court upheld Illinois legislation setting the rates that grain elevator operators could charge customers. The Court held that the statute was within the state's police powers because grain storage businesses served an important public function. Private property "affected with a public interest," such as a grain storage facility, was more readily subject to state regulation. Chief Justice Morrison Waite wrote that property devoted "to a use in which the public has an interest" (*Munn* 127) means that the property owner "grants to the public an interest in that use, and must submit to be controlled by the public for the common good, to the extent of the interest he has created" (*Munn* 126). Therefore, state legislatures had the authority to set prices charged by grain elevators, and the property owner was not deprived of any constitutionally protected right. A vigorous dissent by Justice Stephen Field argued that the state's rate regulations deprived the owners of a property interest. (The Supreme Court would eventually adopt that view toward substantive economic rights under the Fourteenth Amendment.)

Mugler v. Kansas (1887) also illustrates the Supreme Court's initial willingness to defer to state legislation as a valid exercise of the police power. In that case, the Court considered whether a statute prohibiting the manufacture of alcoholic beverages was unconstitutional because it destroyed the significant investment made by owners of breweries. Deferring to the Kansas legislature's determination that manufacturing alcoholic beverages was a "noxious use" of private property, the Court wrote:

> The principle that no person shall be deprived of life, liberty, or property without due process of law, was embodied, in substance, in the constitutions of nearly all, if not all, of the states at the time of the adoption of the fourteenth amendment; and it has never been regarded as incompatible with the principle, equally vital, because essential to the peace and safety of society, that all property in this country is held under the implied obligation that the owner's use of it shall not be injurious to the community. (*Mugler* 665)

The Progressive Era and Labor Legislation

The nature and frequency of legislation affecting economic relations changed significantly in the latter part of the nineteenth century and the early decades of the twentieth century. State legislatures enacted child labor laws, minimum wage laws, maximum workweek hours, worker compensation plans, workplace safety standards, and other legislation directed toward a perceived imbalance of power between corporations and employers, on the one hand, and laborers on the other. This period became known as the Progressive Era, based on the efforts of legislatures to address perceived ills of working conditions in the large-scale industrial settings that were coming to dominate.

Lochner v. New York (1905) is the best-known Supreme Court decision invoking substantive due process to invalidate progressive legislation. The *Lochner* case involved state legislation setting maximum work hours, one component of legislation enacted in many states to improve labor conditions during that time. In *Lochner*, a New York statute limited employment in bakeries to 60 hours per week and ten hours per day. The U.S. Supreme Court held that the New York legislation was unconstitutional because it was an arbitrary interference with the freedom of contract guaranteed by the Fourteenth Amendment's Due Process Clause.

According to the Court, the legislation could not be sustained as a valid exercise of the state's police power to protect the public health, safety, morals, and general welfare. The Court reasoned that bakers, and their employers, ought to be able to contract for as many work hours as they chose:

> There is no reasonable ground for interfering with the liberty of person or the right of free contract, by determining the hours of labor, in the occupation of a baker. There is no contention that bakers as a class are not equal in intelligence and capacity to men in other trades or manual occupations, or that they are not able to assert their rights and care for themselves without the protecting arm of the state, interfering with their independence of judgment and of action. They are in no sense wards of the state. (*Lochner* 57)

The *Lochner* decision was not the first case (or the last) to elevate liberty of contract above a state's police power to protect health and safety.

State courts also engaged in substantive review of economic legislation and often declared their own state's laws to be invalid. For example, in *Ives v. South Buffalo Railway Co.* (NY 1911) the highest court in New York held that state's newly enacted workers' compensation law to be unconstitutional. The New York workers' compensation act, like similar acts in other states, mandated an insurance plan to which employers contributed in order to compensate workers injured in the course of their employment, without the necessity of the employee having to sue the employer to recover costs of workplace injuries. Concerning the validity of the measure, the New York court wrote: "One of the inalienable rights of every citizen is to hold and enjoy property until it is taken from him by due process of law. When our constitutions were adopted it was the law of the land that no man who was without fault or negligence could be held liable for injuries sustained by another" (*Ives* 293). In other words, replacing the usual common law rules to determine liability for workplace injuries with a compensation plan violated a substantive property right of the employer. The same court later reversed itself, and the U.S. Supreme Court upheld the constitutionality of workers' compensation legislation (see *New York Central R.R. v. White* [1917]).

As a number of legal scholars have pointed out, during these years the U.S. Supreme Court in fact upheld more legislation than it overturned, and they argue that the *Lochner*-era judges' reputation as judicial activists is largely undeserved (Urofsky 1985, 63). Yet it is true that contemporaries judged the courts harshly at the time. Newspapers reported significant public reaction to the U.S. Supreme Court's role in striking down state legislation that it judged to violate liberty of contract. The Court's reputation suffered because it was unable to articulate clearly the types of state business regulations that would violate economic due process. Furthermore, at times the Court's decisions appeared to be contradictory. For example, the *Lochner* Court struck down a maximum 10-hour workday for bakers only seven years after it had sustained a state law mandating a maximum eight-hour workday for coal miners (see *Holden v. Hardy* [1898]). Three years after *Lochner*, in *Muller v. Oregon* (1908), the Court upheld another state law establishing precisely the same number of hours per day for women. Only a few years before *Muller v. Oregon*, a New York court had held an eight-hour day for women to be unconstitutional, on a rationale similar to the U.S. Supreme Court's decision in *Lochner*. Furthermore, in *Petit v. Minnesota* (1900), the Supreme Court upheld the right of states to prevent sales on Sundays (so-called *blue laws*) even though such laws completely prevented the kind of economic opportunities the Court was so keen to protect during other days of the week.

The Supreme Court was unable to explain adequately these distinctions. To the casual observer, the distinction was not clear, and the Court itself appeared to vacillate. Adding to the controversy, many decisions were narrow votes with a bare 5–4 majority. Despite *Lochner*, the states' police power was often supported; still, some decisions striking down popular laws caused controversy and resulted in calls for the removal of judges. Many thought that the courts had usurped and thwarted the power of the legislative branch of government.

One scholar has characterized the 1920s-era Supreme Court as "unprecedentedly aggressive" in striking down social and economic regulation (Currie 1987, 504). Similar sentiments were voiced during the *Lochner* era. Noted law professor Roscoe Pound wrote that the judges "exaggerated the importance of property and contract" (Pound 1909, 457). In 1909, Pound claimed that among the state and U.S. Supreme Court decisions applying substantive due process in the preceding 20 years, "the great majority are simply wrong" (Pound 1909, 482).

Critics pointed to a series of cases between 1923 and 1936 in which the Supreme Court struck down minimum wage laws. In the first case, *Adkins v. Children's Hospital* (1923), Congress had enacted a minimum wage law for women in the District of

Columbia. Children's Hospital challenged the wage law on the grounds that it unconstitutionally interfered with the liberty of contract for employment by predetermining the wages that must be paid. Because the legislation originated from Congress and not a state, the Supreme Court invoked the Due Process Clause of the Fifth Amendment. The Court believed that legislators could not determine wages in a free-market economy regardless of the justification that was advanced. Justice George Sutherland asserted that "freedom of contract is . . . the general rule and restraint the exception; and the exercise of legislative authority to abridge it can be justified only by the existence of exceptional circumstances" (*Adkins* 546).

Dissents by Justices William Howard Taft and Oliver Wendell Holmes Jr. argued that legislatures could reasonably limit freedom of contract and that the police power permitted legislatures to regulate minimum wages for women. Holmes wrote in an earlier opinion that the police power "may be put forth in aid of what is sanctioned by usage, or held by the prevailing morality, or strong and preponderant opinion to be greatly and immediately necessary to the public welfare" (*Noble State Bank v. Haskell* [1911], 111). The Supreme Court subsequently cited *Adkins* to overturn state minimum wage laws, including a New York minimum wage law in *Morehead v. New York* (1936).

Other noteworthy cases from the *Lochner* era addressed legislation supporting labor unions. In *Adair v. United States* (1908), the Supreme Court considered an employer's challenge to an 1898 federal statute prohibiting employers from hiring only nonunion employees and protecting union members from discharge for union membership. The Court held the federal law to be an unreasonable restriction of property rights under the Due Process Clause of the Fifth Amendment. As in *Adkins,* this precedent led to the invalidation of similar state laws, including a Kansas labor statute (see *Coppage v. Kansas* [1915]). According to the Supreme Court, an employer's ability to hire only nonunion employees was a fundamental right protected by due process. Many state courts agreed with this analysis.

Federal Legislation during the New Deal

Franklin D. Roosevelt was elected president in 1932 based on the strength of his campaign to bring a "New Deal" to citizens caught in the downward spiral of the Great Depression. For some 50 years prior to that, the Supreme Court had invalidated many state and some federal laws regulating economic matters. However, the New Deal included new initiatives that presupposed the federal government's involvement in helping the economy to recover. The Roosevelt administration placed great faith in the ability of administrative agencies to improve economic conditions. By creating federal agencies such as the Securities and Exchange Commission, the Social Security Administration, and the Food and Drug Administration, the New Deal transformed governmental control over economic matters from the states to the federal government. State regulatory agencies also proliferated during the early decades of the twentieth century.

Almost immediately, the Supreme Court invalidated statutes enacted by Congress at the president's urging. In a series of cases beginning in 1935, the Supreme Court held unconstitutional the National Industrial Recovery Act, the Bituminous Coal Conservation Act (imposing minimum wages and maximum hours for coal miners), and the Agricultural Adjustment Act. The Court also voided legislation establishing a retirement and pension system for railroad workers. Not all of these measures were invalidated on the grounds of substantive due process, but the effect of such decisions added to the perception that the Supreme Court had little respect for the other branches of government, whether federal or state, executive or legislative. Rather than rely on the political process to repeal what might later be determined as unwise economic legislation, the Supreme Court sent the message that there were some areas of economic concern that neither Congress nor the state legislatures would be permitted to address.

THE CONSTITUTIONAL REVOLUTION OF 1937

This series of defeats led Roosevelt in 1937 to announce his intention to increase the number of justices sitting on the Supreme Court—the so-called court-packing plan. Roosevelt's proposal was to enlarge the Supreme Court from nine members to 15; this would allow him to appoint judges who would be more sympathetic to his legislative program and dilute the votes of the sitting conservative justices. That year, however, the Supreme Court began to shift dramatically from its stance with respect to economic legislation. Less than two months after Roosevelt announced his plan, the Supreme Court decided *West Coast Hotel Co. v. Parrish* (1937). In that case, the court upheld minimum wage laws enacted by the California legislature, only one year after it had invalidated a similar measure from New York. Both decisions were based on narrow 5–4 majorities (Justice Owen Roberts switched his vote to uphold the minimum wage laws in *West Coast Hotel*). Later that year, the Court upheld, also by a 5–4 vote, the National Labor Relations Act, which protected the right of employees to organize for purposes of collective bargaining. These two decisions indicated that the Court could move away from its restrictive substantive due process interpretations. Justice Roberts's change of heart (the "switch in time that saved nine") lessened Roosevelt's sense of urgency, and the president did not pursue the court-packing plan.

The Supreme Court's move away from substantive due process was soon confirmed in *United States v. Carolene Products Co.* (1938). In that case, the Court announced that henceforth it would review economic legislation under a less stringent standard than would be accorded to legislation affecting the civil rights of minorities or participation in the political process. The Court wrote that "regulatory legislation affecting ordinary commercial transactions is not to be pronounced unconstitutional unless ... it is of such a character as to preclude the assumption that it rests on some rational basis" (*Carolene Products* 152). In what has become the most famous footnote in any judicial opinion (note 4 in *Carolene Products*), the Court separated economic from other personal liberties. The Court suggested that it would apply relatively strict scrutiny to legislation interfering with the political process or affecting the rights of "discrete and insular minorities" (*Carolene Products* 153). The Court would review economic legislation less strictly, however, asking only whether there was a rational basis for the legislation or some connection between the stated purpose of the legislation and the legislature's chosen path for its implementation. Since then, this two-tiered system of constitutional review has prevailed.

The Contracts Clause, already in decline at the close of the nineteenth century, continued its descent. In *Home Building and Loan Association v. Blaisdell* (1934), the Supreme Court upheld a state mortgage moratorium against the claim that the measure interfered with existing contracts and was thus invalid under the Contracts Clause. The Court disagreed, ruling that an important public purpose could justify state interference with contracts. The Supreme Court did not apply the Contracts Clause again until the late 1970s, when it struck down two state laws as interfering with existing private contracts. Since that time, the Court has not invalidated any state law under the Contracts Clause. However, lower federal and state courts have invoked the Contracts Clause to invalidate legislation, including attempts to alter mortgage foreclosure proceedings, existing leases, and state employee pension plans, indicating that the Contracts Clause remains an important limitation on state governments (Ely 1993).

Whether substantive due process was gone for good, or had merely experienced a brief recession, was not immediately clear even after *Carolene Products*. Congress and state legislatures passed sweeping measures affecting property rights during World War II, including laws that asserted unprecedented governmental control over the economy (Ely 1996). This included the federal Emergency Price Control Act, enacted by Congress in 1942 to enforce rationing and control inflation at the outset of the war. State and local governments enacted rent control measures as well. The Supreme Court sustained these acts and thereby approved broad governmental authority as an exigency of wartime. However, it was not clear whether these kinds of property restrictions (especially price and rent controls) would be upheld after the war was over.

The Supreme Court also articulated a wartime exception to the Takings Clause in *United States v. Caltex, Inc.* (1952). A U.S. oil company owned petroleum facilities in Manila, the Philippines, which the U.S. Army, fearing that the Japanese would make use of the facilities, destroyed as Japanese forces approached. The Court refused to order compensation to the oil company for the destruction of its property, stating: "The terse language of the Fifth Amendment is no comprehensive promise that the United States will make whole all who suffer from every ravage and burden of war. This Court has long recognized that in wartime many losses must be attributed solely to the fortunes of war, and not to the sovereign" (*Caltex* 155–156).

Civil Rights at the Forefront: *Carolene Products*

Where property rights as a boundary to the legitimate scope of government can be said to have dominated the nineteenth century through the Contracts Clause, civil rights and equal opportunity would become more prominent in the twentieth century, as note 4 of *Carolene Products* seemed to suggest. However, it is probably incorrect to view *Carolene Products* as an abrupt change in U.S.

constitutional history because, as later sections of this chapter will suggest, the regulatory takings doctrine fulfills many of the same purposes ascribed to substantive due process. Prior to, and even at times during, the *Lochner* era, exercises of police power often received little more than rational basis-type scrutiny from the Supreme Court. That is, judicial inquiry into the fairness of the legislation was concerned with the establishment of a reasonable purpose behind the legislation, as well as a review of its application to an individual to determine whether the government was acting arbitrarily in a particular case (e.g., by selective enforcement). After economic legislation was relegated to rational basis review, the Takings Clause became the primary constitutional provision to protect private property rights. Yet substantive due process is still invoked on occasion by the Supreme Court today, and substantive due process remains an important component of the Court's review of property regulations under the Takings Clause (see discussion later in this chapter).

However, one transformation resulting from the new approach articulated in *Carolene Products* is clear. In the decades following *Carolene Products,* civil rights laws would limit the traditional property right of exclusion. Title II of the Civil Rights Act of 1964 requires privately owned places of public accommodation—such as hotels, restaurants, and places of entertainment—to provide "full and equal enjoyment of the goods, services, facilities, privileges, advantages, and accommodations" without discrimination "on the ground of race, color, religion, or national origin." Federal and state housing laws also prohibit property owners from discriminating against racial minorities in selecting tenants. The right to exclude persons from private property for any reason, however distasteful the reason might be, traditionally had been associated with private property in the common law. In *Heart of Atlanta Motel v. United States* (1964), the Supreme Court upheld the Civil Rights Act's limitation on traditional property rights as a valid exercise of congressional authority under the Commerce Clause.

The Court rejected the motel owner's argument that the Civil Rights Act was a taking of property rights because the owner was required to rent rooms to African Americans against his will.

More recently, the Americans with Disabilities Act of 1990 also prohibits discrimination against disabled persons in places of public accommodation. The most important provisions of this act with respect to private property include the prohibition of discrimination in access to existing facilities and the requirement that new buildings provide access to persons with disabilities. Older buildings, when renovated, must improve accessibility. Property owners must follow detailed regulations for renovations and new building construction in order to satisfy the requirements of the Americans with Disabilities Act.

The traditional property right to exclude others from privately owned property is also limited to an extent by the First Amendment. In *Martin v. Struthers* (1943), the Supreme Court held that the First Amendment protects door-to-door solicitation from city ordinances that broadly attempt to prohibit it, despite the fact that the solicitor is in a sense trespassing on private property. In other cases, the Supreme Court has ruled that governments may not prohibit free speech, including religious speech, in public areas such as sidewalks and streets, although governments may regulate the activity to maintain order. In *Amalgamated Food Employees Union v. Logan Valley Plaza* (1968), the Supreme Court extended the right of free speech to a privately owned shopping center, so that a private owner could not exclude peaceful picketing of a store to protest its refusal to hire union members, although the Court limited the scope of this decision in *Hudgens v. NLRB* (1976). And in *PruneYard Shopping Center v. Robins* (1980), the Supreme Court ruled that a state constitutional right to free speech can extend to the exercise of that speech on private property that is otherwise open to the public (in this case, an enclosed shopping mall). A concurring opinion by Justice Thurgood Marshall indicates that there are limits on governmental authority to abolish "core" common law rights that protect property owners from intrusions by other private citizens, most notably the common law rules of trespass.

These examples of the priority of other constitutional rights over property rights—suggested in *Carolene Products*—build on the notion that private property put to a public use allows a heightened degree of governmental regulation. Earlier cases such as *Munn v. Illinois* (1876) recognized a broad governmental authority to regulate utilities, railroads, and other business endeavors "affected with a public interest" (*Munn* 127).

The Advent of the Regulatory Takings Doctrine

After *Carolene Products,* it has often been said that property rights receive a lesser degree of constitutional protection than that accorded other individual rights found in the federal Constitution. This generalization, however, does not account for the tremendous expansion of the Takings Clause and the Supreme Court's continued use of substantive due process to invalidate legislation that goes too far in regulating property. Until 1922, the U.S. Supreme Court had interpreted the Takings Clause to apply only to government action that resulted in an intentional, physical invasion of property or a forced transfer of land title by eminent domain. However, in *Pennsylvania Coal Co. v. Mahon* (1922), the Supreme Court for the first time recognized the concept of a *regulatory taking,* or *inverse condemnation.* This transformation in the Court's understanding of the Takings Clause was significant. As Justice Antonin Scalia noted in a 1992 case (*Lucas v. South Carolina Coastal Council*), "Early constitutional theorists did not believe the Takings Clause embraced regulations of property at all" (1028).

The new interpretation of the Takings Clause that began in *Pennsylvania Coal* recognizes that governmental regulation of property may be so substantial that it deprives owners of the value of their property, even though the regulation is not a physical appropriation or an outright transfer of title to the state. An important theory behind the regulatory takings doctrine is that government should not require some individual landowners to be singled out for burdens that the public as a whole, as beneficiaries of the regulation, should pay for through tax dollars.

When considering whether a particular land-use restriction constitutes a regulatory taking, courts balance the public interest underlying the regulation against the extent of diminution in value to the property. In many respects, this balancing is similar to the searching review of economic legislation under substantive due process, with at least one important difference: If the regulation is found to impose a regulatory taking, the statute or regulation itself is not normally voided, but compensation is required if the government wishes to carry out its plans. Courts sometimes invalidate the regulation altogether, rather than simply award compensation, essentially merging the Takings Clause with substantive review of legislation under the Due Process Clause.

Prior to *Pennsylvania Coal,* the Supreme Court had decided very few cases under the Takings Clause. The two most significant cases occurred relatively late in the nineteenth century. *Pumpelly v. Green Bay Co.* (1871) held that property that was flooded as a result of a dam construction project had been taken for public use and that compensation was required to the landowner. *Mugler v. Kansas* (1887) upheld a state statute prohibiting the manufacture and sale of alcoholic beverages against a claim that it constituted a taking of the plaintiff's brewery. One year later, the Court cited *Mugler* as precedent in concluding that the state of Pennsylvania could prohibit the manufacture of oleomargarine as a public health measure, with no compensation due to prior manufacturers even if "the value of the property employed therein would be entirely lost and he be deprived of the means of livelihood" (*Powell v. Pennsylvania* [1888] 682).

Prior to the application of the just compensation requirement of the Fifth Amendment to the states in 1897, state governments, more so than the federal government, undertook eminent domain proceedings, and therefore cases involving federal government takings rarely reached the Supreme Court. Accordingly, many more cases involving compensation for government takings were decided in state courts. At the turn of the twentieth century, one treatise writer reported nearly 13,000 cases on the subject of eminent domain. Many of those involved railroad construction, but increasingly city governments invoked eminent domain to pursue beautification, construction of parks, and preservation of neighborhoods (Friedman 1986, 9).

Pennsylvania Coal changed the landscape of takings analysis. In that case, landowners sued the Pennsylvania Coal Company to prevent it from mining under their property in such a way as to cause the surface of the land to collapse. The right to occupancy had been deeded to the landowners by Pennsylvania Coal, but the company retained the mineral rights, that is, it still possessed the right to remove the subsurface coal. In the deeds, the surface owners had agreed to waive all claims for damages due to mining of the subsurface coal. The surface owners claimed that a 1921 Pennsylvania statute, the Kohler Act, voided those parts of the deeds that permitted the company to damage surface structures. The Kohler Act was ostensibly an exercise of the state's police power to prevent destruction of or damage to homes, streets, and other structures.

In an opinion by Justice Oliver Wendell Holmes Jr., the Supreme Court invalidated the Kohler Act as an improper exercise of the state's police power because it effected a taking of the preexisting property rights of the company. The company had negotiated its right to mine subsurface coal, and the purchasers expressly bought the surface rights to the land subject to the risk that a cave-in of the surface might occur, destroying any buildings erected upon it. Because the Kohler Act interfered with the preexisting contract rights negotiated by the coal company, the Act constituted a taking that would require the state to compensate the coal company (and all of the other affected companies in the state) for the public benefit that the act hoped to procure. Justice Holmes wrote: "So far as private persons or communities have seen fit to take the risk of acquiring only surface rights, we cannot see that the fact that their risk has become a danger warrants the giving to them greater rights than they bought" (*Pennsylvania Coal* 416). *Pennsylvania Coal* is noteworthy, and often quoted, for Holmes's statement of the modern regulatory takings concept:

> The general rule at least is, that while property may be regulated to a certain extent, if regulation goes too far it will be recognized as a taking. We are in danger of forgetting that a strong public desire to improve the public condition is not enough to warrant achieving the desire by a shorter cut than the constitutional way of paying for the change.... When this seemingly absolute protection is found to be qualified by the police power, the natural tendency of human nature is to extend the qualification more and more until at last private property disappears. (*Pennsylvania Coal* 415–416)

Thus, in this decision the Supreme Court inaugurated the concept of a regulatory taking—a recognition that land-use regulations may rise to the level of an actual taking and that in those situations compensation should be paid.

Pennsylvania Coal also established that regulatory takings are not subject to bright-line rules. Whether a particular regulation constitutes a taking of private property, according to Holmes, "is a question of degree—and therefore cannot be disposed of by general propositions" (*Pennsylvania Coal* 416). Justice Holmes meant that courts should determine whether the limits of the police power have been exceeded by considering the nature of the property right involved and the extent of the resulting diminution in value to the property. This ad hoc factual inquiry to determine whether a particular property regulation has gone too far remains the predominant mode of analysis by the modern Supreme Court.

In a dissenting opinion in *Pennsylvania Coal,* Justice Louis Brandeis disagreed that the state had exceeded the scope of its police power. Emphasizing his view that the public interest justified the legislation, he wrote:

> Every restriction upon the use of property imposed in the exercise of the police power deprives the owner of some right theretofore enjoyed, and is, in that sense, an abridgment by the State of rights in property without making compensation. But restriction imposed to protect the public health, safety or morals from dangers threatened is not a taking. (*Pennsylvania Coal* 417)

The Supreme Court had decided a case only a few years earlier, *Hadacheck v. Sebastian* (1915), holding precisely that. In *Hadacheck,* a Los Angeles ordinance prohibited brick manufacturing within designated city limits because of the noise, odors, and inconvenience posed to neighboring property owners. A brick manufacturer, in operation before enactment of the ordinance, challenged on the grounds that it deprived him of the value of his investment in the property in violation of the Fourteenth Amendment. Of the state's police power, the Court wrote: "It is to be remembered that we are dealing with one of the most essential powers of government—one that is the least limitable" (*Hadacheck* 410). The Supreme Court in *Hadacheck* held that the city ordinance was a valid police measure to protect the comfort of neighboring residents. It was neither a deprivation of property without due process nor a taking, and therefore no compensation was due.

Land-Use Planning by Local Governments

Hadacheck signaled an increase in land-use planning, or zoning, by cities and towns at the beginning of the twentieth century. Local governments attempted to organize city growth by dividing areas within city limits into zones—industrial, commercial, residential, mixed use, and so on—as well as by designating sizes of lots, height restrictions, and other building requirements. Zoning ordinances sought to rationalize growing urban populations with the development of industrial areas. Zoning restricted the type of activity that might be pursued in residential areas and imposed restrictions on private property, even in designated residential areas, by classifying some areas for single-family homes, multifamily homes, or apartment buildings. The underlying assumption about zoning has been that all landowners benefit from the enhanced property values secured by an overall plan for an urban area, a plan that protects residential neighborhoods from the incursion of less desirable property uses.

New property owners—those who purchased property in a zoned area *after* enactment of the ordinance—presumably had some advance notice that their use of private property was subject to the limitations imposed by the local government's zoning ordinance. But it was also true that prior owners could find themselves subject to a new use restriction on their property. This was certainly the case for the brick manufacturer in *Hadacheck*, yet in that case the Supreme Court had said that even preexisting rights could be limited by an appropriate exercise of the state's police power: "A vested interest cannot be asserted against it because of conditions once obtaining. To so hold would preclude development and fix a city forever in its primitive conditions. There must be progress, and if in its march private interests are in the way, they must yield to the good of the community" (*Hadacheck* 410).

The first significant constitutional challenge to comprehensive zoning plans reached the Supreme Court in *Village of Euclid v. Ambler Realty Co.* (1926). Euclid had recently enacted ordinances dividing the village into districts zoned for residential, industrial, and commercial uses; it further divided the zones into degrees of residential or commercial use, with specific limitations accompanying the various classifications. Ambler Realty brought a lawsuit challenging the zoning ordinance because it affected the company's unimproved land, which it wished to sell to developers. The company contended that the ordinance reduced the value of its property; that it deprived owners of property without due process; and that it constituted a taking of property without compensation.

The Supreme Court rejected these claims. In sweeping language, the Court accorded wide latitude for police powers in zoning plans, ruling that the Constitution's property provisions were not violated. Citing the upsurge of populations in urban areas, the Court accepted the necessity of restrictions for the use and occupation of private lands in urban communities as an appropriate power of the government, "for reasons analogous to those which justify traffic regulations." Although the Court noted that "the meaning of constitutional guaranties never varies," it wrote that "the scope of their application must expand or contract to meet the new and different conditions which are constantly coming within the field of their operation." As long as zoning ordinances were justified "in some aspect of the police power, asserted for the public welfare," the Court indicated it would find no difficulty in sustaining them (*Euclid* 387).

Interestingly, the Court did not cite *Pennsylvania Coal* for the proposition that a zoning regulation might conceivably go too far in its effect on preexisting property rights. But the Court did indicate it would consider future zoning controversies on a case-by-case basis, and as in *Pennsylvania Coal*, it said that no precise line could be drawn in advance between a valid zoning law and an unconstitutional restriction on property rights. The Court stated: "The line which in this field separates the legitimate from the illegitimate assumption of power is not capable of precise delimitation. It varies with circumstances and conditions. A regulatory zoning ordinance, which would be clearly valid as applied to the great cities, might be clearly invalid as applied to rural communities" (*Euclid* 387).

Thus, few had much reason to doubt that *Hadacheck* continued to represent the Supreme Court's view of a local government zoning powers: A zoning regulation that prohibited a prior use of property would not likely be deemed a compensable taking as long as the zoning restriction promoted health, safety, or general welfare. Nonetheless, two years later, in *Nectow v. City of Cambridge* (1928), the Supreme Court struck down a zoning ordinance as applied to a particular landowner as a violation of due process. Relying on the findings of a special master that the zoning did not promote health, safety, or general welfare, the Court struck down the ordinance as applied because it did not bear a substantial relation to the police power. State courts, where many more zoning cases were considered, for the most part applied their own constitution's property provisions to uphold zoning ordinances, although at times state courts would recognize that some zoning restrictions, at least with respect to prior existing uses, might require compensation.

Courts disallowed zoning ordinances that attempted to preserve racial purity in neighborhoods, including laws that prevented the sale of property to African Americans. In *Buchanan v. Warley* (1917), well before *Carolene Products* and during the era of *Plessy v. Ferguson* (1896), the Supreme Court struck down an ordinance in Louisville, Kentucky, that prohibited property owners in certain neighborhoods from selling their property to nonwhites. The city justified the ordinance as an exercise of police power. Invoking the Fourteenth Amendment's Due Process Clause, the Supreme Court invalidated the ordinance as a deprivation of a fundamental property interest: the right to sell and acquire property. According to one scholar, "*Buchanan* represents both the resolute defense of property owners' rights against regulation and the most significant judicial victory for civil rights during the early decades of the twentieth century" (Ely 1998, 953.)

Zoning ordinances can also be economically exclusionary, but the Property Clauses of the Constitution do not prevent zoning ordinances that create or preserve affluent neighborhoods. For example, zoning measures may require that a neighborhood consist only of large lots for large houses; in general, zoning for such aesthetic reasons is permissible under the federal Takings Clause. In *Village of Belle Terre v. Boraas* (1974), the Supreme Court upheld a zoning law that restricted housing to one-family dwellings, excluding apartments, boardinghouses, and any other housing arrangement in which nonrelated persons lived together. Citing "urban problems" presented by fraternity houses and the like, including more parked cars, traffic, and noise, the Court said: "A quiet place where yards are wide, people few, and motor vehicles restricted are legitimate guidelines in a land-use project addressed to family needs" (*Belle Terre* 9). Accordingly, the Court recognized a wide latitude for local governments to "lay out zones where family values, youth values, and the blessings of quiet seclusion and clean air make the area a sanctuary for people" (*Belle Terre* 9). Some state courts have taken a different view of zoning that restricts property for purely aesthetic reasons.

In *Agins v. City of Tiburon* (1980, 260), the Supreme Court held that a zoning ordinance that restricted construction to single-family dwellings with large open spaces was not a taking. Zoning laws are not a taking, according to the Court, unless "the ordinance does not substantially advance legitimate state interests . . . or denies an owner economically viable use of his land" (*Agins* 260). The Court found that the ordinance in question served a legitimate purpose by preserving the organized development of the residential area. Furthermore, even though the ordinance restricted the number of houses that could be built (and thus resold by the developer), the ordinance was not a taking because it did not completely prohibit use of the land. An important question in Takings Clause cases, the Court said, is whether "the public at large, rather than a single owner, must bear the burden of an exercise of state power in the public interest" (*Agins* 260).

Environmental Legislation

Beginning in the 1960s, Congress and many state legislatures focused on environmental concerns, particularly preservation of natural resources and endangered species and problems caused by pollution. Legislation included the federal Clean Air Act, the National Environmental Policy Act, the Endangered Species Act, the Comprehensive Environmental Reclamation and Control Liability Act, wetlands preservation plans, and other efforts to preserve beaches and green spaces and to maintain and allocate clean water. The Clean Water Act, which became law in 1972, announced "the national goal that the discharge of pollutants into the navigable waters be eliminated by 1985." These new measures gave heightened powers to government agencies to issue detailed regulations and make individual determinations of appropriate land use consistent with the legislative objectives. Property owners who found themselves subject to additional use restrictions on their land challenged the laws as a compensable government taking of property.

State courts initially decided the vast majority of takings claims resulting from this new environmental legislation. For the most part, state courts upheld these laws as legitimate exercises of the police power to pursue environmental protection, even if the law deprived an owner of the opportunity to build on undeveloped land. The justification often given was that the proposed development would harm important community interests. For example, in *Just v. Marinette County* (WI 1972), the Wisconsin Supreme Court ruled against a property owner who had violated a zoning ordinance by filling the shore of designated wetlands on his waterfront property in order to construct a house. The court held that the requirement of just compensation did not apply because the purpose of the restriction was "to protect navigable waters and the public rights therein from the degradation and deterioration which results from uncontrolled use and development of shore lands" (*Just* 765). Furthermore, the court stated that "an owner of land has no absolute and unlimited right to change the essential natural character of his land so as to use it for a purpose to which it was unsuited in its natural state and which injures the rights of others" (*Just* 768).

Some state courts also relied on the doctrine of the public trust to justify certain environmental restrictions. The idea of a public trust in property is that certain natural resources—especially bodies of water such as navigable streams, lakes, and ocean bays—are owned in common (or are subject to an easement for use by the public) and that the government is obligated to preserve this common property for certain purposes. Many land uses along the shores have an adverse effect on public rights to use and enjoy the waters. Ocean beaches are an integral part of the use and enjoyment of the public trust and, as such, became a particular focus of preservation. At least some courts have recognized that restrictions designed to protect property in the public trust are not takings of private property but rather enforce the competing property right of the citizenry as a whole. The public trust doctrine was not new; the U.S. Supreme Court recognized in the late nineteenth century the idea of a public trust in both inland navigable waters as well as ocean shorelines (see *Illinois Central Railroad v. Illinois* [1892]).

The U.S. Supreme Court heard very few challenges to environmental regulations in the 1970s. The most important case, at least in terms of public awareness, was *Tennessee Valley Authority v. Hill* (1978). Known as the snail darter case, *Tennessee Valley Authority* involved the construction of the Tellico Dam with funds appropriated by Congress. The Court considered whether the federal Endangered Species Act required the permanent halting of construction of the dam, which had already cost nearly $100 million. The Court ruled that it did. The Court said that the snail darter, a small fish, must be protected because the Endangered Species Act "shows clearly that Congress viewed the value of endangered species as 'incalculable'" (*TVA* 187). Although this case did not concern the Takings Clause because government property rather than private property was at issue, the Court's decision signaled strong deference to legislative determinations of the value of environmental concerns over development interests.

The U.S. Supreme Court did not address environmental restrictions on property in any comprehensive way until the 1990s (discussed later in this chapter). Prior to that time, state and lower federal courts considered a number of challenges by landowners that environmental regulations had resulted in a regulatory taking. Numerous cases upheld environmental restrictions, as long as the owner was not deprived of all economically viable use of the property. More recently, litigants have challenged as a taking wetlands preservation laws that require the landowner to preserve the land in its natural state. These claims have met with some degree of success, at least when the landowner can show that all of the land, or at least a very significant portion, is subject to a ban on development.

HISTORIC PRESERVATION: *PENN CENTRAL*

The regulatory takings doctrine announced in *Pennsylvania Coal* in 1922 did not immediately affect Supreme Court decisions under the Takings Clause. Until 1978, more than 50 years after *Pennsylvania Coal*, the Court had decided no significant cases construing the regulatory takings doctrine. Local governments continued to enact zoning regulations; the federal and state governments also enacted legislation that reflected the growing public interest in environmental conditions. In addition to environmental and land-use initiatives, cities also enacted historic preservation laws. One such historic preservation effort led to an important regulatory takings case, *Penn Central Transportation Co. v. City of New York* (1978).

In *Penn Central*, the Landmarks Preservation Committee in New York City had designated Grand Central Station as a historic landmark. Because Grand Central Station was so designated, the owners were obligated to maintain its appearance and obtain prior approval for any changes. The Penn Central Transportation Company sought permission to build a 50-story office building above the terminal. When permission was denied by the city, the company brought a lawsuit claiming that the historic preservation law, as applied to its development plans, constituted a taking that would require compensation. The company argued that the ordinance caused a substantial loss of economic value in the property and that the owner of the historic property was unfairly singled out to bear an economic burden that benefited the public as a whole.

The Supreme Court disagreed. Essentially affirming the right of local governments to pursue aesthetic values such as historic preservation, the Court held that the development restriction was not a taking. The Court reasoned that the preservation law did not affect any existing use of the property or unduly "frustrate distinct investment-backed expectations" because the commission had allowed the company to transfer its proposed development to other nearby property that it owned (*Penn Central* 105). Three justices dissented, believing an unconstitutional taking had occurred. Some state courts have held that historic preservation laws require compensation as a taking as a matter of state constitutional law.

Penn Central was the first Supreme Court decision to consider in detail how the regulatory takings doctrine that began with *Pennsylvania Coal* might be applied to future cases. The majority opinion confirmed the ad hoc, case-by-case approach suggested in *Pennsylvania Coal*, because the "Court, quite simply, has been unable to develop any set formula for determining when justice and fairness require that economic injuries caused by public action be compensated by the government, rather than remain disproportionately concentrated on a few persons" (*Penn Central* 124). Because the Court viewed a "clear rule" to be impossible to formulate, the Court set out three factors for consideration of regulatory takings claims: (1) the "economic impact of the regulation on the claimant"; (2) the extent to which the regulation has "interfered with distinct investment-backed expectations"; and (3) the "character of the government action" (*Penn Central* 124).

A number of developments in the 1980s brought renewed interest in the Takings Clause and constitutional protection of private property. In 1988, President Ronald Reagan issued an executive order requiring all federal agencies to undertake a "takings impact analysis" before implementing a regulation to review the potential effects of governmental actions on property owners. Also in the late 1980s, the Supreme Court, in an increasing number of cases, considered in more detail what level of government need must be shown, and found more instances of government takings than it had previously recognized. A few years later, in *Dolan v. City of Tigard* (1994, 392), Chief Justice William Rehnquist declared: "We see no reason why the Takings Clause of the Fifth Amendment, as much a part of the Bill of Rights as the First Amendment or the Fourth Amendment, should be relegated to the status of a poor relation." Rehnquist's statement suggested to many court observers that the Supreme Court may be prepared to abandon the deferential view of economic legislation that began with *Carolene Products.*

The Supreme Court's recent Takings Clause cases have clarified some of the open questions concerning the reach of the regulatory takings doctrine. The remainder of this chapter provides an overview of these developments and summarizes the scope of constitutional protection of private property today.

CONSTITUTIONAL PROTECTION OF PRIVATE PROPERTY: CONTEMPORARY APPLICATIONS

Federal, state, and local governments engage in many endeavors that affect property interests at some level, including environmental preservation, zoning and land-use planning, building-safety regulations, waterfront preservation, green space preservation, and agricultural production quotas, to name only a few. It is nearly impossible to generalize takings rules within these myriad categories of cases because, as the Supreme Court explained, the question of whether a given government activity constitutes a compensable taking is a matter of degree.

To understand the contemporary application of the Takings Clause, it is helpful to categorize the instances in which the Supreme Court has required compensation: (1) when the government acquires title to property through eminent domain; (2) any type of permanent physical invasion, however negligible; and (3) government action that results in the denial of all economically beneficial use of the owner's property. Compensation under the Takings Clause outside these three categories is still relatively rare in state courts (where the majority of compensation claims are heard) as well as in federal courts.

The Supreme Court has continued to decide most challenges to governmental regulation on the basis of the three factors identified in *Penn Central:* (1) the "economic impact of the regulation on the claimant"; (2) the extent to which the regulation has "interfered with distinct investment-backed expectations"; and (3) the "character of the government action" (*Penn Central* 124). These factors are assigned different weights, leading to different outcomes, depending upon the precise factual circumstances in which owners challenge a property restriction. As the Supreme Court noted in *United States v. Riverside Bayview Homes, Inc.* (1985, 126), only "extreme circumstances" lead courts to order compensation for property restrictions that legislatures have deemed to be important for the welfare of society. A broad range of governmental purposes and regulations of property do not implicate the Takings Clause at all.

The Due Process Clause remains an important component of judicial review of any legislation or governmental regulation that is alleged to have an adverse economic impact. State courts, as compared to federal courts, have tended to review economic legislation at a higher level of scrutiny, invoking a substantive due process interpretation under their own state constitutions. Federal courts, following the lead of the U.S. Supreme Court, interpret the federal Due Process Clauses to require that a regulation advance a "legitimate state interest," meaning that courts will consider the purpose of legislation to find a sufficient nexus between the restriction on property use and the reason that the government has sought to impose it. Each of these topics is examined below.

Eminent Domain

The most straightforward application of the Takings Clause occurs when a government exercises its power of eminent domain to obtain title to property for a public use such as the construction of roads or government buildings, or dedication of the acquired land as a park or nature preserve. Also known as *condemnation,* eminent domain proceedings follow a relatively uniform procedure. When a government determines that it wishes to obtain private property for a public use, it negotiates with the affected owners to arrive at a purchase price for the property. The standard is the fair market value of the property. Property owners and government officials frequently do not agree on the fair market value. If the government and the landowner are unable to agree on a price, the government asks a court to determine fair market value in a condemnation proceeding.

At the condemnation hearing, an owner can challenge the government's motives for singling out her property. Usually this means the property owner questions whether, in fact, the government is taking the property for a valid purpose, as the Takings Clause limits the exercise of eminent domain to endeavors with genuine public benefit ("nor shall private property be taken for public use, without just compensation"). But most courts do not question the government's motives and instead interpret "public purpose" quite broadly. In the nineteenth century, for example, state governments commonly delegated eminent domain authority to private corporations such as railroad and canal companies. Although arguably the condemned land would eventually be used for a public purpose (transportation), these private companies clearly benefited. Even earlier, colonial legislatures authorized the taking of land from one private person to award to another private person who was willing to construct a mill, thereby devoting land to the most economically beneficial use for the community.

Courts have generally agreed that the public use requirement prevents the exercise of eminent domain for purely private purposes. In *Calder v. Bull* (1798, 388), Justice Samuel Chase declared that "a law that takes property from A and gives it to B" would be "contrary to the great first principles of the social compact." Many decisions have echoed that sentiment, including a recent opinion by Justice Sandra Day O'Connor in *Eastern Enterprises v. Apfel* (1998). Regardless, "public use" does not mean that all members of the public must be entitled to use or gain some benefit from the property.

In *Hawaii Housing Authority v. Midkiff* (1984), the U.S. Supreme Court held that the public use requirement of the Takings Clause is met if the taking serves a legitimate public purpose, even if the government takes property from one owner (with compensation) primarily for the benefit of new owners. Historical circumstances in Hawaii led to concentration of private property in a small number of landowners. In an attempt to lessen the disparity, the state used its eminent domain power to purchase land from large landowners and resell the lots to the tenants living on them. Upholding the plan, the Supreme Court pointed to the fact that the state's scheme was a rational attempt to remedy a social and economic ill. The legislature merely had to show that it "rationally could have believed" that the act would promote a legitimate interest (*Hawaii* 242).

The public purpose may even be primarily for the benefit of a private corporation. In *Poletown Neighborhood Council v. City of Detroit* (MI 1981), the Michigan Supreme Court approved the city's plan to raze a neighborhood to allow General Motors to construct a manufacturing facility. State and local governments frequently use the power of eminent domain to assist manufacturers and other industries that they wish to attract to their region. Use of eminent domain for urban renewal also can have the effect of transferring property from one owner to another, consistent with a public use.

Thus, the only real question in most eminent domain cases is valuation. How is compensation determined—and how is it challenged by the property owner? Typically, the owner presents evidence of sales of similar properties in the neighborhood, improvements to her own property, and so forth. The property owner has the burden of proof to establish fair market value. The Supreme Court has said that just compensation

> normally is to be measured by the market value of the property at the time of the taking contemporaneously paid in money. Considerations that may not reasonably be held to affect market value are excluded. Deviation from this measure of just compensation has been required only when market value has been too difficult to find, or when its application would result in manifest injustice to owner or public. *United States v. Fifty Acres of Land* (1984, 29)

State laws vary, but the general rule is that no compensation is provided for consequential damages such as relocation costs, sentimental value, and establishing market value in a condemnation proceeding (e.g., hiring experts to testify on value). Lost profits, lost business goodwill, disruption to business, and loss of customers due to relocation of a business (or major thoroughfare) also are not compensable.

Even the potential future use of eminent domain can diminish fair market value. In Georgia in the late 1990s, plans for a major thoroughfare north of suburban Atlanta were publicly discussed, and a route proposed, several years prior to any construction. Property owners in the path of the proposed road saw their property values drop, as potential purchasers knew that the area might soon be taken for the highway. As the political process dragged on, these owners could expect to receive only the fair market value at the time of the actual condemnation proceeding should the highway in fact be built as proposed.

Eminent domain has been used mostly for the construction of roads and government buildings, but it is also used for aesthetic and environmental reasons. The California Supreme Court even approved a contemplated exercise of eminent domain by the city of Oakland over a professional football team to prevent its move from the city and the resulting loss to the economy. Many states also delegate the power of eminent domain to public utilities.

In sum, property owners subject to condemnation may object to the taking on the basis that the proposed use is not a public purpose, but the burden of persuasion is on the property owner to establish that the government's purpose is illegitimate, and the Supreme Court has granted legislatures wide latitude. Therefore, in the typical case the only contended issue is valuation. Provided that fair market value is paid, and absent a clear showing of arbitrary and capricious action by the local government, property owners have no individual right to object to the government's selection of their property for condemnation, as opposed to someone else's. On these grounds, eminent domain remains consistent with its use in the early history of the United States.

Many state constitutions provide a textually broader basis of eminent domain protection for property owners than does the federal Takings Clause. For example, article I, section 13 of the

Minnesota Constitution declares that "private property shall not be taken, destroyed or damaged for public use without just compensation." The federal Takings Clause, by contrast, does not specify that compensation is required for inadvertent destruction or damage to property by governmental action. These state constitutional provisions, added in the late nineteenth century, provided compensation for landowners who sustained physical damage from the construction of roads or other public works adjacent to the property.

Permanent Physical Invasions of Land

One of the clearest rules of the Takings Clause is that government-imposed physical invasions of a permanent or frequent and enduring nature must be compensated, even if the physical invasion has a negligible effect on value or an owner's enjoyment. The physical invasion of private property, such as placement of a communications tower on private land, most closely resembles government acquisition of title to land through eminent domain. Physical invasions of a frequent or enduring nature have been relatively easy cases for courts.

For example, in *Loretto v. Teleprompter Manhattan CATV Corp.* (1982), the U.S. Supreme Court held that a city ordinance authorizing cable TV companies to install cables on residential rental property, against the landlord's wishes, was a taking that required compensation. It held that "any permanent physical occupation authorized by government is a taking without regard to the public interests that it may serve," even if the placement of the cables had no negative impact on the value of the property (*Loretto* 426). In this case, the purported public interest of the ordinance was to allow access by apartment renters to cable TV, argued by dissenting justices to be a form of consumer protection for tenants. But the majority adhered firmly to the categorical rule that any government-authorized physical invasion of more than an occasional or fleeting nature required compensation. This was because the power to exclude others from one's land "has traditionally been considered one of the most treasured strands in an owner's bundle of property rights" (*Loretto* 435). The link between the traditional right of private property owners to exclude others, and the rigid rule developed by the Supreme Court for permanent physical invasions, is an important one.

Compensation for homeowners located directly beneath the takeoff and landing paths at airports is often justified as a frequent and enduring physical invasion of noise and vibration. In *United States v. Causby* (1946, 262), the Supreme Court required compensation for homeowners directly beneath incoming and outgoing flights at an airport, noting that "the land is appropriated as directly and completely as if it were used for the runways themselves." Other neighboring homeowners, however, who may suffer as much noise and vibration, are usually excluded from compensation because the low flights are not directly over their property. The *Causby* framework, as applied by other courts, requires compensation as a taking for homeowners directly beneath the path of flights lower than 500 feet in noncongested areas and 1,000 feet in congested areas.

More recently, courts exhibit a willingness to expand the scope of compensated takings for takeoffs and landings at airports beyond homeowners directly beneath the flight path of a runway. Some courts are now willing to consider whether neighboring landowners are also entitled to compensation if they can show sufficient evidence of disruption to the enjoyment of their land. The leading case supporting this approach is *Argent v. United States* (Fed. Cir. 1997), a decision of the U.S. Circuit Court of Appeals for the Federal Circuit.

The Supreme Court has refused entreaties to expand the categorical rule for physical invasion beyond *Loretto*'s basic protection of the right of a property owner to be free from permanent physical invasions of a tangible nature. In *Yee v. City of Escondido*

(1992), the Supreme Court ruled against owners of mobile-home parks who claimed that a rent control ordinance amounted to physical occupation of their property because it forced them to retain tenants when they might be able to rent to other tenants at a higher rate. The Supreme Court held that this rent control ordinance did not amount to a physical taking of park owners' property, although the Fifth Amendment's Takings Clause generally requires compensation when the government authorizes a physical occupation of property.

Regulatory Takings

If the government's action is not a transfer of title through eminent domain, or a physical invasion of a frequent or enduring nature, courts consider whether compensation is nonetheless required under the doctrine of regulatory takings first described in *Pennsylvania Coal*. Whether a government activity or regulation requires compensation as a regulatory taking is determined on a case-by-case, ad hoc basis, but certain categorical rules have emerged. In addition to the rule of compensation for permanent physical invasions of property, the Supreme Court has set out additional categories in which compensation is likely to be required. These tests inquire whether: (1) an owner has been deprived of certain core property rights, such as the right to exclude; (2) an owner has been deprived of all economically viable use of property; and (3) a government agency has imposed a quid pro quo of "unconstitutional conditions" for certain types of development. The sections that follow describe the range of possible outcomes in regulatory takings cases.

No compensation because the requirement is a valid exercise of police power. Beginning at least with *Mugler v. Kansas* (1887), the Supreme Court has always recognized that a broad range of governmental authority over private property does not implicate the

Takings Clause and thus does not require compensation to affected property owners. A state's police power—its authority to regulate for the health, safety, morals, and general welfare of its citizens—has long been considered an essential attribute of sovereignty. When a state regulates property in furtherance of health and safety, it is not required to compensate owners for property regulations that further these aims.

It is not possible to catalog here the many instances in which state exercises of the police power do not require compensation. A few examples, however, illustrate the range of permissible governmental authority. Governments may intentionally destroy private property for health and safety reasons. In *Miller v. Schoene* (1928), government officials ordered the destruction of a valuable stand of cedar trees on one owner's property to prevent the spread of disease to a nearby orchard. The Supreme Court held that the owner of the cedar trees was not entitled to compensation. Similarly, the destruction of livestock to prevent the spread of disease is also not a taking that requires compensation, even though the financial loss to the affected owner may be substantial.

Governments also may proscribe a form of property altogether. In *Mugler v. Kansas* (1887), the Supreme Court upheld a prohibition statute that rendered essentially worthless an owner's investment in his brewery. More recently, in *Keystone Bituminous Coal Association v. DeBenedictis* (1987), the Supreme Court upheld a Pennsylvania statute protecting surface owners from subsidence caused by coal-mining operations, distinguishing that case from *Pennsylvania Coal*'s ruling that the state could not divest the coal company's prior negotiated rights without paying compensation. Ruling that the state could prevent the "significant threat to the common welfare" that the legislature claimed to exist, no compensation was required because the law "does not merely involve a balancing of the private economic interests of coal companies against the private interests of the surface owners" (*Keystone* 485). The legislature's decision to protect some property owners at the expense of other property owners, without compensation, was a legitimate exercise of its police power authority.

The Supreme Court will generally defer to legislative judgments about health and safety restrictions on property use. For example, in *Queenside Hills Realty v. Saxl* (1946) the Court upheld a New York City ordinance that required the addition of sprinkler systems to existing apartment buildings. No compensation was owed to property owners who, as a result of the new ordinance, had to spend substantial sums of money to renovate older buildings for sprinkler systems. Writing for the court, Justice William Douglas stated: "It is for the legislature to decide what regulations are needed to reduce fire hazards to the minimum. Many types of social legislation diminish the value of the property which is regulated" (*Queenside* 83). More recently, state courts have upheld similar safety regulations that require substantial outlays of money by owners of older buildings. Even if the cost of the modification exceeds the value of the building (e.g., for asbestos abatement), with the result that the owner must cease renting to individuals, compensation is not required.

The general rule, articulated in *Agins v. Tiburon* (1980, 255), is that a regulation does not constitute a taking as long as it "substantially advances legitimate state interests in health, safety, or general welfare." In addition to health and safety regulations, the tendency of the Supreme Court has been to uphold property restrictions that are intended to prevent harm in a more generalized sense. Community notions of harm that may be prevented by state action have long been part of the common law of nuisance. The law of nuisance gives standing to community sentiment concerning the appropriateness of an activity in a given location. Regulations designed to prevent what the public deems a harmful use fall into this category.

The obvious difficulty for the Supreme Court, then, is to determine what is a legitimate state interest and what it will require in order to determine whether a particular regulation substantially advances that interest. Similar to the substantive due process cases during the *Lochner* era, in order to answer these questions courts must have some prior notion of what they consider to be appropriate subjects of regulation. The tendency of the Supreme Court to defer to legislative determinations of the need for health, safety, morals, or general welfare regulations reflects the hesitancy to impede democratic actions to address perceived problems. If local governments were required to pay compensation for every regulation that affected property interests, the cost to the public would be prohibitive.

Valid exercise of police power, but unduly burdensome on individual. Despite the broad range of authority for governmental regulation of property to advance important interests without compensation, at some point the burden on a particular property owner is one that in fairness should be shared by awarding compensation from public funds. This is the "problem of considerable difficulty" noted by *Penn Central*. Regulation that goes too far, as Justice Holmes put it, is a compensable taking of property for public use. The assumption is that when a regulation is deemed to be a taking, the public has acquired something to which it did not previously have a right. The Supreme Court has struggled with this problem ever since *Pennsylvania Coal* was decided 80 years ago.

When is a property restriction so burdensome that to impose it constitutionally compensation must be paid as though the government had acquired the property right itself? The test relies on three general inquiries from *Penn Central*: (1) the economic impact of the regulation on the claimant; (2) the extent to which the regulation has interfered with distinct investment-backed expectations; and (3) the character of the government action. Recently, the U.S. Supreme Court elaborated on the elements required for compensation for property restrictions that take away all economically viable use of an owner's property, even when the restriction is deemed a necessary environmental measure by the government. The Court has also disallowed local development regulations that require landowners to give up, without compensation, a core property right. In addition, the Court has interpreted the Takings Clause to require compensation for temporary use restrictions in some situations.

All economically viable use: *Lucas v. South Carolina Coastal Council.* One more categorical rule for a per se taking—obviating the open-ended balancing test otherwise used for regulatory takings—was announced by the Supreme Court in *Lucas v. South Carolina Coastal Council* (1992). In *Lucas,* the Court held that excessive government interference with private property occurs, and compensation is thus required, when governments impose a use restriction that causes a property owner to lose all economically viable use of property regardless of the state's interest.

In Lucas, the South Carolina Coastal Council imposed a construction ban on any buildings along beachfront property in order to preserve the shoreline. David Lucas bought two oceanfront lots in 1986. At the time he purchased the lots, there were no restrictions that would have affected his plans to build two single-family homes. Moreover, other houses already had been built on neighboring lots. In 1988, before Lucas began construction, a state law went into effect that prohibited construction in certain coastal areas, which included Lucas's lots. The Supreme Court of South Carolina held that the use restriction was not a taking because, as the legislature had stated, beachfront construction threatened the coastline and the measure was intended to prevent a serious public harm.

Lucas appealed his case to the U.S. Supreme Court. The Court reversed the South Carolina court because the law effected a "total deprivation of beneficial use" of Lucas's property and thus was "the equivalent of a physical appropriation" (*Lucas* 1017). Reasoning that the regulation required the owner to grant a "benefit" to the public—beach preservation—the public ought to pay for the benefit by compensating the affected landowner. Lucas's case was different from government action to prevent a "noxious use" or a nuisance, because prior to enactment of the 1988 law, Lucas had the right to construct a home on the lots, and the legislature had not yet determined that construction would harm other owners or the community.

The majority opinion also noted, however, that no compensation is required even if an owner is deprived of all economically beneficial use if the restriction prevents the owner from engaging in an activity for which he never had a legal right. Justice Antonin Scalia wrote: "Where the State seeks to sustain regulation that deprives land of all economically beneficial use, we think it may resist compensation only if the logically antecedent inquiry into the nature of the owner's estate shows that the proscribed use interests were not part of his title to begin with" (*Lucas* 1027).

Some legal scholars suggest that the decision in *Lucas* may be consistent with a position advocated by professor Richard Epstein. Epstein maintains that all government restrictions on private property that could not be obtained by individuals bringing common law nuisance actions require compensation (Epstein 1985). Writing for the majority, Justice Scalia seemed to equate permissible government restrictions with the common law of nuisance, at least for those regulations that deny an owner all economically beneficial use. But the Supreme Court's categorical rule does not apply to regulations that leave *some* economically viable use for property. In *Lucas,* the lower court had previously established that the use restriction left the owner with no economically viable use of his land.

Property interests are not defined by the federal Constitution or created by the federal government. Instead, the Supreme Court looks to state law, including common law, to define the range of interests that qualify for protection as property under the Takings Clause. The federal Constitution permits traditional common law rights to limit absolute property rights. For example, property owners may not arm spring guns against intruders (e.g., the gun is rigged to fire automatically), and property owners generally have some duty to keep their property in a safe condition for others. Still, the Supreme Court has indicated that there are limits on governmental authority to abolish core common law rights that protect individual owners from intrusions on their property rights by other private citizens, most notably the common law rules of trespass. A total deprivation of a beneficial use that the state's common law had previously recognized, according to *Lucas*, requires compensation.

In *Palazzolo v. Rhode Island* (2001), the Supreme Court considered a takings claim by a developer who had purchased property with prior notice that the tract of land was subject to use restrictions. Unlike David Lucas in South Carolina, the developer bought the property knowing that it was subject to an environmental regulation that barred development on 18 acres of oceanfront wetlands in Rhode Island and thus, arguably, had no legitimate "investment-backed expectation" in his proposed use of the land. The lawsuit sought more than $3 million in damages to account for the profit the developer said he would have made by building and selling single-family homes. The developer's request for a permit to fill the wetlands had been denied, leaving the developer the ability to build only one single family house on an upland part of the property, not the 74 homes he wanted to build.

An important question in the case was whether a property owner who acquired land after the regulation was in place was barred from claiming compensation for a taking. The *Lucas* decision had indicated this possibility in its statement that for "regulations that prohibit all economically beneficial use of land ... any limitation so severe cannot be newly legislated or decreed (without compensation)" (*Lucas* 1029). In *Palazzolo*, however, the Supreme Court ruled that subsequent purchasers may still raise takings claims. The Court stated: "Just as a prospective enactment, such as a new zoning ordinance, can limit the value of land without effecting a taking because it can be understood as reasonable by all concerned, other enactments are unreasonable and do not become less so through passage of time or title" (*Palazzolo* 2462). Compensation may still be required if the property restriction is "so unreasonable or onerous as to compel compensation" (*Palazzolo* 2462). The judgment of reasonableness of the property restriction, in turn, is apparently a judgment for courts to make, not a political majority. Dissenting justices rejected that view.

Another important question in the case was whether the coastal protection measure had denied the developer all economically beneficial use of the land, which the *Lucas* court had indicated would be considered a per se taking. The Rhode Island courts had rejected the developer's claim because he was still permitted to build a house on the upland portion of the property. Although the Supreme Court remanded the case to state court to determine whether a taking had actually occurred, the Court indicated that the per se rule in *Lucas* need not apply when some economically viable use remained. Although the Supreme Court noted that "a State may not evade the duty to compensate on the premise that the land owner is left with a token interest," the developer in this case was not in that position (*Palazzolo* 2464).

The categorical rule announced in *Lucas*, then, seems to be restricted to cases in which a property owner's legitimate expectations for use of his property are subject to a restriction that denies all economically beneficial use, defined as something more than a mere token of remaining value. Property restrictions are less likely to require compensation as a taking if the diminution in value is minimal. Even if the diminution in value is substantial, as long as the regulation prohibits a property use that was never part of the owner's rights in the first place, or is justified by a sufficiently strong public interest in protecting the public from harm, no compensation is required (Singer 2001, 679). In these situations, the *Penn Central* balancing test is applied.

Unconstitutional conditions. The Supreme Court has also interpreted the Takings Clause to prohibit governments from exacting benefits as a condition for permission to develop land that it could not gain outright without paying for the benefit through an exercise of eminent domain. In *Nollan v. California Coastal Commission* (1987), the commission had required that any beachfront property owner who wished to increase the size of existing structures on his land must grant a public easement—public access along the beachfront parallel to the water—in order to obtain permission. The Nollans, who built a larger structure without obtaining prior permission, challenged this requirement as a taking without just compensation. The U.S. Supreme Court, in a 5–4 decision, agreed with the property owners.

In essence, the Court held that if the state wishes to condition development upon a grant of public access through private land, it must pay compensation to the property owner. The Court asserted that the easement over the beachfront land parallel to the water was a property right that could not be taken away from a private owner except through the exercise of eminent domain. As such, the state could not condition the building permit on the owner's giving up that property right without compensation. Therefore, this *unconstitutional condition* required compensation to the landowner, as would other similar conditions if the government were unable to show a sufficient relation between the condition and its legitimate government exercise of police power. For example, building permits conditioned upon a height restriction could be a legitimate effort to preserve public views of the beach. Requiring lateral access to beachfront property, in the majority's view, was not. However, the Court noted that "a broad range of governmental purposes and regulations" does not implicate the Takings Clause (*Nollan* 835).

Nollan involved the dedication of a portion of an owner's property in order to gain permission to build a house at variance with size limits. Many cities also require impact fees of developers to recoup (from the developers and, ultimately, new residents) the costs that local governments incur for providing infrastructural improvements and additional city services. Most state courts routinely uphold impact fees as long as the development creates or exacerbates the need for a government service and if the charges imposed have some relation to the burdens created by the development.

In *Dolan v. City of Tigard* (1994), the Supreme Court specified that the government must show that the required dedication or impact fee is "roughly proportional" with the costs attributable to the development (Kendall et al. 2000, 305–306). In *Dolan,* a storeowner sought permission to enlarge a store, construct an additional building, and pave a gravel parking lot. As a condition for issuing the requested building permit, the city required that the owner dedicate approximately 10 percent of the land to the city for use as green space in order to construct a bicycle path and control flooding from runoff due to the increased paved area. The city argued that the measures were reasonable exactions to compensate the public for costs the city must bear for increased traffic and exacerbated flooding problems.

The Supreme Court held that the city had imposed unconstitutional conditions on the building permit. The city, the Court said, could have addressed the flooding issue by refusing to permit the additional development of the owner's property. Furthermore, the city had not shown that a bicycle path actually would alleviate traffic congestion that the city feared would result from increased traffic to the store. Therefore, the Court reasoned, the requirement that the property owner give up a portion of her land to the city was an unconstitutional condition because that portion would otherwise have to be purchased by the city through eminent domain.

Temporary takings. Governments may have to pay compensation for temporary restrictions on land use, even if those restrictions are not permanent limitations on the use of the property. In *First English Evangelical Lutheran Church v. Los Angeles* (1987), property owned by a church had been destroyed in a flood. An ordinance adopted as a temporary measure prohibited construction within the floodplain. As a result, the church was unable to construct new buildings on its land for several years. The Supreme Court held that the Takings Clause may require compensation for the period during which the church was unable to rebuild the structures on its property, even though the ordinance was later withdrawn. Thus, if an ordinance is found to be a taking, the government must pay for the temporary taking while the regulation was in place if the regulation denied the owner all use of the property. However, the Court was careful to note that it did not intend its decision to cover government-supervised functions such as the usual delays in obtaining building permits.

A more recent case by the U.S. Supreme Court rejected a takings claim brought by more than 400 families who were denied permits to build on their lots near Lake Tahoe from 1981 to 1984. The moratorium on building had been imposed due to fears that runoff from the hillsides adversely affected the lake. In *Tahoe-Sierra Preservation Council v. Tahoe Regional Planning Agency* (2002), the property owners contended that the total prohibition on building, which lasted nearly three years, deprived them of all economically viable use of their land for that period and that they should be compensated. Justice John Paul Stevens, writing for the majority, said: "A rule that required compensation for every delay in the use of property would render routine government processes prohibitively expensive or encourage hasty decision making" (*Tahoe* 1485). Refusing to recognize a categorical rule for temporary takings, the Court explained: "In our view the answer to the abstract question whether a temporary moratorium effects a taking is neither 'yes, always' nor 'no, never': the answer depends on the particular circumstances of the case" (*Tahoe* 1478).

The Court thus reaffirmed its case-by-case approach to temporary takings rather than a categorical, fixed rule. *Lucas* was limited to the "extraordinary case in which a regulation permanently deprives property of all value" (*Tahoe* 1469). The temporary moratorium question is important to city planners as well. Municipalities often impose temporary bans on development. For example, in fast-growing communities land-use planners can suspend development until a new sewage plant is built or other city services are available.

The Court in *Lake Tahoe* also made clear that the distinction between a physical invasion and a regulatory taking would remain important. For both due process and takings considerations, Justice Stevens affirmed the "fundamental distinction" (*Tahoe* 1480) between a government seizure of private property and regulation that limits an owner's use of land:

> Land-use regulations are ubiquitous and most of them impact property values in some tangential way—often in completely unanticipated ways. Treating them all as *per se* takings would transform government regulation into a luxury few governments could afford. By contrast, physical appropriations are relatively rare, easily identified, and usually represent a greater affront to individual property rights. (*Tahoe* 1479)

Finally, the Supreme Court affirmed an earlier rule that it had developed to determine regulatory takings claims. Under the so-called parcel-as-a-whole rule, the Court's analysis of whether a particular land-use restriction constitutes a taking must consider the impact on the property as a whole, not only the affected portion. Thus, if a wetlands or wildlife protection restriction on development affects only a portion of an owner's property, the Court will consider the economic effect of the restriction on the entire property, using its traditional inquiry into the extent of the diminution in value of the land, the effect on distinct investment-backed expectations, and the government's interest in imposing the restriction.

Judicial takings. The Constitution's property clauses traditionally have been viewed to limit the actions of the legislative and executive branches of government. In the closing decades of the twentieth century, an increasing number of legal scholars and judges questioned whether the Constitution's property protections also apply to actions by the judicial branch and thus prohibit so-called judicial takings. The concern with judicial takings is whether changes by state courts in common law property rules may deprive an owner of a property interest without due process of law or constitute a taking of private property without paying just compensation. The U.S. Supreme Court has not explicitly endorsed the view that a state court's abandonment or modification of common law property rules may constitute a taking or violate due process. In 1994, however, Justices Antonin Scalia and Sandra Day O'Connor dissented from the denial of certiorari in *Stevens v. City of Cannon Beach*, on the ground that the Oregon Supreme Court's recognition of the doctrine of custom may have effected an uncompensated taking.

Speculation that the Supreme Court in the modern era might recognize a judicial taking by a state court stems primarily from a concurring opinion by Justice Stewart in 1967 in *Hughes v. Washington*. In that case, a landowner challenged a state court's ruling that newly accreted lands at the shoreline did not become part of her property. The Supreme Court reversed the state court ruling. The Court held that the question was one of federal law, not state law, because the owner's land originally came from a federal grant. Federal law, the Court said, gave title to the newly accreted lands to the adjacent landowner. Writing separately, Justice Stewart would have recognized a judicial taking by virtue of the state court's construction of its common law:

To the extent that the decision of the Supreme Court of Washington on that issue arguably conforms to reasonable expectations, we must of course accept it as conclusive. But to the extent that it constitutes a sudden change in state law, unpredictable in terms of the relevant precedents, no such deference would be appropriate. For a State cannot be permitted to defeat the constitutional prohibition against taking property without due process of law by the simple device of asserting retroactively that the property it has taken never existed at all. Whether the decision here worked an unpredictable change in state law thus inevitably presents a federal question for the determination of this Court. (*Hughes* 296)

Although the issue of judicial takings remains largely an academic debate, a few lower federal and state courts have appeared receptive at least to the possibility of a judicial taking, and with increasing frequency attorneys raise judicial takings arguments in litigation. The primary issue of contention is whether a state court abandonment or alteration of precedent presents a federal question such that federal courts may scrutinize state court determinations of state common law.

Due Process and Forfeiture of Property

The renewed interest in property protection under the Takings Clause, evident in Supreme Court decisions, legal commentary, and state legislative initiatives, should not lead one to overlook the procedural aspect of the Due Process Clause as an important protection for private property. Procedural due process is a constant feature of court work and remains centrally important to the protection of property.

Private property, including land, homes, cars, and cash, may be subject to forfeiture to the government because of its use in the commission of a crime. Property that itself is declared unlawful to possess (e.g., drug manufacturing equipment) may be subject to summary forfeiture. Many criminal laws also provide for forfeiture of property used in connection with (or proceeds derived from) the commission of a crime. Examples of forfeited property include land, houses, cars, and cash. Procedural due process, not the Takings Clause, applies in such cases.

In *United States v. James Daniel Good Real Property* (1993, 62), the Supreme Court held that "absent exigent circumstances, the Due Process Clause of the Fifth Amendment requires that the Government give notice and an opportunity to be heard prior to its seizure of real property subject to civil forfeiture." Unlike the prior notice and hearing procedures required for seizure of real estate, personal property (movable items such as cars, boats, and the like) may be seized for unlawful conduct without prior notice and hearing. In such cases, the Due Process Clause requires that the owner have some opportunity to contest the seizure while the property is in the government's custody.

Innocent owners of property used in connection with a criminal activity have limited rights. The Supreme Court has held that even when the property was used in connection with unlawful conduct without the actual owner's knowledge or participation, civil forfeiture does not violate constitutional due process or constitute a taking. In *Calero-Toledo v. Pearson Yacht Leasing Co.* (1974), the owner of a yacht leased to another person who used it to transport marijuana without the owner's knowledge claimed that forfeiture of the yacht unconstitutionally deprived the owner of property without just compensation. The Supreme Court rejected that claim, noting that forfeiture statutes that authorize the taking of innocent parties' property had been held to be constitutional in prior cases. But the Court also implied that it would be difficult to reject a takings claim by an owner who could prove he was not only uninvolved in and unaware of the wrongful activity but also had done all that reasonably could be expected to prevent the proscribed use of the property. In a subsequent case, the Supreme Court held that a state's forfeiture as a public nuisance of an automobile used by one of its owners to pick up a prostitute did not violate the due process rights of the co-owner of the car, in this case his wife (see *Bennis v. Michigan* [1996]).

Another controversial issue is government seizure of property that a criminal defendant wishes to use to pay for a lawyer in defense of the criminal charge, including bank accounts and other assets. The Supreme Court has held that accused persons do not have a due process right to use forfeitable property for this purpose (see *Caplin & Drysdale v. United States* [1989]).

Property Rights Legislation

During the 1990s, some states enacted legislation designed to bolster the rights of individual property owners against government regulatory takings. In Congress, several measures were proposed with a similar goal in mind. The congressional measures were not enacted (although the proposed Private Property Protection Act passed in the House; it would have created a statutory right to compensation when federal actions under certain federal programs reduce the value of private property by more than a specified percentage).

Recent state legislation with respect to property rights falls into two general categories. First, at least 18 states have enacted planning bills modeled after President Ronald Reagan's executive order, which required federal government agencies to perform a takings impact analysis prior to the promulgation of regulations that might adversely impact property values. These states have enacted similar laws to require state government agencies to know and plan for the cost of new rules. Second, a few states have enacted laws to define a regulatory taking and to provide procedures for landowners to challenge state actions alleged to constitute a regulatory taking. In a few states (Mississippi, Louisiana, and Texas), statutes create a right to compensation when certain types of land-use restrictions reduce the value of private property by more than a specified percentage. The proposed Private Property Protection Act, as well as examples of recent state legislation on regulatory takings, are excerpted in Chapter 6.

In 2000, citizens in Oregon narrowly approved a constitutional amendment that would require compensation for any reduction in value to property as the result of a land-use restriction such as zoning. The measure read in part: "If the state or a local government passes or enforces a regulation that restricts the use of private real property, and the restriction has the effect of reducing the value of a property upon which the restriction is imposed, the property owner shall be paid just compensation equal to the reduction in the fair market value of the property." Soon after the election, municipal corporations and county governments filed a lawsuit challenging the validity of the ballot initiative. At roughly the same time, a property owner filed a lawsuit against local government officials, claiming entitlement to $50 million under the new constitutional provision for a land-use restriction that prevented the owner from constructing a mining operation near the town of Jacksonville. In October 2002, the Supreme Court of Oregon invalidated the measure on the grounds that the initiative failed to comply with Oregon's election laws.

Conclusion

The U.S. Supreme Court has made clear that no one is constitutionally entitled to the most profitable use of her property. Governments are charged by their citizens with furthering public goals. Governments are also charged by the Constitution with protecting private property. As Justice Oliver Wendell Holmes Jr. noted, not every diminution in value of property can be compensated, because governments would never have enough money to pursue legitimate aims. In a democratic government, the popular will may prefer some property uses over others in order to further interests deemed to be beneficial to all.

The vast majority of legislators are property owners themselves and accountable to the public for the laws they enact. James Madison expected factions in representative governments to attempt to appropriate property for themselves. The main issues of the modern debate about constitutional property rights have not changed much from the longer historical experience in which the Supreme Court has considered the limits of governmental authority over private property rights. The authority of state and local governments to define and regulate property use requires some view of the appropriate reach of the police power, in an era in which environmental interests, city planning, and historic preservation increasingly have appeared on the legislative agenda.

From *Pennsylvania Coal* through *Penn Central,* the Supreme Court laid out in broad design the foundations of modern takings law. The three factors that it identified for consideration in each case remain the basis for the Court's review of most regulatory takings claims. The Court has clarified that it will require compensation for any government activity that takes away all economically viable use of property. But there is a large area between the extreme of no economically viable use and no government-imposed restriction at all. The effect of government restrictions on property use might range from trivial to severe in terms of the property owner's prior expectations about use of private property and yet not take away all economically viable use. The challenge for the Supreme Court, if possible, is to articulate more precise boundaries to determine when governments must compensate property owners for regulations intended to benefit the public as a whole.

The predominant theme emerging from the Supreme Court's Takings Clause decisions is the difficulty of balancing democratically enacted laws with the adverse impact those laws might have on individual property owners. As the Supreme Court frequently states, the Takings Clause was "designed to bar Government from forcing some people alone to bear public burdens which, in all fairness and justice, should be borne by the public as a whole"

(*Penn Central* 123–124). Any hesitance the Court might have in second-guessing legislative judgments of public need may be overcome in instances in which individual landowners have been unfairly singled out for heavy burdens. If the public good indeed requires that individuals surrender their property rights entirely, compensation to those individuals from public tax dollars best ensures that the public pays for the benefits it obtains.

Courts must consider on a case-by-case basis whether an unconstitutional taking has occurred, an approach that necessarily restricts the ability to fashion more generally applicable rules that would apply to all of the myriad forms of governmental regulation of property. The law of takings is ultimately a question of whether a government-imposed limit on property use should be paid for by taxpayers as a whole rather than borne individually by the affected property owner. But the law of takings is also, ultimately, a question of the legitimate boundaries of legislation and the extent to which the judiciary should defer to the policymaking branches when representative bodies deem property restrictions to be necessary.

References and Further Reading

Bederman, D. J. 1996. "The Curious Resurrection of Custom: Beach Access and Judicial Takings." *Columbia Law Review* 96:1375–1455.

Chapman, T. E. 1997. "To Save and Save Not: The Historic Preservation Implications of the Property Rights Movement." *Boston University Law Review* 77:111.

Clegg, R., ed. 1994. *Regulatory Takings: Restoring Private Property Rights.* Washington, DC: National Legal Center for the Public Interest.

Congressional Budget Office. 1998. *Regulatory Takings and Proposals for Change.* Washington, DC: Congressional Budget Office. Available online at *http://purl.access.gpo.gov/GPO/LPS2350*. Publication of the Congress of the United States.

Coyle, D. 1993. *Property Rights and the Constitution: Shaping Society Through Land Use Regulation.* Albany: State University of New York Press.

Currie, D. 1987. "The Constitution in the Supreme Court: The New Deal, 1931–1940." *University of Chicago Law Review* 54: 504–555.

Eagle, S. 1996. *Regulatory Takings.* Charlottesville, VA: Michie.

Ely, J. W. 1998. *The Guardian of Every Other Right.* 2d ed. New York: Oxford University Press.

———. 1996. "Reflections on *Buchanan v. Warley,* Property Rights, and Race." *Vanderbilt Law Review* 51:953.

———. 1996. "Property Rights and the Supreme Court in World War II." *Journal of Supreme Court History* 1: 19–34.

———. 1993. "The Enigmatic Place of Property Rights in Modern Constitutional Thought." In J. Bodenhamer and J. W. Ely, eds., *The Bill of Rights in Modern America: After 200 Years.* Bloomington: Indiana University Press, pp. 87–100.

Epstein, R. 1985. *Takings: Private Property and the Power of Eminent Domain.* Cambridge, MA: Harvard University Press.

Epstein, R., ed. 2000. *Constitutional Protection of Private Property and Freedom of Contract.* New York: Garland Publishing.

Erickson, N. S. 1989. "*Muller v. Oregon* Reconsidered: The Origins of a Sex-Based Doctrine of Liberty of Contract." *Labor History* 30:228.

Fischel, W. 1995. *Regulatory Takings: Law, Economics, and Politics.* Cambridge, MA: Harvard University Press.

Friedman, L. 2002. *American Law in the Twentieth Century.* New Haven: Yale University Press.

———. 1986. "A Search for Seizure: *Pennsylvania Coal v. Mahon* in Context." *Law and History Review* 4: 1–22.

Harrington, M. P. 2002. "'Public Use' and the Original Understanding of the So-Called 'Takings' Clause." *Hastings Law Journal* 53:1245.

Horwitz, M. 1992. *The Transformation of American Law: 1870–1960.* Cambridge, MA: Harvard University Press.

Kendall, D., Dowling, J., and Schwartz, A. 2000. *Takings Litigation Handbook.* Cincinnati, OH: American Legal Publishing.

Meltz, R., Merriam, D., and Frank, R. 1998. *The Takings Issue: Constitutional Limits on Land Use Control and Environmental Regulation.* Washington, DC: Island Press.

Michelman, F. 1988. "Takings, 1987." *Columbia Law Review* 88:1600.

———. 1967. "Property, Utility, and Fairness: Comments on the Ethical Foundations of 'Just Compensation' Law." *Harvard Law Review* 80:1165.

Paul, E. F. 1987. *Property Rights and Eminent Domain.* New Brunswick, NJ: Transaction Books.

Paul, E. F., and Dickman, H. 1990. *Liberty, Property, and the Future of Constitutional Development.* Albany: State University of New York Press.

Peterson, A. L. 1989. "The Takings Clause: In Search of Underlying Principles." *California Law Review* 77:1299.

Phelan, M. 1995. "The Current Status of Historical Preservation Law in Regulatory Takings Jurisprudence: Has the *Lucas* 'Missile' Dismantled Preservation Programs?" *Fordham Environmental Law Journal* 6:785.

Pound, R. 1909. "Liberty of Contract." *Yale Law Journal* 18: 454–487.

Radin, M. 1988. "The Liberal Conception of Property: Cross Currents in the Jurisprudence of Takings." *Columbia Law Review* 88:1667.

Sax, J. L. 1993. "Property Rights and the Economy of Nature: Understanding *Lucas v. South Carolina Coastal Council.*" *Stanford Law Review* 45:1433.

———. 1971. "Takings, Private Property, and Public Rights." *Yale Law Journal* 81:149.

———. 1964. "Takings and the Police Power." *Yale Law Journal* 74:36.

Schultz, D. 1992. *Property, Power, and American Democracy.* New Brunswick, NJ: Transaction Publishers.

Siegan, B. 1997. *Property and Freedom: The Constitution, the Courts, and Land-Use Regulation.* New Brunswick, NJ, and London: Transaction Publishers.

Siemon, C. L. 1985. "Of Regulatory Takings and Other Myths." *Journal of Land Use and Environmental Law* 1:105.

Singer, J. W. 2001. *Introduction to Property.* Gaithersburg, MD: Aspen Law and Business.

Stoebuck, W. B. 1990. "Police Power, Takings, and Due Process." *Washington and Lee Law Review* 37:1057.

Talmadge, P. 2000. "The Myth of Property Absolutism and Modern Government: The Interaction of Police Power and Property Rights." *Washington Law Review* 75:857.

Thompson, B. H. 1990. "Judicial Takings." *Virginia Law Review* 76:1449–1544.

Treanor, W. M. 1995. "The Original Understandings of the Takings Clause and the Political Process." *Columbia Law Review* 95:782.

Urofsky, M. 1985. "State Courts and Protective Legislation During the Progressive Era: A Re-Evaluation." *Journal of American Legal History* 72: 63–91.

Waldron, J. 1988. *The Right to Private Property.* Oxford, UK: Clarendon Press.

Walston, R. E. 2001. "The Constitution and Property: Due Process, Regulatory Takings, and Judicial Takings." *Utah Law Review* 2001:379–438.
White, G. E. 2000. *The Constitution and the New Deal.* Cambridge, MA: Harvard University Press.
Wright, D.C., and Laughner, N. 2002. "Shaken, Not Stirred: Has *Tahoe-Sierra* Settled or Muddied the Regulatory Takings Waters?" *Environmental Law Reporter* 32:11177.

4

INTO THE TWENTY-FIRST CENTURY: ISSUES AND PROSPECTS

> *[Property] in its particular application means "that dominion which one man claims and exercises over the external things of the world, in exclusion of every other individual." In its larger and juster meaning, it embraces every thing to which a man may attach a value and have a right; and which leaves to every one else the like advantage.*
> —JAMES MADISON, "PROPERTY" (1792)

At the beginning of the twenty-first century, several critical questions remain about the extent of constitutional protection of private property. Property rights advocates urge more court intervention in government activity, not less. Other political groups advocate a greater role for legislatures to protect environmental and other interests against individual uses of private property that they perceive to be wasteful or destructive of larger public interests. The U.S. Supreme Court has not explicitly endorsed a heightened degree of scrutiny of economic legislation under the Due Process Clause, but many property rights advocates believe that it should. Opponents cite the excesses of the *Lochner* era to argue that substantive due process inevitably means that courts replace legislative policy decisions with their own preferences. Also critical is the question of the future direction of the Supreme Court's ad hoc evaluation of government action to determine whether a regulatory taking has occurred. As noted in Chapter 3, the Supreme Court now considers two categories of cases to be per se takings requiring compensation to the property owner without the need to balance the government's interest. Will more per se categories be added? Once again, this question divides property rights advocates and other political groups, particularly environmentalists.

Another continuing debate concerns the fundamental question of defining the constitutional property to be protected in the first instance. State and federal courts have encountered a dramatically increased number of takings claims following the Supreme Court's regulatory takings decisions in the 1980s and 1990s. The vast majority of those cases involved land, but the Supreme Court's new emphasis on the Takings Clause suggests that lower courts can expect more cases with issues affecting other forms of property as well. This chapter will consider the extent to which intellectual property and biotechnological processes are subject to constitutional protection. Privately owned intellectual property is an important source of wealth for individuals and corporations. The chapter will conclude with a consideration of the resource allocation of air and water as a property right traditionally associated with private landownership. The extent to which courts will consider air and water to be a public resource, or capable of private ownership, will affect future efforts by the government to protect environmental resources.

What Is "Property" for Purposes of Constitutional Protection?

In order to present a valid case for a compensable taking, a claimant must prove that she (1) has a specific property interest; and (2) that the government has appropriated that interest in some way. The U.S. Constitution does not define the property that is to be protected from governmental interference. In the years immediately following ratification of the Constitution, land was the most important marketable commodity. U.S. courts were especially vigilant to protect investment expectations with respect to land transactions, as the Supreme Court's opinion in *Fletcher v. Peck* (1810) reflects. But courts also protected less tangible forms of property, including debts owed to creditors, liens, and other contracts. At one time, slaves were considered to be a constitutionally protected form of property. Over the course of U.S. history, new economic interests have constantly emerged to claim status as property, demonstrating that property definitions must be dynamic. The role of the courts in determining what may be counted as property for the Constitution's guarantees is thus critically important.

The Supreme Court has said that in most cases it must defer to state definitions of what constitutes property for purposes of the federal Constitution's property guarantees, as it did in *Phillips v. Washington Legal Foundation* (1998). But the Court has also suggested that there are limits to the latitude afforded to state legislatures to redefine property rights in such a way as to retroactively impair an investor's expectations. We have yet to consider in detail how courts, as an initial matter, have determined what economic or other interests qualify as property. Yet the future direction of constitutional protection of property rights must increasingly confront that question. Property in land remains the primary focus of the Supreme Court's takings jurisprudence because real estate represents the most important economic investment for most

U.S. citizens. The per se regulatory takings rule followed in *Lucas*—the deprivation of all economically viable use of an owner's land—appears to be limited to land-use regulations.

The Supreme Court generally considers property not to be limited to objects that a person may possess but to be anything to which a bundle of rights attaches—including the right to exclude others from interference and the right to pass on the interest to others upon death. In *United States v. General Motors Corp.* (1945, 378), the Supreme Court defined property as "the group of rights inhering in the citizen's relation to the physical thing, as the right to possess, use and dispose of it." Property need not be a physical thing, however. The Supreme Court has viewed liens and other contract rights, interest from funds deposited by attorneys in client trust funds, and intangible proprietary information to be property protected by the Takings Clause. Moreover, property is more than mere economic value. Even when the property interest may have no economically realizable value to its owner, the Supreme Court has recognized that constitutional property rights may nonetheless be at stake (*Loretto v. Teleprompter Manhattan CATV Corp.* [1982]). Therefore, property is said to be potentially anything for which individuals can exclude others, with state backing, against the rest of society. A key criterion is historical tradition, but another key is the observation by Justice Oliver Wendell Holmes Jr. that "property depends upon exclusion by law from interference" by others—something of a cyclical definition because a society must first define what interests it is willing to protect (*International News Service v. Associated Press* [1918], 246).

In 1964, Charles Reich published an important article, "The New Property," in which he suggested that government benefits—including, for example, social security and welfare benefits—should be viewed as a new type of property to be accorded constitutional protection. Reich suggested that courts should safeguard the receipt of public benefits by individuals from arbitrary deprivation, because for many those public benefits had become an important means of livelihood. The Supreme Court has not equated public benefits programs with the traditional property rights protected under the Constitution, but the concept of new property is an apt one to describe generally the idea that society's expectations about forms of property are not static but may change over time.

The Supreme Court in recent years has invoked seemingly inconsistent methods to identify interests that may be considered constitutional property (Merrill 2000, 889). Property definitions are important because the scope of constitutional protection depends upon them. If the Supreme Court should return to a stricter review of economic legislation, as some have advocated that it should, any interest that might be conceived of as property could greatly restrict the authority of governing bodies.

The importance of this question—what is property?—for the future of constitutional protection is examined first in two areas of growing commercial importance. First, intangible intellectual property such as a patented invention constitutes a significant source of wealth in the United States. The scope of constitutional protection depends upon the scope of governmental authority to determine what may qualify as intellectual property. Second, governmental regulation of biotechnology is an unsettled area of law implicating questions of property rights in the human body. To the extent a property model is chosen to determine rights in the human body and products derived from it, takings issues may result.

This chapter concludes with a consideration of competing theories of property rights in the area of environmental law. James Madison, in his essay on the subject of property excerpted at the beginning of this chapter, regarded property as a set of individual interests apparently bounded by the equivalent interests of others in the community, *"which leaves to everyone else the like advantage"* (Madison 1907, 101, emphasis in original). How one defines property interests in environmental resources—as an individual or a community right, for instance—will determine the future direction of constitutional rights of property owners.

Intellectual Property: Takings Implications

The term *intellectual property* refers to ideas, inventions, and forms of expression that are accorded some degree of property status. In the United States, that status is conferred by federal statutes awarding patent, trademark, and copyright protection to applicants. For a term of years set by Congress, owners of patents and copyrights are given exclusive rights in the commercial use of their inventions or ideas, rights that may be enforced against interference by others through the award of monetary damages or equitable relief by courts. Patents and copyrights confer a monopoly right not permitted in other commercial activities, thereby providing an incentive for the creation of new inventions, technologies, and expressive works.

The U.S. Constitution contains a separate intellectual property clause in Article I, section 8. That clause awards Congress the power "to promote the Progress of Science and useful Arts, by securing for limited times to authors and inventors the exclusive right to their respective writings and discoveries." The clause permits, but does not require, Congress to create legal protections for copyright and patents. Congress determines the duration of the legal status, what qualifies for this legal status, and what actions by others constitute interference with the intellectual property right such that a court will order the payment of damages or injunctive relief.

For example, Congress has specified that patents may be awarded to "whoever invents or discovers any new and useful process, machine, manufacture, or composition of matter, or any new and useful improvement thereof." In the twentieth century, Congress added patent protection to new plant varieties, subject to confirmation by the U.S. Department of Agriculture that the patent application be for a plant that is in fact "new" in the sense that it is not naturally occurring.

Congress also determines the number of years that the creator of an expressive work may hold an exclusive copyright. The Copyright Term Extension Act of 1998 enlarged the duration of copyrights by 20 years, so that copyrights owned by individual persons expire 70 years after the author's death, and copyrights owned by corporations expire 95 years from publication or 120 years from the date of creation. In 2003, the Supreme Court considered a challenge to Congress's authority to expand the term of years for copyright protection to such lengths. In *Eldred v. Ashcroft* (2003), the Supreme Court ruled that the Copyright Term Extension Act did not violate the constitutional requirement that copyrights endure only for "limited times." The Court also ruled that the act did not violate First Amendment rights of those persons wishing to use the copyrighted works.

For many corporations and individuals, intellectual property rights are their most important form of economic wealth. Patents for pharmaceutical drugs, for example, can be worth billions of dollars because of the right to exclude others from marketing the product claimed in the patent. The immense wealth generated by Microsoft is another example of the potential commercial effect of exclusive rights to inventions and ideas. The many current controversies about the extent of intellectual property rights—international piracy, achieving an international consensus on enforcement, Internet property, and digital music copying, to name only a few—involve government management of private rights of individuals and businesses against other individuals and businesses.

The lengthy tradition of constitutional property rights lies in the background of these debates. As acknowledged by the U.S.

Court of Claims in *DeGraffenried v. United States* (Fed. Cl. 1993, 387), "The patent laws create substantial private property rights," including "the right to exclude others from making, using, or selling the patented invention throughout the United States." In *Florida Prepaid v. College Savings Bank* (1999, 642), the U.S. Supreme Court said that patents "have long been considered a species of property," citing an 1876 case for the proposition that "a patent for an invention is as much property as a patent for land" (*Consolidated Fruit-Jar Co. v. Wright* [1876], 96).

With respect to government action, the Constitution's property clauses are potentially significant in two ways. First, although Congress is not required to create intellectual property rights at all, once it has done so there may be some constitutional constraint upon retroactive modifications to those rights. Intellectual property rights differ from property rights (primarily land) traditionally viewed in the Lockean sense of a natural or preexisting right, because the existence of an intellectual property right is created by legislation. Patents and copyrights are more in the nature of a contract benefit, conferred by the government in exchange for disclosure of the original work. The fact that the owner can exclude others from interference with this form of property is purely a creation of statute. Yet Locke's labor theory of property might suggest a strong property interest to be respected by the government due to the intellectual effort and monetary resources required to create new technologies and inventions.

The Supreme Court has long recognized that the federal government, as well as the states, ought not change expectations retroactively, particularly to impair previously conferred benefits supported by investment-backed expectations. The Court has not yet definitively addressed the extent to which either the Takings Clause or the Due Process Clause may limit Congress's ability to change intellectual property laws so as to retroactively effect existing patents and copyrights. The Supreme Court has suggested that settled expectations of patent holders are entitled to great respect when courts consider whether to change judicially created patent doctrines (see *Festo Corp. v. Shoketsu* [2002]). Some scholars have suggested that new regulations that affect existing patent rights may constitute a taking and thus require compensation (Ackiron 1991, 175). Other scholars suggest that Congress has plenary power to impose conditions on the use of intellectual property and that no person has a vested right in a patent.

Second, in instances in which the government itself makes use of intellectual property owned by others, without permission, compensation is generally considered analogous to a taking of a property right, just as a private person would be subject to payment of damages for the unauthorized use of another's intellectual property. Claims that the federal government has made use of a patent or other intellectual property are heard in the federal Court of Claims in Washington, D.C., the forum for other property and compensation claims against the federal government. Congress has enacted what might be termed a just compensation statute to permit suits against the federal government for its infringement of a private citizen's patent or copyright. This statute (28 USC 1498) specifies that "reasonable and entire" compensation is required for the government's unauthorized use of patents or copyrights. Whether compensation is required in a given case depends upon the type of intellectual property, the extent of the government's use, and other considerations. As one scholar has characterized the issue, "If the law of takings as applied to real and personal property is the 'muddle' that many commentators insist it is, the law of takings with regard to intellectual property can only be characterized as a muddle within the muddle" (Cotter 1998, 529).

Because Congress permits the creation of property rights in inventions but is not required to do so under the U.S. Constitution, the federal government possesses broad authority to determine what may be patented. Recently, scholars have debated whether a business method should or should not be patentable. Patents for medical methods, for example, have significant implications for the costs of health care. In 1996, Congress amended the patent code to limit the enforceability of any medical method patent used in the course of performing medical services (35 USC 287). The amendment followed a lower federal court's decision (*Pallin v. Singer* [Dist. VT 1996]), holding a doctor liable for infringement of another doctor's patent in a surgical method. The case was widely denounced by the American Medical Association and in Congress. Accordingly, the 1996 amendment exempts doctors and other health care providers from liability for infringement of medical procedure patents that do not involve drugs or medical devices. Owners of previously issued medical method patents have argued that Congress's action constitutes a taking under the Fifth Amendment, and some scholars agree (see, e.g., Brinckerhoff 1996).

Congress can specify categories of inventions that would normally be patentable as outside the scope of patent protection, as it has done by denying or revoking previously issued patents under the Atomic Energy Act for inventions useful solely in an atomic weapon. The decision to deny a patent application on the basis that the subject matter of the application does not meet the standards set by Congress does not deny a constitutional property right, unless the government has arbitrarily treated an individual application differently from others. Equal protection permits no distinctions among applicants based upon race or gender, for instance, but the denial of a patent application is not viewed to be a taking of a preexisting property right. If the government has an important government objective for doing so, there is no taking to deny a patent application on public policy grounds.

Use of Patented Inventions by the Federal Government

The view that the Fifth Amendment's Takings Clause applies to the government's use of privately owned intellectual property has a long pedigree. In *James v. Campbell* (1882), the Supreme Court considered a claim by an inventor against a postmaster for unauthorized use of an invention that printed a postmark and canceled the postage stamp at the same time. Although the inventor's patent was determined to be invalid, and thus the inventor could assert no property right against the postmaster, the Supreme Court considered the general question whether the use of a patented invention by the government requires compensation to the owner. The Court compared the government's unauthorized use of a patented invention to a taking of land:

> That the government of the United States when it grants letters-patent for a new invention or discovery in the arts, confers upon the patentee an exclusive property in the patented invention which cannot be appropriated or used by the government itself, without just compensation, any more than it can appropriate or use without compensation land which has been patented to a private purchaser, we have no doubt. If it could use such inventions without compensation, the inventors could get no return at all for their discoveries and experiments. It has been the general practice, when inventions have been made which are desirable for government use, either for the government to purchase them from the inventors, and use them as secrets of the proper department; or, if a patent is granted, to pay the patentee a fair compensation for their use. (*James* 357–358)

In England, the Court noted, the sovereign was said to reserve the prerogative to use inventions without compensation as a condition for granting the patent. The situation was different in the United States. In this country, the Court maintained, "the government of the United States, as well as the citizen, is subject to the Constitution" (*James* 358).

Lower courts have debated the extent to which 28 U.S.C. sec. 1498, the compensation statute for unauthorized governmental use of intellectual property, is equivalent to an eminent domain proceeding. That statute confers upon the federal government the absolute right to use any patented invention without notice to the owner. The government's use of a patented invention is considered to be a compulsory, nonexclusive license. But if the government does appropriate privately owned intellectual property, the statute requires "reasonable and entire compensation" for the government's use. The Clean Air Act also authorizes Congress to institute compulsory licensing of patented products and technologies useful for air pollution control, with reasonable compensation to be paid to the inventor (42 USC 1857). In this sense, the government's authority to appropriate intellectual property over the objection of the owner is like the government's authority to take privately owned land through eminent domain.

In order to receive compensation for the federal government's appropriation of a patented invention or technology, a claimant must prove ownership of a valid patent issued by the U.S. Patent and Trademark Office and that the government infringed the patent. As is the case in eminent domain actions for real property, a government agency cannot be enjoined from using a patented invention, but it must pay reasonable and entire compensation, which under the statute includes a reasonable royalty rate for the patent, along with incidental costs to the owner such as attorney fees. The amount due the patent holder also includes compensation for delayed payment of those royalties.

For example, in the 1950s the U.S. Navy used a privately patented process to remove accumulations of rust, marine growth, and other corrosion from the ballast tanks of ships. The owner of the patent brought suit to obtain payment for the Navy's use of the patented process. In *Amerace Esna Corporation v. United States* (Ct. Cl. 1972), the company proved that it owned a valid patent for this process and that the government had used it for a number of years without paying royalties. The patent owner was awarded $25,000 in lost royalties and additional delay damages at a rate of 4 percent of the royalties dating back to the government's first use of the patented process.

The calculation of a reasonable royalty is often contentious. The Court of Claims has often stated, as it did in *Amerace Esna*, that the reasonable royalty rate is "what the parties would have agreed upon, if both were reasonably trying to reach an agreement" (*Amerace Esna* 1780). As part of this consideration, courts will consider established royalty rates that other licensees may have paid to the owner. In cases in which it is difficult to determine a reasonable royalty, courts may choose to award the lost profits of the patent owner or the savings to the government from its use of the invention.

Although claims by patent owners against the government are governed by the language of the statute, the Fifth Amendment's Takings Clause guides these compensation rules. In *Tektronix, Inc. v. United States* (Ct. Cl. 1977, 346–347), for example, the Court of Claims wrote: "It is settled that recovery of reasonable compensation under §1498 is premised on a theory of eminent domain taking under the Fifth Amendment. The Supreme Court has in many cases emphasized that basic equitable principles of fairness are the governing consideration in determining just compensation for an *eminent domain* taking." Citing cases involving government appropriations of real estate, the court concluded that those principles include "the full monetary equivalent of the property taken," calculated as the fair market value of the property at the time of the taking (*Tektronix* 347).

THE INVENTIONS SECRECY ACT AND FEDERAL EXPORT REGULATIONS

In most cases, the government's unauthorized use of a patented invention does not restrict the patent owner's ability to market the invention to others. However, in some instances the federal government can acquire an exclusive right to the use of a technology or invention submitted for a patent. The government can also delay the patent application under a secrecy order—preventing the disclosure or use of the technology in the interest of national security or some other compelling government purpose. The federal government has wide-ranging authority to restrict exports of patented technology, as well as to determine whether it wishes to appropriate new technology proposed in a patent application exclusively for government use. The extent to which these government actions constitute a compensable "taking" is unclear.

In 1951, Congress enacted the Inventions Secrecy Act, which authorizes government agencies to delay a patent application if the technology or invention would be detrimental to the national security of the United States. Upon application by a government agency, the commissioner of patents may issue a secrecy order preventing disclosure or publication of the information contained in the patent application for one year. The secrecy order may be renewed for additional one-year periods, at the government's discretion, for potentially unlimited duration. The patent application remains pending during this time, and the government may itself appropriate the technology described in the patent application.

Inventors whose patent applications are subject to a secrecy order have no means to challenge the patent commissioner's decision, but they can apply to the head of any department or agency that caused the secrecy order to be issued for compensation for damages. They may also apply to the same agency for compensation for any government use of the invention or technology. Failing a settlement, the applicant can bring suit in the Court of Claims to obtain compensation. Among other things, the applicant must establish the fair market value for the delay—a difficult proposition at best.

One study reported that although the number of secrecy orders issued by the U.S. Patent Office was relatively constant in the two decades following enactment of the Inventions Secrecy

Act, beginning in 1979 the number of secrecy orders steadily increased (Hausken 1988, 202). Following the attacks on the World Trade Center in 2001 and the ensuing war on terrorism, it seems likely that government agencies concerned with national security will increasingly invoke the authority of the Inventions Secrecy Act to scrutinize more closely the technology ramifications of some patent applications. The federal government also has wide-ranging authority to restrict the export outside of the United States of patented technology for reasons of national security, foreign policy, nonproliferation of arms, and short supply. Related definitions are broad, and the agencies responsible for determining what technologies should be restricted have substantial discretion to make decisions. In the 1990s, encryption technology in software was broadly prohibited from export on the grounds that it impeded national security investigations of suspected terrorists.

It is unlikely that any export restriction on these grounds would implicate the Takings Clause given the stated interests of the government in national security and other compelling purposes. Yet the issue of whether a secrecy order furthers a legitimate government interest in the nature of a police power, or is more similar to an exercise of eminent domain, has not been definitively resolved. The Inventions Secrecy Act itself provides for compensation in certain cases. For those instances in which compensation is not expressly provided by statute, courts will most likely avoid finding a constitutional taking in the face of the stated government objective of national security. In 1980, a House committee hearing into the application of the Inventions Secrecy Act questioned whether the act is an exercise of the power of eminent domain, but the committee did not attempt to resolve this issue (Hausken 1988, 203). Arguably, if a secrecy order issued during the patent application process keeps the patent from issuing, then no patent right exists, and thus it cannot be taken.

State Government Immunity for Patent Infringement

Today we have a rather anomalous state of affairs with respect to government takings of patent rights. When the federal government uses a patented invention, compensation is usually required. However, when a state government violates an intellectual property right, it may not be required to compensate the owner because of the doctrine of sovereign immunity (the concept that governments are immune from lawsuits against them by citizens). Sovereign immunity has emerged as an important consideration when state government agencies use a patented technology without compensating the owner. The principle was recognized in this country as early as the colonial era. The federal government has waived its sovereign immunity to permit individuals to sue the federal government for specified claims through the Federal Tort Claims Act of 1946. The reasonable-and-entire-compensation statute for federal government use of patents and copyright (28 USC 1498) also waives the federal government's sovereign immunity for these types of claims. The principle of sovereign immunity does not prevent suits against specific government officials accused of wrongdoing.

State governments also possess sovereign immunity. The Eleventh Amendment (1798) prohibits suits against states in federal court. Congress can abrogate this state immunity in some cases. In the Patent Remedy Act of 1992, Congress attempted to abrogate state immunity to allow claims for patent infringement against state governments. However, the U.S. Supreme Court invalidated that legislation in *Florida Prepaid v. College Savings Bank* (1999).

The key question in *Florida Prepaid* was whether the Patent Remedy Act was a valid exercise of the federal government's responsibility to secure the Fourteenth Amendment's protections against deprivation of property without due process of law. The Court identified the property issue at stake to be state infringement of patents and the use of sovereign immunity to deny patent owners compensation for the invasion of their patent rights, conduct that Congress sought to remedy through the Patent Remedy Act. The Court affirmed that patents "have long been considered a species of property"; as such, "they are surely included within the 'property' of which no person may be deprived by a State without due process of law" (*Florida Prepaid* 642). But the majority of the Court invalidated the act on the ground that "Congress identified no pattern of patent infringement by the States, let alone a pattern of constitutional violations" (*Florida Prepaid* 640). In other words, Congress may abrogate state immunity when state conduct makes clear the necessity for doing so, as it did by documenting the record of racial discrimination by states when Congress abrogated state immunity in voting rights cases. The Supreme Court, however, did not believe that state patent infringement occurred with enough frequency to justify congressional intervention.

Critics of the Supreme Court's decision in *Florida Prepaid* argue that the Takings Clause, and not the Fourteenth Amendment's Due Process Clause, is the appropriate vehicle to solve the problem of state government violations of intellectual property rights (Ghost 1999). For the time being, at least, intellectual property owners with a grievance against a state government agency for uncompensated use of intellectual property must rely on state law to determine whether the claim will be heard. In some states, general eminent domain statutes setting forth procedures for compensation may be construed to permit suits about intellectual property as an inverse condemnation claim. Some states specifically permit suits for intellectual property claims against state agencies, but the majority, like Florida, do not. However, following the Supreme Court's decision in *Florida Prepaid,* several states have enacted legislation to put such protections in place.

Regulatory Takings and Intellectual Property

For patented inventions used by the government, courts have considered the requirement of compensation to be analogous to the exercise of eminent domain—the power to take private property for public use. The analogy is a physical appropriation of property by the government, which in the context of real estate results in a per se taking that requires compensation. Regulatory takings (see Chapter 3) concern the degree of governmental regulation of the use of property. Unduly burdensome regulations may also result in a compensable taking. A looming question is whether the Supreme Court will review regulation of intellectual property in the same manner as land-use restrictions. The Supreme Court has confronted this question in only one case to date (*Ruckelshaus v. Monsanto* [1984]). Because *Ruckelshaus* considered a special form of intellectual property (a trade secret), the decision may not be an indication of the likelihood that regulatory takings analysis will extend to other forms of intellectual property such as patents.

A trade secret is a form of intellectual property recognized by state and federal laws. Unlike a patent, trademark, or copyright, a trade secret is not a government-granted, exclusive property right. Rather, a trade secret may include proprietary information of a company pertaining to processes, technology, or know-how for production of a product or business method that provides an advantage over competitors. The value to the owner of a trade secret is the ability to keep the information confidential from competitors. Against the government, the owner of a trade secret may have constitutional property rights with respect to unauthorized disclosure to others. This form of intellectual property, however, is not covered under a specific compensation statute, as is the case with patents and copyrights.

In *Ruckelshaus,* the Supreme Court addressed the question whether a trade secret is property to which the Takings Clause applies to remedy government interference. The Court ruled that it is and that regulatory use of a trade secret could be a taking. The Court reasoned that because trade secrets have long been recognized in state law to be a property interest, the Takings Clause therefore applies to proprietary information as it does to contracts, liens, and other intangible forms of property. According to the Court, the property right in a trade secret depends upon the "extent to which the owner of the secret protects his interest from disclosure to others" (*Ruckelshaus* 1002). In other words, the property right exists only as long as the owner does not disclose the information publicly or to any person who has no obligation not to reveal the secret. If the government reveals the trade secret, the value of the proprietary information is lost.

In *Ruckelshaus*, the Monsanto Corporation challenged Environmental Protection Agency (EPA) regulations that required disclosure of health, safety, and environmental data submitted to the EPA in applications for registration of pesticides under the federal Insecticide, Fungicide, and Rodenticide Act. That statute requires that a pesticide must be registered with the EPA to be sold in the United States. The company submitted applications designating certain information as trade secrets. Under a prior version of the law, the EPA was prohibited from revealing trade secrets publicly or using trade secret information to evaluate other applications. But the EPA *did* disclose publicly some of the company's proprietary information. Because the statutory scheme promised confidentiality at the time the company's trade secrets were disclosed, the Court found that a compensable taking had occurred.

Monsanto also challenged a 1978 amendment to that act that permitted more government use and disclosure of proprietary information submitted for a product registration. Monsanto contended that these new regulations also constituted a taking of its property. To determine whether the new rules constituted a compensable taking, the Court applied the regulatory takings analysis articulated in *Penn Central v. New York* (1978). The *Penn Central* inquiry to determine whether a restriction on the use of land requires compensation directs courts to consider three factors: (1) the economic impact of the regulation on the claimant; (2) the extent to which the regulation has interfered with distinct investment-backed expectations; and (3) the character of the government action.

The Supreme Court believed that Monsanto did not have "reasonable investment-backed expectations" with respect to the 1978 amendments because the company was "on notice of the manner in which EPA was authorized to use and disclose any data turned over to it by an applicant for registration" (*Ruckelshaus* 1006). The property rights that companies must give up in order to register pesticides for sale in the United States are not an "unconstitutional condition," according to the Court, because the government is charged with regulating products such as pesticides that are potentially harmful to persons and the environment. The conditions placed on the company were thus "rationally related" to a "legitimate" government interest (*Ruckelshaus* 1007). Congress's purpose in passing the law was to make useful products available to the public more quickly by avoiding duplication of research and thereby approving applications more efficiently. The disclosure to the general public of the information applicants submitted for registration directly benefits the public. The Supreme Court therefore upheld the trade secret disclosure provisions of the 1978 statute against Monsanto's claim that the compelled disclosures constitute a taking.

Ruckelshaus is important because it is the only Supreme Court opinion to date to address the question whether government regulations that affect intellectual property rights may constitute a regulatory taking. Some scholars have suggested that *Ruckelshaus* may have overruled cases that considered *all* unauthorized government uses of intellectual property, including patents, to be equivalent to the exercise of eminent domain and that a case-by-case regulatory takings analysis will now be the preferred approach for any government use of intellectual property (Cotter 1998, 555). Other scholars suggest *Ruckelshaus* should not be read to stand for a broad rule that government interferences with intellectual property should always be evaluated under regulatory taking principles (Heald and Wells 1998, 868). *Ruckelshaus* could also mean that the government's use or regulation must virtually destroy the value of a patent for the owner to receive any compensation. However, it is clear that the Supreme Court will balance the owner's right to confidentiality in a trade secret against the asserted government need to interfere with that right. Whether this public-need inquiry will extend to other forms of intellectual property, such as patents and copyrights, remains to be seen.

Property Rights and the Human Body

Biotechnology and medical-related processes—specific forms of intellectual property that have become increasingly important commercially—raise issues for property rights that are not implicated in the usual intellectual property case. Biotechnology may be defined to include technologies and products related to genetic material, genetically engineered organisms, and the like. The consequences of granting extensive private property rights in these technologies is viewed to be undesirable by some. Biotechnology critics, for instance, have urged that nations ban patents on living things and on parts of living things such as genes or cells. Recent debates in the United States over whether gene sequences may be patented, and President George W. Bush's stated objective in 2001 to limit federal financing of human embryonic stem-cell research and to ban cloning of human embryos, call into question the extent to which products and technologies originating from the human body may implicate property rights and, accordingly, whether they deserve a measure of constitutional protection.

Determining the limits of the government's police power to regulate commercial developments in biotechnology is complicated by competing views of the appropriateness of classifying one's interest in the human body, or products derived from the human body, as a property interest. Federal and state laws prohibit the commercial sale of human organs. Courts in the past have considered the human body to constitute quasi-property at best, meaning that for some purposes (e.g., donating organs) human body components are treated like other forms of property. But for other purposes—most notably the ability to sell organs—human body components are *not* treated like other forms of property. Rights of personal autonomy and privacy play a large role in the debate over human tissue as a potential commodity. Yet if the human body and its components are not considered to be property, the scientific use and commercial profit from human cells present difficult issues.

Should products derived from living organisms be the subject of private property rights and thus constitutionally protected? If so, the Takings Clause would operate as a check on the power of government in the way that the federal property clauses have protected more traditional forms of property. The Supreme Court considers significant investment-backed expectations to be an important factor in regulatory takings cases. Biotechnology is a multibillion-dollar industry. The U.S. Patent Office has issued many patents for human genes, new cell lines, genetically modified animals, pharmaceutical products, and bioengineered plants—all representing significant investments. With respect to these commercial developments in biotechnology, constitutional property rights potentially pose two issues: first, whether retroactive changes to regulations substantially impair investment-backed expectations; and second, whether there are limits to the power of the federal government, primarily the U.S. Food and Drug Administration, to regulate or to prohibit the development of biotechnology processes.

Courts and legal scholars have often said that there can be no property rights in human bodies (Singer 2001, 772). One of the few cases to consider the issue suggests that a person does not retain a property interest in organs, tissues, or cells removed from his or her body for use by others. In *Moore v. Regents of the University of California* (CA 1990), a former patient, John Moore, sued his physicians for their use of blood and tissue samples taken over a series of visits, which the physicians used to establish a cell line for which they received a patent estimated to be worth more than $3 billion. The physicians had not disclosed their intended use of the tissue and blood samples taken in connection with Moore's treatment for leukemia. Moore claimed he was owed compensation for the conversion of his genetic property.

The California Supreme Court ruled that Moore had no property interest in the cells after their removal from his body. To prevail on his claim, Moore would have to show that the physicians had interfered with his "ownership or right of possession" in the tissue and blood samples (*Moore* 136). Because Moore had no reasonable expectation of maintaining "ownership or possession" after their removal, the Court said, Moore was not entitled to any compensation from the commercial exploitation of his cells. The court left open the possibility that a person could retain a property right by contract if a patient expresses a clear intent to maintain control over cells after their removal. In John Moore's case, however, the physicians had not disclosed their intended use.

Biological materials taken in medical procedures are often used for research purposes. Although the American Medical Association's code of ethics suggests that consent of the patient should be obtained before biological materials are used for research purposes, the association does not believe such consent is legally required because patients do not retain property rights for tissues removed while they are alive. One scholar has suggested that there are strong public policy reasons for this position, proposing a policy in which "tissue is used with permission where possible, and without permission when the public interest in use is significant and the possible dignitary or pecuniary harm to the individual is de minimis" (Alta Charo 2002, 442). Alternatively, human cells and other body tissues could be viewed as "common property" rather than personal property, thus recognizing the significant public interest in continuing research and development of medical therapies.

Presumed-Consent Statutes and Due Process

The ability to recycle human body tissue and organs for use as transplants for living persons creates a market (noncommercial, in theory) that relies upon voluntary donations from the relatives of deceased persons. In a few countries, the legal system considers a person's body after death to revert to the government for the limited purpose of harvesting tissue suitable for transplant. A dead body is, in essence, the property of the state, although relatives retain control over the ultimate disposition of the body for burial purposes. In the United States, the human body at death is not considered the property either of the next of kin or the state. The next of kin retain some interest—short of a property right—in the disposition of remains of deceased relatives. State governments have at least a limited possessory interest in cadavers, and dead bodies are subject to state control for some purposes. For example, state laws specify where a body may be buried and, if not cremated, how the body is to be prepared for burial. Other laws grant to medical examiners the right (and sometimes the obligation) to perform autopsies in certain circumstances.

Although the persons most closely related to a deceased person do not own the body as property, courts have recognized a quasi-property right in the next of kin to the bodily integrity of remains. This quasi-property right generally prevents medical providers from harvesting organs from dead persons without either the consent of the person while alive or the consent of the next of kin after death. The fact that U.S. courts have considered human bodies, at best, to be merely quasi-property is important for the question of organ donation for transplantation to living persons. The United States relies on voluntary donations of human organs for transplantation. Transplant procedures have become so successful, in fact, that there is a shortage of organs and other tissues available for this purpose. If cadavers were considered to revert to the government as the property of the state, as some countries recognize, the legal status of organ and tissue harvesting would be more clear.

The status of human body tissues and cells as quasi-property has led to conflicting opinions between state and federal courts over the constitutionality of presumed-consent statutes for harvesting corneas from cadavers. On occasion, medical examiners or coroners receive unclaimed bodies, and sometimes the next of kin are not immediately available for consultation about donation of usable tissue from the body. A number of states have enacted presumed-consent statutes to permit medical examiners during a death investigation to harvest corneas for later use by others, in the absence of any indication that the donor or the donor's next of kin would have objected. Cornea transplants are extremely successful, but the supply of transplantable corneas remains low because corneal tissue must be removed from a body within ten hours of death. In order to obtain corneas for transplant, the statutes permit medical examiners, while conducting an autopsy, to remove corneal tissue if no objection by the next of kin of the decedent is known by the medical examiner.

For body parts other than corneas, most states have enacted the Uniform Anatomical Gift Act, which authorizes removal of organs when no knowledge of objection is known and after "a reasonable effort has been made to locate and inform [the next of kin] of their option to make, or object to making, an anatomical gift." The difference between presumed consent statutes for corneas and those for all other organs is that the medical examiner, under the Uniform Anatomical Gift Act, must make a "reasonable effort" to question the next of kin prior to removal, and corneas may be removed if the medical examiner merely "has no knowledge of objection to the removal."

The supreme courts of Florida and Georgia upheld their respective presumed-consent statutes against challenges that the statutes permit a taking of private property by state action for a nonpublic purpose. The courts based their decisions on the position that next of kin have no property right in the remains of a decedent, although these courts recognized that generally the common law confers a right on the next of kin to bury a relative without mutilation to the body. In *Florida v. Powell* (FL 1986, 1192), the court explained that rights of the next of kin in a person's remains are based upon "the personal right . . . to bury the body rather than any property right in the body itself." The court stated: "The view that the next of kin has no property right but merely a limited right to possess the body for burial purposes is universally accepted by courts and commentators."

The Florida court also considered whether next of kin have a due process right to control the disposition of the remains of a relative, claimed in that case to be a "fundamental right of personal liberty protected against unreasonable governmental intrusion by the due process clause" (*Florida* 1193). The argument is that taking corneas without confirmed knowledge of the family's preference infringes upon a right characterized as a liberty interest. The court also rejected this constitutional challenge. The court said that freedom of choice concerning personal matters exists only for ongoing relationships among living persons. The court also noted that there was no evidence that the next of kin's objections to the removal of the corneal tissues for human transplants were based on any fundamental tenets of their religious beliefs. The decision turned, instead, on the balance between the public health interest in cornea donation and the "infinitesimally small intrusion" of their removal (*Florida* 1191).

Similarly, in *Georgia Lions Eye Bank v. Lavant* (GA 1985), the Georgia Supreme Court held that Georgia's presumed-consent statute violated no constitutionally protected right in a decedent's body. In that case, the parents of an infant were not given specific notice of the intended removal of the deceased infant's corneas. The lower court had held that the statute violated the parents' due process right because it deprived the next of kin of a "property right in the corpse" without notice and an opportunity to object. The Georgia Supreme Court disagreed. It held that common law interests such as this could be modified or abrogated by the legislature in view of the state's responsibility for the public welfare and its specific goal to preserve corneas for later use.

However, three federal courts have disagreed with this analysis. Two decisions of the Sixth Circuit Court of Appeals in the 1990s recognized a property interest in the next of kin that could not be taken without due process of law. And the Ninth Circuit Court of Appeals in *Newman v. Sathyavaglswaran* (9th Cir. 2002) reached the same result. The court held that California's presumed consent statute violates due process when corneas are harvested without providing the next of kin an opportunity to object. Determining that both the law of California and "national common law" gave to next of kin the exclusive right to possess bodies of deceased relatives for burial, the parents thus had a property interest that could not be deprived without procedural due process.

The presumed-consent statute at issue in *Newman* allowed the coroner to remove corneal tissue without any effort to notify and obtain the consent of the next of kin, "if the coroner has no knowledge of objection to the removal" (*Newman* 795). The stated purpose of the act was to provide California nonprofit eye banks an adequate supply of corneal tissue. In considering whether the coroner's implementation of the statute deprived the parents of property, the court defined *property* as "the group of rights inhering in the citizen's relation to the physical thing, as the right to possess, use and dispose of it" (*Newman* 795). The court rejected the argument that because California forbids the trade of body parts for profit, the next of kin lack a property interest in the tissue of a deceased relative. Because the court believed California law recognized the next of kin's interest in a relative's body to be a property right, it ruled that the legislature may not constitutionally authorize the deprivation of such an interest without appropriate procedural safeguards. "At bottom," the court said, "property rights serve human values. They are recognized to that end and are limited by it" (*Newman* 798). Property rights were necessary in such cases, the court reasoned, because as a property right the "dignity of the human body in its final disposition" is preserved. According to the court, California's significant interest in obtaining corneas or other organs of the deceased in order to contribute to the living did not outweigh this property right in the next of kin.

Courts in the United States undoubtedly would protect the right of religious freedom in next of kin who would view any removal of tissue as a desecration of the body according to the tenets of their religion. Those issues, however, were not presented in any of these cases. Instead, three federal appellate courts have determined that one's property interest is violated if no procedures are in place to allow next of kin an opportunity to object to the removal of any body tissue from a deceased relative. Two state supreme courts—in Georgia and Florida—have ruled differently. The U.S. Supreme Court has not addressed this issue and, indeed, has not directly confronted any question concerning the extent to which a person retains a property right in her own organs or tissue.

Stem Cells and Cloning

Stem cells—cells from the human body that have the ability to become specialized cells to generate new tissue and organs—potentially can replace damaged tissue and organs in living persons, lessening the need to rely on donated organs and tissue from deceased persons. Stem-cell research is also used to create new cell therapies and to test new drugs. Researchers have reported significant progress in experiments on stem cells for therapeutic cloning and other cell therapies, including potential cures for Parkinson's and diabetes, among other diseases.

However, embryonic stem-cell research is controversial because it relies on human embryos and fetuses. Some abortion opponents believe that embryonic research, as well as research on aborted fetuses, should be prohibited entirely. In 1996, Congress prohibited federal financing of embryo experiments. President Bill Clinton subsequently issued an executive order prohibiting federal financing for human cloning research. During the presidency of George W. Bush, the federal government further limited research involving aborted fetuses and imposed strict regulations to discourage the destruction of embryos.

In a TV address in August 2001, President Bush, in order to create a "moral line" with respect to the use of human embryos in research, said scientists could use federal funds to study only those cell lines that had already been extracted from human embryos. Most existing stem-cell lines are commercially owned through patents, which give the owners the right to exclude others from using the cell line absent commercial agreements for use by other researchers. The result has been that very few cell lines are available to researchers, particularly those who rely on funding from the National Institutes of Health.

Related to the political debate concerning embryonic stem-cell research is the issue of reproductive or therapeutic cloning of human embryos. Cloning of embryos provides additional research opportunities, and cloning of adult human tissue potentially could provide therapies with the same genetic makeup as a patient. In 2002, Congress extensively debated whether and how to impose a ban on human cloning. The House passed a ban on all forms of human cloning, whether to produce a baby for an infertile couple or to conduct research on potential therapies. The Senate debated proposals that would allow therapeutic cloning research to proceed, banning only the implantation of a cloned embryo to create a person. The issue was not resolved by Congress in early 2003, but at least four states had already enacted laws prohibiting human reproductive cloning.

An unresolved question is the extent to which human embryos or aborted fetuses can be considered property, either of the human contributors or the researchers who acquire them. Most states have enacted statutes criminalizing the commercial sale of aborted fetuses along with other human body parts. In Georgia, for example, a statute (Human Body Traffic, OCGA sec. 16–12–160) states: "It shall be unlawful for any person, firm, or corporation to buy or sell, to offer to buy or sell, or to assist another in buying or selling a human body or any part of a human body or buy or sell a human fetus or any part thereof." The statute provides exceptions for hair, blood, and "other self-replicating body fluids," payments of processing fees and reimbursement of expenses for donations of bodies or body parts, and "the purchase or sale of human tissue, organs, or other parts of the human body for health sciences education."

Prior state and federal case law suggests conflicting answers to the question whether human embryos or aborted fetuses are property. Some courts have considered stored human embryos to be the property of the couple who contributed the egg and sperm. With respect to aborted fetuses, however, the considerable moral issues surrounding the abortion debate admit no clear resolution about whether an aborted fetus should be considered property. The U.S. Supreme Court's decision in *Roe v. Wade* (1973) recognized the potential for human life of a fetus. Under this view, an aborted fetus could be treated as a cadaver, with the quasi-property status accorded both the state interest and the next of kin. The ban on the commercial sale of aborted fetuses, however, appears to have more to do with fear of encouraging abortions than the fear of commercial exploitation of donated human organs.

These issues illustrate the importance of whether a property model is chosen for embryos and fetuses. To some extent, the property model has already been chosen for stem-cell lines and other genetically created living organisms, because they may be patented. The U.S. Patent Office has issued patents on individual genes and genetically modified animals, in addition to nearly 2,000 patents for plant varieties. The Supreme Court has held that the Patent Act of 1952 permits the creation of property rights in living organisms and other genetically engineered creations, including patents derived from human tissue research. In *Diamond v. Chakrabarty* (1980), the Supreme Court considered the language of the Patent Act to be broad enough to include genetically engineered microorganisms (in this case, a new form of bacteria useful for cleaning oil spills). "The relevant distinction," the Court said, is not "between living and inanimate things, but between products of nature, whether living or not, and human-made inventions" (*Diamond* 313). Because the Court's inquiry was limited to whether the language of the statute could be construed to cover this proposed subject matter, it did not discuss some of the more extreme claims raised by organizations interested in the outcome of the case, including the claim that "genetic research may pose a serious threat to the human race" (*Diamond* 316). The Supreme Court affirmed its view in *Diamond* that living things may be patented under the Patent Act in *J.E.M. Ag Supply v. Pioneer Hi-Bred International* (2001).

At a much earlier point in U.S. history, Supreme Court Justice Joseph Story recognized a "public policy" exception for the validity of patents under the Patent Act. In *Lowell v. Lewis* (C.C.D. MA 1817, 1019), Justice Story stated that a court could determine a patent to be invalid if it was "frivolous or injurious to the well-being, good policy, or sound morals of society." Although subsequent Supreme Court decisions cast doubt on the existence of a public policy exception for the validity of patents, the U.S. Patent and Trademark Office has suggested it might deny applications for animal or human embryo patents, citing the *Lowell* case (Yelpaala 2000, 204.)

In biotechnology generally, the question of what constitutes property is not clearly defined. The right to develop genetically modified human body tissues remains unresolved because of the underlying conflict about whether any part of a human body, or anything derived from it, should be considered property. Furthermore, even though owners of patents for genetic technology and products have some property interest, the extent of permissible governmental regulation is broad. The U.S. Food and Drug Administration extensively regulates pharmaceuticals, medical devices, and medical processes, and its authority to do so does not constitute a regulatory taking of property because of its obligation to ensure safety and to protect the public health. The Food and Drug Administration has even claimed the authority to prohibit human cloning research (Cohen 2002, 526).

Redefining Property for Community Rights: Implications for Environmental Law

Environmental law presents a third area in which the definition of property for purposes of determining a constitutional right is critical. Several scholars have identified different conceptual starting points to determine the specific land uses that ought to be constitutionally protected property rights (for summaries, see, e.g., Munzer 2001, 36; Schultz 1992, 173–174). Two visions of property rights compete with each other. One is the classical individualist model, which relies on a particular historical tradition of preexisting natural rights to define the extent of one's future rights in property. A competing model, the common property rights model, suggests that whatever constitutes property does not originate in preexisting natural rights but is subject to change from the historical tradition when democratic processes reflect different communitarian values. One view or the other is necessarily chosen when courts decide the appropriate limits on governmental authority over land use, although most often courts do so without explicit recognition of any theory of what is a justified property right (Radin 1993, 163).

The classical individualist view of landownership focuses upon what rights an individual owner may assert against the community in which the land is located. It is a Lockean notion that natural property rights exist before any governmental authority to regulate them. The best-known advocate of this model is Richard Epstein, who argues that the Constitution prohibits the government from changing any traditional property use without compensation (Epstein 1985). The best understanding of the Constitution's property clauses, according to Epstein, is that the government may not prevent landowners from engaging in any land use that did not historically constitute a nuisance to a neighboring landowner. According to this view, the Constitution strictly protects preexisting natural rights to property use from interference by the majority, and historical tradition is the most important guide in determining the content of the natural right. Any legislative curtailment of this historical tradition is thus a compensable taking under the eminent domain clause.

In contrast, some scholars suggest the need for recognizing a greater community or public interest in property uses, particularly in the effect that individual land-use decisions may have on common property resources. Joseph Sax, for example, suggests that we have an overly limited conception of property rights with respect to private resource users and that current takings law "stands as an obstacle to rational resource allocation" (Sax 1971, 150). Other scholars challenge the notion that a prepolitical natural right to land use excludes recognition of community values or freezes community values at some point in the past. This competing model emphasizes that landowners may not use their land in such a way as to inflict harm on the community, allowing community definitions of harm to be stated by the current political process, not restricted solely to historical views of land uses that in the past were considered to constitute a harm to the community. These scholars point to the need to redefine property to include community rights in common resources. They suggest that to some extent this has already occurred, and some scholars attempt to show that community rights have always been recognized at some level historically.

The idea that evolving notions of appropriate property uses, rather than a fixed historical tradition, should play some role in evaluating the government's interest in regulating land use is apparent in cases like *Penn Central v. New York* (1978) and *Tahoe-Sierra Preservation Council v. Tahoe Regional Planning Agency* (2002). But the counterprinciple is the constitutional protection of the vested rights and settled expectations of an individual property owner. If a society determines certain historical property uses should no longer be supported, can it change them? Conservatives and libertarians maintain that the majority may do so only with compensation, at least when the government's actions fall disproportionately on one person or a small group of individuals. On the other side, however, is the reality that "government could hardly go on if to some extent values incident to property could not be diminished without paying for every such change in the general law," as Justice Holmes wrote in *Pennsylvania Coal v. Mahon* (1922, 413).

The most important historical example of this conundrum is slavery. Abraham Lincoln, agreeing with most judges and legal thinkers of the mid-1800s, believed that slavery could not be abolished without compensation to slave owners because the Constitution prevented interference with anything that in historical practice had been considered to be a property right. This view prevailed despite the fact that a majority of citizens viewed property in human beings to be immoral. Following the Civil War, the

Thirteenth Amendment (1865) declared that human beings could no longer be considered property, freeing all persons held as slaves without compensation to their former owners, including a significant number of slave owners in states that had remained loyal to the Union. Section 4 of the Fourteenth Amendment prohibited the federal and state governments from paying any claims for the emancipation of slaves, specifying that "all such debts, obligations and claims shall be held illegal and void." Without these constitutional amendments, the government would have been obligated to pay billions of dollars to the slave owners in order to accomplish emancipation. The tradition that the Constitution protects historical expectations about property, then, is strong. It is difficult to fathom the idea that property rights in slaves would be protected by the U.S. Constitution, but if constitutional property is always to be defined by historical practices, this fact becomes part of our constitutional tradition.

One of the central debates in environmental law is the extent to which the historical view of individual property rights restricts the government's authority to require landowners to preserve land in its natural state when altering that natural state produces adverse effects on a larger community. In *Just v. Marinette County* (WI 1972), a state supreme court held that landowners have no inherent natural right to change their land from its natural state when community interests are adversely affected. But in *Lucas v. South Carolina Coastal Council* (1992), the U.S. Supreme Court indicated that individual landowners may have this right even if the owner's proposed use of the property creates environmental problems for the adjacent community. This would mean that in order to preserve shorelines and other ecological systems, for example, a state must purchase the land from a private owner rather than restrict the traditional right of the landowner to build or develop—regardless of the effect on any larger community interest. The difference between these two decisions might be said to illustrate the classic individual rights model versus the common property model. This conflict is essentially whether a common interest in the preservation of biodiversity and ecosystems allows governments to regulate land use by requiring the landowner to maintain property in its natural state when those natural functions may be important to the ecosystem (Sax 1993, 1438).

Beach property illustrates the growing recognition of a common property model by courts in unique land resources. In *Lucas*, although the Supreme Court sided with the landowner against the state's concern to protect shoreline erosion, it did so because neighboring property owners already had been permitted to construct houses along the shore, as David Lucas planned. Some state courts have moved away from a strict private property regime toward recognition of common rights and a public trust idea in beaches (Radin 1993, 167). Common law in the nineteenth century permitted individual property owners to assert full exclusion rights to beach areas above the high-tide mark. State courts have now recognized a competing customary right of public access to beaches, viewing beaches to be a special public resource necessary to preserve and not properly subject to all of the traditional privileges of private property. In a sense, courts have recognized a competing property interest of the public in a unique natural resource.

When interests in common resources are viewed as a competing property right of the general public, the governmental purpose is strengthened. Some state constitutions explicitly recognize this interest. The Pennsylvania constitution, for example, was amended in 1970 to include the following provision:

> The people have a right to clean air, pure water, and to the preservation of the natural, scenic, historic and esthetic values of the environment. Pennsylvania's public natural resources are the common property of all the people, including generations yet to come. As trustee of these resources, the Commonwealth shall conserve and maintain them for the benefit of all the people. (PA Const., art. I, sec. 27)

WATER AND AIR AS COMMON PROPERTY

An important potential application of the common property view lies in the recognition of water and air as the property of all citizens in a community. Some political groups associated with environmental causes urge a strengthened basis for more governmental action to protect the fundamental rights of everyone to breathe air that does not harm them and to have access to sufficient supplies of clean water for human consumption and for preservation of aquatic life. Air and water, they argue, are common property rights. Governments should be allowed substantial room to regulate individual behavior in order to preserve these fundamental rights. If water and air are considered a fundamental common right, then the liberty of an individual to pollute or consume common resources competes with the equal—and possibly stronger—property right of others.

Urban settings interfere with such rights because of excessive individual use of property. One's right to drive a car, for example, adversely affects everyone's right to breathe clean air. Air pollution from automobile exhaust is so severe that many cities issue warnings to curtail outdoor activities, especially for children and the elderly. If air is a common property right held by all citizens, then two competing property rights conflict with each other. Car owners assume a liberty interest to use their property as they wish. The "owners" of the air might be viewed to have a liberty interest to engage in outdoor activities as they wish. Governments rely on industry emission standards to address air pollution problems, an authority well within governmental police powers. But governments rely more heavily on voluntary arrangements to lessen the effects of car exhaust on the environment (e.g., by encouraging the use of public transportation and dedicating highway lanes for carpools). In all major cities it is apparent that an unrestricted right to drive makes it unhealthy to breathe.

In the nineteenth century, the common law recognized clean air as a property right through the law of nuisance. For example, an individual landowner could sue a neighboring factory for the effects of air pollution on her own property. Proof of the source of the pollution and proof that it caused harm to one's own property were essential elements of the case. But in situations with many potential contributors to air pollution, it is difficult to identify every contributor's contribution. The inability of nuisance law to protect public health from the adverse effects of multiple sources of air pollution led Congress to enact the Clean Air Act of 1970. Along with the Clean Water Act of 1972, it authorized significant governmental involvement and control in setting absolute limits for all potential sources of pollution. Constitutional challenges claimed that these statutes would force some existing companies out of business and thus take a vested property right, but the statutes have been upheld as a lawful purpose of government to protect the public.

Currently, the U.S. Environmental Protection Agency grants pollution rights by setting an upper limit on the total amount of emissions per region—the so-called bubble concept that allows regulators to treat several existing air pollution sources within a region as a single source. This EPA policy allows companies to trade propertylike rights of air pollution, and new companies whose activities would add to the air pollution of a region may obtain emissions credits from existing sources of pollution. Such commercial trading practices suggest that even air has become privately owned to some degree. Perhaps, then, the concept of air as a property right of all citizens is not a far-fetched possibility for future recognition by courts. This view would support more stringent regulation of individual property uses that might, at present, be considered too onerous based upon the historical belief that natural resources were unlimited.

Competing demands on finite water supplies have also raised issues of constitutional protection for property interests. The increasingly limited availability of clean water illustrates the conflict between historically permitted individual use and common property rights in natural resources that are affected by that use.

State law governs the allocation of natural water sources within a state. In general, eastern states follow a riparian rights model to allocate ownership of water in streams and rivers. That doctrine permits private landowners adjacent to surface water to divert it for their own use, but only to the extent that this use is reasonable with respect to downstream users. In other words, the upstream landowner must preserve a reasonable flow for downstream users, so the property owner does not truly own the adjacent stream. In western states, most states follow the first-in-time or prior appropriation doctrine, in which the first property owner to use adjacent surface water has the right to take all of it, regardless of the needs of downstream owners. In these states, water rights are said to be first-come, first-served, at least with respect to privately owned property abutting the river or stream.

The first-in-time rule in most of the western states directly contradicts the view that water is common property. In eastern states, although the property interest in water is only one of reasonable use by an adjacent property owner, courts encounter considerable difficulty determining what is reasonable. Demands for water include power generation, drinking water supplies, and minimum natural stream flows for environmental and recreational purposes. To determine a reasonable use, courts consider the purpose of the use; the suitability of use to the remaining water supply; the economic value of the use; the social value of the use; the extent and amount of harm the use causes; and the practicality of avoiding harm to downstream users by adjusting another owner's use. There are, in fact, so many different opinions about what is a reasonable use that a court cannot possibly choose among them on any objective basis.

Whatever the particular choice of rule to govern private ownership of water in streams and rivers, most courts seem to recognize that water may qualify as an individual property right (Meltz et al. 1999, 458). This view emerged early in the nineteenth century. In *Gardner v. Village of Newburgh* (Ch. Ct. NY 1816), a New York court protected a landowner's right to water from an adjacent stream from uncompensated appropriation by a city government. Individual ownership of naturally flowing water as a constitutionally protected interest obviously poses great difficulty for government efforts to allocate and preserve sources of water. If surface water were to be considered incapable of private ownership—similar to the public trust doctrine for tidal areas—the Takings Clause would not be implicated when the government limits individual water use in order to preserve the supply.

Some state courts have taken the view that whatever private property rights may exist to the resource, water rights are incapable of private ownership for constitutional protection (Meltz et al. 1999, 459). Yet some federal and state courts have given greater attention to claims that a state's (or the federal government's) reallocation of water use priorities constitutes a taking of private property without compensation. Although a number of courts have rejected these claims, the Supreme Court of Oklahoma struck down state legislation that changed the state's prior allocation of water rights. In *Franco-American Charolaise, Ltd. v. Oklahoma Water Resource Board* (OK 1990), the court held that prior water rights were violated by a legislative change, and therefore the legislature's action constituted a taking for public use without compensation. Academics have also suggested that the Takings Clause, particularly the regulatory takings doctrine, applies to attempts to change existing water distribution schemes. One author claims that it is "virtually certain that the number of Takings Clause–based attacks on water rights determinations will increase in the coming years" (Meltz et al. 1999, 457).

In the early twentieth century, the U.S. Supreme Court considered private landowners' rights to appropriate water to be less substantial than constitutional protections afforded for real estate.

In *Hudson County Water Co. v. McCarter* (1908, 356), Justice Holmes wrote:

> Few public interests are more obvious, indisputable, and independent of particular theory than the interest of the public of a state to maintain the rivers that are wholly within it substantially undiminished, except by such drafts upon them as the guardian of the public welfare may permit for the purpose of turning them to a more perfect use. The private right to appropriate is subject . . . to the initial limitation that it may not substantially diminish one of the great foundations of public welfare and health.

Several state constitutions, in fact, specify that water is the property of the public at large, rather than of private persons, and some courts have suggested that flowing water is commonly owned by citizens as a public trust. Although most courts recognize that governments have a higher degree of control over water rights than real estate generally, it is not clear whether naturally flowing surface water is entirely public property in the sense that a government may impose any restriction it wishes.

The following example illustrates the problems posed by limited water resources in the face of demand for use from many groups. The dramatic expansion of population around the city of Atlanta, Georgia, has taken much of the water flow from the Chattahoochee River, while many downstream uses include drinking supply, fisheries, agriculture, recreational, and preservation in Alabama and Florida. Continued residential and commercial development in the Atlanta area threatens to consume even more water resources and poses additional downstream shortages that may cause environmental changes. But there is no legal mechanism to resolve competing claims to the water (neither the first appropriation rule nor the reasonable use rule provide a solution).

If the issue of water ownership were purely a matter of state law, the tendency would be for courts in upstream states to protect their state's interests at the expense of downstream users. Federal regulation is therefore necessary for interstate disputes, but this will also require some theory on the ownership of water. Defining finite water supplies as common property seems to be the only appropriate starting point. Environmental advocates—and those interested in maintaining water resources for consumption, the environment, and recreation—agree on the need for more stringent, innovative laws to address this problem. They argue that it may be necessary to encroach on the traditional property rights of some persons in order to sustain the environment's finite ability to absorb pollution of air and water and to sustain usable water resources in the future. However, as yet there is no right to protect water resources, or the environment generally, in the same way that courts have historically recognized real estate development to be constitutionally protected.

Conclusion

This chapter has examined three areas in which constitutional protection of property depends to a great extent on how an individual property right is defined in the first instance. The U.S. Constitution's property clauses do not define which interests qualify as property, but the Constitution has historically been read to protect expectations in the form of vested rights to property that are not limited to land. In the three issues considered—intellectual property, biotechnology, and the environment—constitutional tradition teaches only that legitimate past expectations about property may be protected from violation by the government in the future.

But what are legitimate expectations regarding property rights? With respect to real estate, courts have tended to view the historical pedigree of a proposed land use as an indication that the use is subject to constitutional protection, against which the government's interest must be compared. In turn, the government's interest in regulating land use is viewed to be highest when a clear detriment to larger public interests would otherwise result. For property other than land, the path is less clear. The current unsettled state of takings law recognizes that governments rearrange property rights constantly and that not every government action can be considered a taking.

Critics of contemporary takings jurisprudence come from all sides of the political spectrum. Conservatives, generally associated with a property rights movement that favors limited government, tend to view the Takings Clause as an absolute barrier to governmental regulation of any property use in the public interest for which compensation is not paid. Some liberals, by contrast, criticize the U.S. Supreme Court's recent takings cases on the grounds that they tend to adopt a constricted historical view that constitutionally sanctions all property uses that were approved in the past. Some fear that efforts at environmental and natural resource protection will be considered takings of prior property uses, such that democratically enacted measures cannot be enforced because the government could not possibly afford to compensate all affected landowners. If the government is required to compensate property owners for every environmental regulation, the concern is that the government would not act to protect the environment because of the prohibitive costs involved in compensating affected landowners.

Another underlying tension relates to one's beliefs about the democratic process in the United States. Skeptics of government do not view enacted laws necessarily to reflect majority will or to further the common good. Rather, they view the political process to be dominated by special interest groups that have the political clout to enact legislation solely for their own benefit. This view of the political process is not far from that of James Madison, the author of much of the federal Constitution as well as the Takings Clause. Madison feared that factions would gain control of local governments and enact laws for their own benefit at the expense of property owners. For this reason, Madison relied heavily on the structure of the federal government to diffuse the tendency of factions to redistribute property in their own favor.

It cannot be doubted that the Takings Clause of the federal Constitution is to some extent an antimajoritarian rule designed to protect individuals from government confiscations of property without compensation. Yet scholars will argue, and the Supreme Court has recognized, that the founding generation never envisioned a regulatory takings interpretation of the Takings Clause. Moreover, we have no way of knowing what the Framers would have thought about environmental protection laws, property in human-derived organisms, and so on. As Milton Friedman wrote,

> The notion of property, as it has developed over centuries and as it is embodied in our legal codes, has become so much a part of us that we tend to take it for granted, and fail to recognize the extent to which just what constitutes property and what rights the ownership of property confers are complex social creations rather than self-evident propositions. (Friedman 1962, 26)

What will be constitutionally protected property in the twenty-first century is open to debate.

References and Further Reading

Ackerman, B. 1977. *Private Property and the Constitution.* New Haven, CT: Yale University Press.

Ackiron, E. 1991. "Patents for Critical Pharmaceuticals: The AZT Case." *American Journal of Law and Medicine* 17: 145.

Alta Charo, R. 2002. "Skin and Bones: Post-Mortem Markets in Human Tissue." *Nova Law Review* 26:421.

Arnold, C. A. 2002. "The Reconstitution of Property: Property as a Web of Interests." *Harvard Environmental Law Review* 26:281–364.

Becker, L. 1993. "Deserving to Own Intellectual Property." *Chicago-Kent Law Review* 68:609.

Bederman, D. J. 1996. "The Curious Resurrection of Custom: Beach Access and Judicial Takings." *Columbia Law Review* 96:1375.

Brinckerhoff, C. 1996. "Medical Method Patents and the Fifth Amendment: Do the New Limits on Enforceability Effect a Taking?" *University of Baltimore Intellectual Property Journal* 4:147.

Cohen, D. M. 2002. "Cloning and the Constitution." *Nova Law Review* 26:511.

Coombe, R. J. 1991. "Objects of Property and Subjects of Politics: Intellectual Property Laws and Democratic Dialogue." *Texas Law Review* 69:1853.

Cotter, T. F. 1998. "Do Federal Uses of Intellectual Property Implicate the Fifth Amendment?" *Florida Law Review* 50:529–572.

Coyle, D. 1993. *Property Rights and the Constitution: Shaping Society Through Land Use Regulation*. Albany: State University of New York Press.

Eagle, S. 1996. *Regulatory Takings*. Charlottesville, VA: Michie.

Ellickson, R., Rose, C. M., and Ackerman, B. A., eds. 1995. *Perspectives on Property Law*. 2d ed. New York: Little, Brown.

Ely, J. W., ed. 1998. *Main Themes in the Debate Over Property Rights*. New York: Garland Publishing.

———. 1997. *Contemporary Property Rights Issues*. New York: Garland Publishing.

Epstein, R. 1985. *Takings: Private Property and the Power of Eminent Domain*. Cambridge, MA: Harvard University Press.

Epstein, R., ed. 2000. *Private and Common Property*. New York: Garland Publishing.

Fischel, W. 1995. *Regulatory Takings: Law, Economics, and Politics*. Cambridge, MA: Harvard University Press.

Friedman, M. 1962. *Capitalism and Freedom*. Chicago: University of Chicago Press.

Ghost, S. 1999. "Reconciling Property Rights and States' Rights in the Information Age: Federalism, the Sovereign's Prerogative, and Takings after College Savings." *University of Toledo Law Review* 31:17.

Gordon, W. J. 1993. "A Property Right in Self-Expression: Equality and Individualism in the Natural Law of Intellectual Property." *Yale Law Journal* 102:1533.

Hausken, G. L. 1988. "The Value of a Secret: Compensation for Imposition of Secrecy Orders under the Invention Secrecy Act." *Military Law Review* 119:201.

Heald, P., and Wells, M. 1998. "Remedies for the Misappropriation of Intellectual Property by State and Municipal Governments Before and After *Seminole Tribe:* The Eleventh Amendment and Other Immunity Doctrines." *Washington and Lee Law Review* 55:849.

Hernandez, T. 1999. "The Property of Death." *University of Pittsburgh Law Review* 60:971.

Hilmert, L. 2002. "Cloning Human Organs: Potential Sources and Property Implications." *Indiana Law Journal* 77:363.

Kirsch, M. T. 1997. "Upholding the Public Trust in State Constitutions." *Duke Law Journal* 46:1169.

Madison, J. 1907 (G. Hunt, ed.). *The Writings of James Madison, Volume 6: 1790–1802.* New York: G. P. Putnam's Sons.

McCartney, J. J. 2002. "Embryonic Stem Cell Research and Respect for Human Life: Philosophical and Legal Reflections." *Albany Law Review* 65:597.

McGrath, R. J. 2000. "Patent Infringement Claims Against the United States Government." *Federal Circuit Bar Journal* 9:351.

Meltz, R., Merriam, D., and Frank, R. 1999. *The Takings Issue: Constitutional Limits on Land Use Control and Environmental Regulation.* Washington, DC: Island Press.

Mercuro, N., and Samuels, W. J., eds. 1999. *The Fundamental Interrelationships Between Government and Property.* Stamford, CT: JAI Press.

Merrill, T. W. 2000. "The Landscape of Constitutional Property." *Virginia Law Review* 86:885–999.

Michelman, F. I. 1987. "Possession vs. Distribution in the Constitutional Idea of Property." *Iowa Law Review* 72:1319.

Munzer, S. R. 2001. *New Essays in the Legal and Political Theory of Property.* Cambridge, UK: Cambridge University Press.

———. 1990. *A Theory of Property.* Cambridge, UK: Cambridge University Press.

Nelson, R. H. 1995. *Public Lands and Private Rights.* Lanham, MD: Rowman and Littlefield Publishers.

Paul, E. F. 1987. *Property Rights and Eminent Domain.* New Brunswick, NJ: Transaction Books.

Paul, E. F., and Dickman, H. 1990. *Liberty, Property, and the Future of Constitutional Development.* Albany: State University of New York Press.

Radin, M. J. 1993. *Reinterpreting Property.* Chicago: University of Chicago Press.

Rao, R. 2000. "Property, Privacy, and the Human Body." *Boston University Law Review* 80:359.
Reich, C. A. 1964. "The New Property." *Yale Law Journal* 73:733–787.
Rose, C. 1996. "Property as the Keystone Right?" *Notre Dame Law Review* 71:329.
———. 1994. *Property and Persuasion: Essays on the History, Theory, and Rhetoric of Ownership.* Boulder, CO: Westview Press.
———. 1984. "Mahon Reconstructed: Why the Takings Issue Is Still a Muddle." *Southern California Law Review* 57:561.
Ryan, E. 2001. "Public Trust and Distrust: The Theoretical Implications of the Public Trust Doctrine for Natural Resource Management." *Environmental Law* 31:477.
Salkin, P. E., and Freilich, R. H., eds. 2000. *Hot Topics in Land Use Law: From the Comprehensive Plan to* Del Monte Dunes. Chicago: American Bar Association.
Sax, J. 1993. "Property Rights and the Economy of Nature." *Stanford Law Review* 45:1433.
———. 1971. "Takings, Private Property, and Public Rights." *Yale Law Journal* 81:149–186.
———. 1970. "The Public Trust Doctrine in Natural Resource Law: Effective Judicial Intervention." *Michigan Law Review* 68:471.
Schultz, D. 1992. *Property, Power, and American Democracy.* New Brunswick, NJ: Transaction Publishers.
Schulz, C. W., and Weber, G. S. 1988. "Changing Judicial Attitudes Towards Property Rights in California Water Resources: From Vested Rights to Utilitarian Reallocations." *Pacific Law Journal* 19:1031.
Siegan, B. 1997. *Property and Freedom: The Constitution, the Courts, and Land-Use Regulation.* New Brunswick, NJ, and London: Transaction Publishers.
Singer, J. W. 2001. *Introduction to Property.* Gaithersburg, MD: Aspen Law and Business.
Volokh, E. 2000. "Sovereign Immunity and Intellectual Property." *Southern California Law Review* 73:1161.
Whitehead, R., and Block, W. 2002. "Environmental Takings of Private Water Rights: The Case for Water Privatization." *Environmental Law Reporter* 32:11162.
Williams, J. 1998. "The Rhetoric of Property." *Iowa Law Review* 83:277–361.

Winters, S., and Blomgren, J. 2002. "How the U.S. Government Controls Technology." *Computer and Internet Lawyer* 1:1.

Yelpaala, K. 2000. "Owning the Secret of Life: Biotechnology and Property Rights Revisited." *McGeorge Law Review* 32:111.

5

Key People, Cases, and Events

Adverse Possession

Originating in the common law, *adverse possession* is the circumstance in which a property owner may lose ownership rights if, for a period of years, another person lives on the property or engages in some other substantial open use and the original owner does not enforce his right to evict the trespasser. The time period required to establish adverse possession varies according to legislation in each state. In general, to establish adverse possession, the possession must be (1) *exclusive*; (2) *actual and uninterrupted*; (3) *open and notorious*; and (4) *hostile and under a claim of right made in good faith*.

Agins v. City of Tiburon, 447 U.S. 255 (1980)

In this 1980 decision, the U.S. Supreme Court held that a zoning ordinance that restricted development of land to single-family dwellings with large open spaces was not a taking. Zoning laws constitute a taking only if "the ordinance does not substantially advance legitimate state interests . . . or denies an owner economically viable use of his land." The Court found that the ordinance in question served a legitimate purpose by preserving the organized development of the residential area. Furthermore, even though the ordinance restricted the number of houses that could be built (and thus resold by the developer), the ordinance was not a taking because it did not completely prohibit use of the land. An important question under the Takings Clause, according to the Court, is whether "the public at large, rather than a single owner, must bear the burden of an exercise of state power in the public interest."

Alien Land Laws

In the eighteenth and nineteenth centuries, many state courts enforced common law rules that denied noncitizens certain property rights with respect to land. Aliens could not inherit real estate, and any land that they had purchased remained subject to state confiscation. In the United States today, approximately half of the states have laws that restrict to some degree the rights of noncitizens to own real property. Many of these restrictions affect only nonresident aliens or are merely reporting requirements, although a few states completely prohibit aliens from owning land. Some states also limit the right of aliens to inherit real property, usually providing a window of several years within which an alien who has inherited land may sell the land to a U.S. citizen in order to avoid forfeiture. Some states retain alien land restrictions primarily for agricultural land. A large number of states guarantee that aliens enjoy the same rights as citizens with respect to landownership or have no constitutional or statutory law on the subject at all. Federal statutes also regulate some alien property rights. Treaties between the United States and some nations mutually exempt the citizens of those nations from state-imposed real property restrictions.

Allgeyer v. Louisiana, 165 U.S. 578 (1897)

This U.S. Supreme Court case recognized the concept of *economic due process* as a constitutionally protected liberty interest against state intrusion. A Louisiana law prohibited Louisiana residents from obtaining insurance from out-of-state companies not authorized by the legislature to conduct business in Louisiana. In its decision, the Court held that the Due Process Clause of the Fourteenth Amendment protected the right to "enter into contracts which may be proper" without legislative interference. The Court's decision effectively prohibited state interference with contractual rights, a view that received its most prominent recognition in *Lochner v. New York*, 198 U.S. 45 (1905).

Articles of Confederation

Submitted by the Continental Congress in 1777 and ratified in March 1781, the Articles of Confederation became the governing instrument of the 13 original states until ratification of the U.S. Constitution in 1789. The Articles of Confederation established a federal system of government in which sovereign power was divided between central and local governments, but Congress was not given the ability to tax or to control interstate commerce. Congress's power in foreign affairs was greatly limited by veto rights possessed by each state. Many Federalists viewed the Articles of Confederation to be a flawed instrument. Accordingly, the U.S. Constitution gave the federal government greater powers with respect to commerce, foreign affairs, and other matters. The Contracts Clause of the Constitution prevented states from retroactively impairing the obligation of contracts through debtor-relief laws, actions that were viewed by the Federalists to impede economic growth.

Barron v. Baltimore, 32 U.S. 243 (1833)

This case recognized that the original Bill of Rights, and in particular the Fifth Amendment's Takings Clause, applied only to the federal government and not to state and local governments, the primary authorities over the private property of most U.S. citizens. At the close of the nineteenth century, the U.S. Supreme Court held that the Fourteenth Amendment (ratified in 1868) "incorporated" most of the provisions of the Bill of Rights to limit state action as well as the federal government. In *Chicago, Burlington & Quincy Railroad Co. v. Chicago,* 166 U.S. 226 (1897), the Supreme Court held that state takings of private property must be compensated under the federal Constitution, abrogating *Barron v. Baltimore.*

Bill of Rights

The first ten amendments to the federal Constitution. The amendments were added to the Constitution in 1791, two years after the Constitution was ratified. The Bill of Rights was modeled upon similar provisions in state constitutions. A bill of rights generally is understood to be a statement of specific individual rights against the government, designed to limit governmental power. In the founding period, lists of individual rights were not viewed to express all of the rights that an individual possessed. The Ninth Amendment, for example, states that "the enumeration in the Constitution, of certain rights, shall not be construed to deny or disparage others retained by the people."

Blackstone's *Commentaries on the Law of England*

English jurist William Blackstone published his *Commentaries on the Law of England* from 1765 to 1769. Widely available in the

American colonies, the *Commentaries* presented Blackstone's distillation of English common and statute law, with a particular emphasis on liberties and rights of English subjects. Blackstone's writings were extremely influential in the formation of American common law, particularly with respect to property rules. After independence from Great Britain, newly formed state legislatures directed that the common law should provide the rules of decision in court cases in the absence of statutes applicable to the subject. As a result, lawyers and judges frequently consulted the *Commentaries* for evidence of common law rules throughout the nineteenth century.

Calder v. Bull, 3 U.S. 386 (1798)

Calder v. Bull was the first occasion for the U.S. Supreme Court to address the meaning of the Ex Post Facto Clause in Article I, section 10, of the U.S. Constitution. Among other restrictions on state action, this section prohibits states from enacting any ex post facto law. The justices concluded that the term *ex post facto* applied to laws imposing retroactive punishment by creating criminal sanctions for conduct that was previously legal. The Ex Post Facto Clause does not apply to civil matters, such as disputes about a state law affecting property rights.

This case is important for Justice Samuel Chase's statement that "the very nature of our free Republican governments" placed limits on governmental authority, such as the basic proposition that "a law that takes property from A and gives it to B" is void. This opinion is often cited as representative of the early view that courts might appropriately limit legislative action on the basis of natural laws or unwritten fundamental laws in addition to specific constitutional provisions.

Chicago, Burlington & Quincy Railroad Co. v. Chicago, 166 U.S. 226 (1897)

This was the first U.S. Supreme Court decision to establish that the Constitution requires states to compensate private property owners when their property is taken for public use. The Supreme Court held that the Due Process Clause of the Fourteenth Amendment required compensation for state takings of private property for public use, because the Fourteenth Amendment, which limits state governments, "incorporated" this specific guarantee from the Bill of Rights. Prior to this time, compensation for state and local government takings of private property was strictly a matter of state law, although all states recognized the just compensation requirement in principle.

Civil Rights Act of 1964

Several civil rights statutes limit the traditional property right of exclusion. Title II of the Civil Rights Act of 1964 requires privately owned places of public accommodation to provide "full and equal enjoyment of the goods, services, facilities, privileges, advantages, and accommodations" without discrimination "on the ground of race, color, religion, or national origin."

Commerce Clause

Article I, section 8, clause 3 of the U.S. Constitution; gives Congress the power "to regulate Commerce with foreign nations, among the several States, and with the Indian tribes." The Commerce Clause is today one of the most important powers of the federal government. State legislation that interferes with interstate commerce is invalid under the clause. Federalist judges in the early national period interpreted the Commerce Clause broadly. For example, in *Gibbons v. Ogden* (1824) Chief Justice John Marshall interpreted the Commerce Clause to prohibit a state's grant of a shipping monopoly on its waters.

Common Law

The Anglo-American style of judicial reasoning based upon prior court decisions. Cases decided in the past become precedent for future judicial decisions unless a legislative enactment governs the specific controversy before the court. In the founding period, property law in the states consisted extensively of the received English common law. William Blackstone's summary of English common law rules had great influence on the development of American common law. The common law of property continues to play an important role in the determination of constitutional property rights. For example, in *Lucas v. South Carolina Coastal Council* (1992), the Supreme Court indicated that property rights subject to the just compensation requirement may be determined from prior common law.

Constitutional Revolution of 1937

When the U.S. Supreme Court used substantive due process and federalism concerns to strike down significant legislative efforts by Congress during the New Deal, President Franklin Roosevelt charged that the justices were activists who projected their own economic views and preferences into their decisions to thwart democratic government. Roosevelt's so-called court-packing plan—an effort to change the outcome of these cases by increasing the number of justices on the Supreme Court—grew out of the president's frustration with the number of legislative measures invalidated by the court. In the so-called constitutional revolution of 1937, the Court changed its substantive due process approach to review of economic legislation. The Court's new approach, apparent in *West Coast Hotel Co. v. Parrish* (1937), effectively reversed a host of prior substantive due process decisions.

Contracts Clause

Article I, section 10 of the Constitution; the Contracts Clause prohibits states from passing any law that would "impair the obligation of contracts," a phrase that came to have great significance in the early nineteenth century. The Contracts Clause was the basis for the most important instances of judicial review of state legislation by the U.S. Supreme Court in the early decades following independence. While garnering little discussion at the Constitutional Convention, this provision was interpreted by the Court under John Marshall to mean that contractual expectations were a form of property to be protected against retroactive impairment by states. Among other types of legislation, state debtor-relief laws were struck down as contrary to the Contracts Clause because they delayed or prevented collection of debts based upon prior contracts. The use of the Contracts Clause to protect property rights gradually declined in significance toward the end of the nineteenth century, coinciding with the rise of substantive due process and the regulatory takings doctrine. Since the New Deal era, the Contracts Clause rarely has been used to invalidate state legislation. The Contracts Clause does not apply to the federal government.

Dartmouth College v. Woodward, 17 U.S. 518 (1819)

In *Dartmouth College,* the U.S. Supreme Court extended the protections of the Contracts Clause to private corporations. In the first decades of this country's history, corporate charters were granted by special enactments of state legislatures. Dartmouth College was created in 1769 by a royal charter establishing the private college. In 1817, in response to an internal dispute between the trustees and the president of Dartmouth, the New Hampshire legislature passed a statute repealing the 1769 charter and creating a new governing structure for the college. The Supreme Court invalidated this legislative act, holding that a charter for a private corporation was a contract deserving of constitutional protection and that the legislature had passed a law impairing the obligation of contract in violation of the Contracts Clause of the federal Constitution. The *Dartmouth College* decision protected acts of incorporation involving private property from legislative interference.

Debtor-Relief Laws

Following the American Revolution, many state legislatures enacted measures to aid farmers and others who had fallen into debt, in an effort to ameliorate the dire economic conditions of the time. Common examples of debtor-relief laws included laws requiring creditors to accept newly issued paper money for debts, extending the time of repayment on debts, or preventing foreclosures and other court actions for debts for a period of time. Federalists, who supported ratification of the new U.S. Constitution, wanted to prohibit debtor-relief laws because of the perceived adverse effect on the economy and the unwillingness of lenders to extend credit. Largely to prohibit these laws, Federalists supported the Contracts Clause in the U.S. Constitution, which restrained state legislatures from enacting laws that impaired the obligations of contracts already in existence. Congress is expressly given the power to create a "uniform law of bankruptcy," and the federal government is not subject to the Contracts Clause. Congress enacted the first permanent bankruptcy statute in 1898.

Dolan v. City of Tigard, 512 U.S. 374 (1994)

In *Dolan*, a local zoning board approved a building permit for expansion of a retail facility on the condition that the owner appropriate part of the land to the city for a public greenway and bicycle path. Noting that the burden of proof was on the city to justify the regulation, the Court held that there must be a "rough proportionality" between such exactions and the foreseen public costs of the building project. The city failed to meet its burden, and the Supreme Court thus held that the regulation constituted a taking of private property without just compensation in violation of the Takings Clause.

Dred Scott v. Sandford, 60 U.S. 393 (1856)

In the years preceding the Civil War, some Southerners defined their liberty to include the right to own slaves with no governmental interference. These slave owners viewed Congress's attempts to prevent slavery in federal territories as a violation of the Constitution. They claimed the right to emigrate to the territories with their slave clause, citing, among other provisions, the fugitive slave provision in the Constitution as a recognition that slaves were constitutionally protected property. The U.S. Supreme Court in *Dred Scott v. Sandford* endorsed this view. Chief Justice Roger Taney, writing for the majority, held that Congress was without authority to ban slavery in federal lands. More important, *Dred Scott* essentially recognized slave ownership as a vested right of property and hence subject to constitutional protection. Abraham Lincoln's and the Republican Party's stated intention to disregard the *Dred Scott* decision is cited as one of the contributing factors leading to secession and the Civil War.

Due Process

The principle that no individual may be deprived of life, liberty, or property, without due process of law is of ancient origin. In the founding period, state constitutions routinely included this provision as a limitation upon governmental authority. The concept was drawn from English law dating back to the English Magna Carta, a compact between King John and English feudal barons in 1215. The U.S. Constitution contains two relevant clauses, in the Fifth Amendment (applicable to the federal government) and the Fourteenth Amendment (applicable to state governments).

The requirement of due process is said to have two aspects: procedural and substantive. *Procedural due process* is a requirement that government provide a fair procedure when it imposes burdens on individuals. Due process is designed to prevent arbitrary or mistaken application of laws and to provide individuals the opportunity to respond to charges against them before a neutral arbitrator. *Substantive due process* is a limitation on the subject matter of laws that governments may enact. From the late nineteenth through the early twentieth centuries, the U.S. Supreme Court invalidated a number of state economic regulations under the view that substantive due process restricted state authority to govern private business transactions. Substantive due process was viewed with disfavor after the 1930s as inappropriate judicial activism by the courts, although to a lesser degree it remains a limitation on legislation today.

Eastern Enterprises v. Apfel, 524 U.S. 498 (1998)

Eastern Enterprises challenged the federal Coal Industry Retiree Health Benefit Act, which required the company to pay additional medical benefits to former employees even though it no longer conducted mining operations. The Supreme Court held that the law as applied to Eastern Enterprises was unconstitutional because it imposed a severe, retroactive financial burden on the company. The justices did not agree whether the act was invalid because it was a taking in violation of the Takings Clause or because it violated due process. Five justices concluded that the Takings Clause does not apply to government actions that simply impose a financial obligation without affecting a specific, identified property interest.

Eminent Domain

Eminent domain is a government's power to obtain private property for government or public use. The Just Compensation Clause of the Fifth Amendment requires that governments must pay the fair market value of private property taken for public use. Prior to the Revolution, colonial governments exercised powers of eminent domain frequently. State governments continued to invoke eminent domain to construct roads, canals, and other public works in the early nineteenth century. Considered an inherent power of government, the right to take property for public use is not specified in the federal or most state constitutions. However, the principle that governments must pay just compensation for takings of private property has long been a part of the common law and state constitutions. State governments in the nineteenth century (and to some extent today) routinely delegated eminent domain authority to private companies authorized by the state, most notably for the construction of railroads and public utilities.

English Declaration of Rights (1689) and Petition of Right (1628)

Origins of property rights in the United States can be traced to England. The 1628 Petition of Right included a prohibition against requiring English subjects to quarter soldiers in private homes. The Declaration of Rights, approved by the English Parliament in 1689, included a list of 13 "undoubted Rights and Liberties" of English subjects, including parliamentary approval prior to taxation, freedom from excessive fines or bail, and the right to a jury trial before forfeiture of property.

Ex Post Facto Clause

Article I, section 10 of the U.S. Constitution, among other restrictions on state action, prohibits states from enacting any ex post facto law; Article I, section 9, clause 3 prohibits Congress from enacting ex post facto laws. Literally translated as "after the fact," an ex post facto law retroactively punishes as a crime an act that was not an offense when committed, or any law that creates a harsher punishment than those that existed at the time of the act.

The U.S. Supreme Court interpreted the ex post facto prohibitions in the Constitution to apply only to criminal statutes and penalties, not to civil laws that might have a retroactive effect.

Federalists and Anti-Federalists

Federalists and anti-Federalists refer to participants in the debates over the ratification of the U.S. Constitution in the 1780s. Federalists were proponents of the Constitution, consisting largely of market economy participants, creditors, exporting farmers, and learned professionals. Federalists supported a strengthened centralized government whose control of commerce and foreign relations, they hoped, would help to curb many of the economic problems plaguing the various states at that time. They viewed a strong central federal government as the best way to secure private property rights in order to create a stable economy and thereby promote national prosperity. In an effort to persuade others of the benefits of the proposed U.S. Constitution, Alexander Hamilton, James Madison, and John Jay composed a series of essays known as the *Federalist Papers*. These essays explained the importance of the various constitutional provisions and urged ratification as a means for securing economic stability.

Anti-Federalists were opposed to the ratification of the Constitution and tended to be small farmers and persons not heavily involved with commercial activity. Anti-Federalists feared that a strong centralized government would re-create many of the abuses perceived under colonial rule, including increased taxes and policies that would favor an aristocracy. They were also concerned that a strong centralized government would lead to a restriction of state sovereignty and individual civil liberties, which led many anti-Federalists to call for a federal Bill of Rights. The addition of the Bill of Rights to the U.S. Constitution in 1791 is largely due to the influence of the anti-Federalists.

Fee Simple

Also known as *fee simple absolute*; a property rights classification that denotes personal ownership in land with unconditional power of disposition. To own land in *fee simple* means that an owner has the exclusive power to transfer ownership, by sale or gift, during the owner's lifetime, and at death the property may be inherited by the owner's designation in a will or to relatives under a state's laws of intestate succession. Fee simple is sometimes referred to as outright ownership of land with the possibility of perpetual existence. If land owned in fee simple is sold or passed to the person's heirs upon death, the ownership interest continues to be unlimited in duration and disposition.

First English Evangelical Lutheran Church v. Los Angeles, 482 U.S. 304 (1987)

This case established the proposition that governments may be required to provide just compensation for temporary land-use restrictions. A county ordinance prohibited new construction in an area affected by a recent flood that had destroyed the church's buildings. The church challenged the ordinance as a taking that required compensation. The ordinance was eventually rescinded to permit construction, but the church pursued its claim for compensation for the period in which the ordinance had restricted the church's use of its property. The U.S. Supreme Court required the county government to compensate the church for the temporary taking. Following this decision, the Supreme Court has attempted to define the circumstances that will amount to a temporary taking, as well as the criteria for determining the amount of compensation to be paid for excessive restrictions on property use that are not permanent (see *Tahoe-Sierra Preservation Council v. Tahoe Regional Planning Agency*, 535 U.S. 302 [2002], Chapter 6).

Fletcher v. Peck, 10 U.S. 87 (1810)

For a description and excerpt from this case, see Chapter 6.

Gardner v. Village of Newburgh, 2 Johns. Ch. 162 (Ch. Ct. NY 1816)

Newburgh attempted to divert a stream running across the plaintiff's property for the purpose of obtaining drinking water for the village. Citing principles of natural law and equity, the New York Court of Chancery found in favor of the property owner, enjoining the village's actions. The court held that the prior use of the stream by the property owner created a property interest that could not be taken by the village government without compensation. Although the New York constitution did not contain a takings clause, the court stated that compensation is "a clear principle of natural equity" and that it would be "unjust, and contrary to the first principles of government," to take from the landowner his use and enjoyment of the stream of water on his property without compensation.

Gibbons v. Ogden, 22 U.S. 1, 53–54 (1824)

In *Gibbons v. Ogden,* the U.S. Supreme Court determined that the Commerce Clause permitted Congress to override state-created monopolies on steamboat travel. The New York legislature awarded a monopoly for steamboat navigation on New York's waters. Challenges to this exclusive property right involved Aaron Ogden, who held a state-mandated license, and Thomas Gibbons, who held a federal license. Chief Justice John Marshall, writing for the Court, ruled in favor of Gibbons on the ground that the federal commerce power prevailed over contrary state laws, including those that created property rights in the form of a state-granted monopoly. Marshall recognized that "the right to use all property, must be subject to modification by municipal law.... It belongs exclusively to the local state legislatures, to determine how a man may use his own, without injuring his neighbor." According to Marshall, the federal government's enhanced supervisory role with respect to interstate commerce did not displace the broad range of state and local authority over private property, but it did supercede state law in the event of a conflict involving interstate commerce.

Hawaii Housing Authority v. Midkiff, 467 U.S. 229 (1984)

This case stands for the proposition that the requirement of a public use in eminent domain cases is quite broad. In *Hawaii Housing Authority,* the Supreme Court held that if the state's use of its eminent domain power is "rationally related to a legitimate state purpose," the public use requirement is satisfied. Historical circumstances in Hawaii led to concentration of private property in a small number of landowners. In an attempt to lessen the disparity, the state used its eminent domain power to purchase land from large landowners and resell the lots to the tenants living on them. Upholding the plan, the Court pointed to the fact that the state's strategy was a rational attempt to remedy a social and economic ill. As in any case in which a state's police power is in question, the legislature simply had to show that it "rationally could have believed" that the act would "promote a legitimate interest."

Heart of Atlanta Motel v. United States, 379 U.S. 241 (1964)

In *Heart of Atlanta,* the U.S. Supreme Court upheld Title II of the Civil Rights Act of 1964, which requires privately owned places of "public accommodation" to provide services without discrimination "on the grounds of race, color, religion, or national origin."

The act limited the traditional property right of exclusion. The Court held that the Civil Rights Act was a valid exercise of congressional authority under the Commerce Clause. The Court rejected the motel owner's argument that the Civil Rights Act was a taking of private property because the owner was required to rent rooms to African Americans against his will.

Holmes, Oliver Wendell, Jr.

During his 30 years as an associate justice on the U.S. Supreme Court (1902–1932), Holmes became known as the "Great Dissenter" because of his pithy dissenting opinions, particularly in *Lochner*-era economic due process cases. With respect to the Takings Clause, however, Holmes's most significant contribution was his majority opinion in *Pennsylvania Coal v. Mahon* (1922). Holmes stated that "while property may be regulated to a certain extent, if regulation goes too far it will be recognized as a taking." The reasoning found in Holmes's opinion in *Mahon* emerged in regulatory takings cases decided by the Supreme Court more than half a century after that decision.

Intellectual Property

Ideas, inventions, and forms of expression that are accorded some degree of property status. In the United States, that status is conferred by federal statutes awarding patent, trademark, and copyright protection to applicants. For a term of years set by Congress, owners of patents and copyrights are given exclusive rights in the commercial use of their inventions or ideas, a right that may be enforced against interference by others through the award of monetary damages by courts. Patents and copyrights confer a monopoly right not permitted in other commercial activities to provide an incentive for the creation of new inventions, technologies, and expressive works. A trade secret is another form of intellectual property, recognized by both federal and state law. Unlike a patent, trademark, or copyright, a trade secret is not a government-granted exclusive property right. Rather, a trade secret may include proprietary information of a company pertaining to processes, technology, or know-how for production of a product or business method that provides an advantage over competitors who do not know or use it. The value to the owner of a trade secret is the ability to keep the information confidential from competitors.

Inventions Secrecy Act

Enacted in 1951, the federal Inventions Secrecy Act applies to prospective patents in which the government believes the award of a patent could constitute a danger to national security. The act permits the commissioner of patents to order the invention be kept secret and withhold the grant of a patent for a period of at least one year. The act does not set a maximum time period to withhold the patent; theoretically it is possible for the government to extend the secrecy order indefinitely. The act sets out the specific circumstances in which compensation is to be paid to the inventor due to the inability to use the invention. The inventor is entitled to compensation if the government uses the invention during the period in which a patent is withheld.

Inverse Condemnation

The technical term for a claim that a government's property use restriction is a regulatory taking. The term is best explained in a Supreme Court dissenting opinion:

> The phrase "inverse condemnation" generally describes a cause of action against a defendant in which a land owner may recover just compensation for a "taking" of his property under the Fifth Amendment, even though the formal condemnation proceedings in exercise of the

sovereign's power of *eminent domain* have not been instituted by the government entity. In the typical condemnation proceeding, the government brings a judicial or administrative action against the property owner to "take" the fee simple or an interest in his property; the judicial or administrative body enters a decree of condemnation, and just compensation is awarded. In an "inverse condemnation" action, the condemnation is "inverse" because it is the land owner, not the government entity, who institutes the proceeding. *San Diego Gas & Electric Co. v. City of San Diego,* 150 U.S. 621, 638 n.2 (1981) (Brennan, J., dissenting)

Johnson v. M'Intosh, 21 U.S. 543 (1823)

Johnson v. M'Intosh is one of a series of cases decided by the U.S. Supreme Court in the early 1800s that established several propositions with respect to Indian land. The most important holding was that the U.S. government, not the states, succeeded to the rights of the British crown with respect to Indian land. Under the European doctrine of discovery, the European power that first discovered land in America had the exclusive right to appropriate for itself any lands claimed by existing native inhabitants, either through conquest or purchase. The British crown, and subsequently the U.S. government, obtained fee simple interest in these lands, subject to a vague occupancy right of Native Americans. The Supreme Court held that although Native Americans may have possession of the land on which they lived, they did not have title to it and could not convey title to other persons. One result of the court's holding was that a title to land derived from the federal government, or from one of the states, had priority over an earlier purported grant from an Indian tribe.

Land Patent

When the federal or a state government first conveys public lands to a private person, the grant is referred to as a *patent*.

Legal Tender Cases (1870–1871)

Three U.S. Supreme Court decisions recognizing broad powers of Congress over currency and monetary policy. During the Civil War, the federal government issued paper currency not redeemable in gold or silver in order to finance the war effort. In 1862, Congress passed the Legal Tender Act, which declared the so-called greenbacks to be lawful tender for all debts, thus compelling creditors to accept payment in devalued paper money. In *Hepburn v. Griswold*, 75 U.S. 603 (1870), the Supreme Court held that the Legal Tender Act violated the Due Process Clause of the Fifth Amendment and impaired the obligation of contract. Following the nomination of two judges to fill court vacancies, the Supreme Court reconsidered its position in the combined cases *Knox v. Lee* and *Parker v. Davis*, 79 U.S. 457 (1871). The reconstituted court overruled *Hepburn* and upheld the Legal Tender Act with respect to both preexisting and future contracts.

Liberty of Contract

Beginning in the mid-1880s, the U.S. Supreme Court (and many state courts) interpreted the Fourteenth Amendment's Due Process Clause to impose substantive limits on state laws regulating economic activity, often termed *liberty of contract*. The Supreme Court used this new doctrine of substantive due process over the next 50 years to strike down a number of state laws that it viewed as impinging private property rights. Liberty of contract represented the view that the judiciary should review the content of legislative acts to determine whether they transgressed the economic thought extolling the virtues of free-market exchanges without government intervention in economic matters, including labor contracts. The Supreme Court's decisions in cases such as *Allgeyer v. Louisiana* (1897) and *Lochner v. New York* (1905) weakened states' attempts to regulate the employment sector. The liberty-of-contract doctrine was abandoned by the Supreme Court in the 1930s (see *Constitutional Revolution of 1937* on page 189).

Lochner v. New York, 198 U.S. 45, 53 (1905)

For a description and excerpt from this case, see Chapter 6.

Locke, John

In his *Second Treatise on Government* (1689), John Locke set forth a natural rights philosophy holding that all individuals possessed certain inherent and inalienable rights prior to the formation of any government. Locke believed that a legitimate government is formed only by consent of individuals, whose allegiance to that government is given in exchange for the protection of their natural rights. Locke attributed particular importance to the protection of property rights, professing that each person inherently possessed a natural right to acquire and protect property. Locke associated the protection of these natural property rights with liberty and believed it was the principal purpose of government to protect individual liberty. Accordingly, for the government to arbitrarily confiscate property without the consent of the governed was an invasion of individual liberty, an idea that heavily influenced subsequent property rights debates in the early years of the republic.

Loretto v. Teleprompter Manhattan CATV Corp., 458 U.S. 419 (1982)

In *Loretto*, the U.S. Supreme Court affirmed the rule that if the government authorizes a permanent physical invasion of private property, such action is a taking, even if interference with the owner's use is minimal and is supported by a countervailing governmental interest. The Court distinguished cases in which a governmental regulation merely prescribes how the owner may use her property versus cases of permanent physical occupation. The latter category was "qualitatively more intrusive than perhaps any other category of property regulation." Therefore, regardless of the public benefit or the minimal financial impact on the owner, compensation is required.

Lucas v. South Carolina Coastal Council, 505 U.S. 1003 (1992)

For a description and excerpt from this case, see Chapter 6.

Magna Carta

This charter, granted by King John of England in 1215, consisted of 38 chapters defining the liberties of English subjects. The charter introduced two property rights concepts that were central to the justifications given for American independence from Great Britain. First, representative consent was required prior to the imposition of taxes. Second, no person's property could be seized "except by the lawful judgment of his peers and the law of the land." The law-of-the-land clause appeared in many early state constitutions and came to be known as *due process*, that is, governments may not deprive persons of their life, liberty, or property without due process of law.

Mugler v. Kansas, 123 U.S. 623 (1887)

In this case, the U.S. Supreme Court recognized that states possess broad authority under the police power to enact laws that affect property rights. Peter Mugler manufactured beer after the Kansas state legislature enacted a prohibition law. The state fined and imprisoned Mugler and confiscated his brewery and beer inventory for violation of the statute. The Supreme Court upheld the prohibition law as a valid exercise of the state police power to protect health and morals, even though the law essentially rendered worthless Mugler's investment in his brewery.

Munn v. Illinois, 94 U.S. 113 (1877)

Grain elevator operators challenged an Illinois law setting the prices that the owners could charge customers. The owners invoked the Due Process Clause of the Fourteenth Amendment, arguing that the fixed rate deprived them of property without due process of law. The U.S. Supreme Court upheld the law because it fell within the state's police power. Grain elevators, the Court reasoned, were a type of private property "affected with a public interest," meaning that the state had a greater interest in the uses of that property. The majority opinion recognized that under some circumstances regulatory statutes could violate a property owner's due process rights. A strong dissent by Justice Stephen Field argued that the Illinois statute was unconstitutional and set forth a rationale for the conclusion that later courts would adopt as substantive due process.

Nollan v. California Coastal Commission, 483 U.S. 825 (1987)

In this case, the U.S. Supreme Court interpreted the Takings Clause to prohibit a local government from exacting benefits as a condition for permission to develop land that it could not gain outright without paying for the benefit or invoking eminent domain. The ordinance in *Nollan* conditioned the issuance of a permit to enlarge a structure on beachfront property on the owners' grant of a public easement over a portion of the property. By a 5–4 margin, the Court held that a taking occurred because the condition did not relate to any problem caused by the development. The Court stated that a logical nexus is required between the permit condition and the alleged harm caused by the development. In this case, the grant of a public easement over the land could not be a condition for permission to construct a larger home but instead was a property right that could not be taken away from the owner except through the exercise of eminent domain.

Northwest Ordinance

Legislation enacted by Congress in 1787 under the Articles of Confederation to establish a system of government for the vast area of land not yet organized into state governments. The Northwest Ordinance protected property rights in several ways and served as a model for the property clauses later included in the U.S. Constitution. The ordinance included a due process clause ("No man shall be deprived of his liberty or property, but by the judgment of his peers of the law of the land"); a takings clause ("Should the public exigencies make it necessary, for the common preservation, to take any person's property, or to demand his particular services, full compensation shall be made for the same"); and a contracts clause ("In the just preservation of rights and property, it is understood and declared, that no law ought ever to be made, or have force in the said territory, that shall, in any manner whatever, interfere with or affect private contracts or engagements, bona fide, and without fraud, previously formed"). The ordinance prohibited slavery in the territories, thus eliminating one category of property.

Nuisance

A common law doctrine that restricts use of one's property that adversely affects the use or enjoyment of neighboring property. The common law of nuisance reflects relative property rights: historically, whether a particular use of property constituted a nuisance with respect to neighbors depended upon whether that use was deemed appropriate for the location. A property owner whose use of his property constitutes a nuisance can be prevented from that use. A landowner can sue a neighbor for use of land that endangers the life and the health of others, is in violation of a law, or obstructs the reasonable and comfortable use of one's property. Courts have found nuisances in the diversion of water from a mill, smoke from a foundry, noxious gases or unpleasant odors (such as keeping pigs in an urban area), the pollution of a stream, or unsightly premises. State and local governments may also enjoin an individual landowner for activity on his land that constitutes a *public nuisance.* A public nuisance is an interference with the rights of the community, remedied by either a criminal prosecution by local authorities, or abatement of the nuisance by an injunctive decree or court order.

Offsetting Benefits Doctrine

State courts in the nineteenth century developed the doctrine of offsetting benefits to evaluate claims for compensation for takings of property by eminent domain. The idea of an offsetting benefit was that a landowner who was required to give up a portion of his land for construction of a railroad or highway gained a benefit from the proximity of the new transportation route; that benefit should be subtracted from the amount of compensation due to the property owner. Legislatures frequently delegated eminent domain power to private companies constructing railroads and other transportation projects. The reduction of just compensation for land condemned for a transportation route by the supposed offsetting benefit to the landowner worked to subsidize the projects, because the companies were not required to pay the full fair market value of the land. The doctrine of offsetting benefits is absent from modern eminent domain law.

Palazzolo v. Rhode Island, 533 U.S. 606 (2001)

This case addressed the important question whether a property owner who acquired land knowing that a use restriction was in place was barred from claiming compensation for a taking. *Lucas v. South Carolina Coastal Council*, 505 U.S. 1003 (1992), had indicated this possibility in its statement that for "regulations that prohibit all economically beneficial use of land . . . any limitation so severe cannot be *newly* legislated or decreed (without compensation)." In *Palazzolo*, however, the U.S. Supreme Court ruled that subsequent purchasers may still raise takings claims: "Just as a prospective enactment, such as a new zoning ordinance, can limit the value of land without effecting a taking because it can be understood as reasonable by all concerned, other enactments are unreasonable and do not become less so through passage of time or title." Compensation may still be required if the property restriction is "so unreasonable or onerous as to compel compensation." Although the Court remanded the case on this issue, it indicated that the per se rule of compensation in *Lucas* need not apply when some economically viable use remained. The decision appeared to limit the *Lucas* rule to cases in which a property owner's legitimate expectations for use of his property are subject to a restriction that denies "all economically beneficial use," defined as something more than a "mere token of remaining value."

Parcel-as-a-Whole Rule

First articulated in Justice William Brennan's majority opinion in *Penn Central v. New York* (1978); requires that courts must consider an owner's entire property holding in order to determine whether a regulation imposes a taking. Justice Brennan wrote that takings jurisprudence does not divide a parcel into segments to determine whether the value of one of those portions has been entirely abrogated. Instead, the extent of diminution of value considers "the character of the action and on the nature and extent of the interference with rights in the parcel as a whole." Under this rule, the Court's analysis of whether a particular land-use restriction constitutes a taking must consider the impact on the property as a whole, not merely the affected portion.

Penn Central Transportation Co. v. City of New York, 438 U.S. 104 (1978)

In *Penn Central*, the U.S. Supreme Court held that a New York City ordinance that prevented modification of a designated historic structure did not constitute a taking of private property. The owners of Grand Central Station wished to build a high-rise office building on top of the original structure. A commission designated the property as a historic landmark, preventing the owner from modifying the structure as proposed. Although the Court upheld the city's historic preservation law as applied in this instance, the Court indicated that a regulation designed to preserve a historic structure could result in a compensable taking in other situations. The Court identified three factors for determining whether a taking has occurred: the nature of the governmental action; the regulation's economic impact on the property owner; and the extent to which the regulation interfered with "distinct, investment-backed expectations." These three factors continue to form the standard inquiry in most regulatory takings claims.

Pennsylvania Coal v. Mahon, 260 U.S. 393 (1922)

For a description and excerpt from this case, see Chapter 6.

Police Power

A state government's authority to protect the health, welfare, and safety of its citizens through legislation designed to restrict certain conduct. Historically considered an essential attribute of state sovereignty, the police power encompasses a range of subjects. This power is subject to federal and state constitutional limitations, most notably the Takings Clause and the Due Process Clause of the Fourteenth Amendment. Most state and local laws regulating use of property, including zoning ordinances, are justified as an exercise of this power. The extent to which an exercise of the police power unconstitutionally deprives an owner of a property right is the central debate in modern takings law.

Private Property Protection Act of 1995 (U.S. House of Representatives)

For a description and excerpt from this proposed legislation, see Chapter 6.

PruneYard Shopping Center v. Robbins, 447 U.S. 74 (1980)

This case is important for the proposition that a physical invasion of one's property does not necessarily constitute a taking if the reason for the intrusion is supported by another important constitutional interest. The Court found that no taking occurred when a state law required shopping centers to accommodate students distributing literature on its property during business hours. In rendering its decision, the Court considered the importance of freedom of speech and the quasipublic nature of the private property involved. As a result, a state constitutional right to free speech can extend to the exercise of that speech on private property that is otherwise open to the public, even though the owner's right to exclude others from private property is impaired.

Public Trust Doctrine

A common law category of property owned in common (or subject to an easement for use) by all citizens. Land that is considered to be in the public trust requires the government to maintain the land for all citizens, and it may not alienate the land to private owners. U.S. courts first recognized a public trust in tidal land—the land between high tide and low tide. The state acts as trustee for the people, and in connection with its police power, the state retains the responsibility to protect and preserve the land for future public uses. In *Illinois Central Railroad v. Illinois*, 146 U.S. 387 (1892), the U.S. Supreme Court recognized the public trust doctrine in a large area of submerged land along the Chicago waterfront. In 1869, the Illinois legislature granted this land to a railroad company. The legislature later repealed the grant and sought to reclaim the land. The Supreme Court rejected the railroad's claim that this action violated the Contracts Clause and the Court's earlier holding in *Fletcher v. Peck* (1810). The Court held that any purported grant of land constituting a public trust is revocable by the government.

Pumpelly v. Green Bay Co., 80 U.S. 166 (1871)

A landowner brought suit against the Green Bay and Mississippi Canal Company for flooding 640 acres of his land following the construction of a dam authorized by the Wisconsin legislature. Although the Takings Clause applied only to the federal government at this time, the Wisconsin constitution contained an almost identical provision requiring compensation for takings of private property. The Court recognized that physical invasions of land constitute a taking equivalent to an exercise of the governmental power of eminent domain. The Court stated that "a serious interruption to the common and necessary use of property may be . . . equivalent to the taking of it, and under the constitutional provisions it is not necessary that the land should be absolutely taken." Thus, the concept of a taking that required compensation was not limited to actual exercises of eminent domain by a governmental authority but could include physical invasions as well.

Quasi-property

Rights that are not expressly characterized as property rights yet are so analogous to other property rights that some protection is afforded. The term *quasi-property* has been used to describe rights associated with organ donation, disposition of human bodies after death, and tissues and cells derived from the human body. States recognize certain quasiproperty rights in dead bodies, where the right of disposition for burial, organ donation, and so forth is said to reside in the next of kin.

Regulatory Takings

Governmental regulation of private property that deprives an owner of substantial value of the property. A regulatory taking requires compensation under the Takings Clause even though no physical invasion or transfer of property to the government has occurred. *Pennsylvania Coal v. Mahon* (1922) was the first U.S. Supreme Court decision to recognize the possibility of a regulatory taking. This case announced that the Takings Clause may require compensation for excessive regulatory measures, in addition to outright takings of property under a government's exercise of eminent domain. The regulatory takings doctrine generally balances the public interest in and need for regulation against the decline or impairment of value to an individual's property. Regulatory takings are determined on a case-by-case, ad hoc basis with two exceptions: If the regulation results in a permanent physical invasion of one's land, or if the regulation deprives a landowner of "all economically viable use" of the land, a court will likely find that a taking has occurred without the need to balance the government's asserted need for the regulation. The regulatory takings doctrine is based on the view the Takings Clause requires courts to consider whether the public at large, rather than a single owner, must bear the burden of an exercise of state power in the public interest.

Slaughterhouse Cases, 83 U.S. 36 (1873)

In one of the first cases construing the Fourteenth Amendment's Due Process Clause, the U.S. Supreme Court refused to invalidate a Louisiana law granting monopoly rights to operate slaughterhouses. The Court rejected the argument that the monopoly deprived other butchers of property rights under the Fourteenth Amendment by preventing them from pursuing their trade. The Court reasoned that legislation of this sort was within the state's police power to promote health and safety, and economic rights per se were not intended for federal oversight through the Fourteenth Amendment. In the following decades, this initial view of the Fourteenth Amendment changed quite radically, evidenced in *Allgeyer v. Louisiana* (1897) and culminating in *Lochner*-era decisions extolling liberty of contract, a property right to be protected by federal courts from state legislative interference (see *Liberty of Contract*).

State Property Rights Legislation

For a description and excerpts from recent state legislation, see Chapter 6.

Tahoe-Sierra Preservation Council v. Tahoe Regional Planning Agency, 535 U.S. 302 (2002)

For a description and excerpt from this case, see Chapter 6.

Vested Rights

The concept of a vested right in property signifies an ownership interest that has become complete, such that depriving a person of property would upset settled expectations. The vested rights doctrine of the nineteenth century was based largely on a natural rights view of property ownership. The notion of a vested right in property entitled to constitutional protection received its first clear articulation by the U.S. Supreme Court in *Fletcher v. Peck* (1810). Chief Justice John Marshall refused to allow the Georgia legislature to rescind land grants resulting from a bribery scandal because the land had already been resold to innocent purchasers, whose ownership in the land had vested. Modern courts use a similar concept of vested rights in property to distinguish ownership rights with settled expectations from a mere expectancy of an economic benefit.

Village of Euclid v. Ambler Realty Co., 272 U.S. 365 (1926)

The *Euclid* case resolved doubts about the constitutionality of use zoning, whereby a municipality is divided into districts where only certain uses of land are permitted. The U.S. Supreme Court held that a zoning measure would be found to be constitutional unless it was "clearly arbitrary and unreasonable, having no substantial relation to the public health, safety, morals, or general welfare." The zoning scheme in *Euclid* passed the Court's test because, among other things, it was designed to reduce traffic and noise in residential areas and aid fire prevention. After the Court's clarification in *Euclid* of the constitutionality of use zoning, similar ordinances proliferated in cities across the country. The division of a municipality into separate use districts is often referred to as Euclidean zoning in reference to this case.

West Coast Hotel v. Parrish, 300 U.S. 379 (1937)

This case represents the U.S. Supreme Court's retreat from substantive due process review of economic legislation in the *Lochner* era (see *Constitutional Revolution of 1937*). In this decision, the Court upheld a Washington State minimum wage law for women and minors, only one year after it invalidated a similar measure from New York. The *West Coast Hotel* decision signaled the effective end of economic due process and laissez faire as a constitutional norm.

Wynehamer v. The People, 13 N.Y. 378 (1856)

For a description and excerpt from this case, see Chapter 6.

Yee v. City of Escondido, 503 U.S. 519 (1992)

For a description and excerpt from this case, see Chapter 6.

6

Documents

This chapter presents 16 primary documents. Included first are the property clauses of the U.S. Constitution, followed by an excerpt from James Madison's *Federalist No. 10.* In that essay, Madison explains the importance of the proposed structure of the new federal government to protect private property rights. Madison's essay is followed by excerpts from important U.S. Supreme Court decisions that address constitutional property rights, beginning with *Fletcher v. Peck* (1810) and ending with *Tahoe-Sierra Preservation Council v. Tahoe Regional Planning Agency* (2002). One state court decision, *Wynehamer v. The People* (NY 1856), is included to illustrate the vested rights doctrine in the nineteenth century. This chapter concludes with examples of legislation on the subject of property rights. These documents include the Private Property Protection Act of 1995, proposed but not enacted by Congress, and examples of recent legislation from two states, Florida and Texas, designed to enhance remedies for regulatory takings.

The U.S. Constitution: Property Clauses

The Constitution contains several provisions that address property rights. These provisions—the Contracts Clause, the Takings and Due Process

Clauses of the Fifth Amendment, and the Due Process Clause of the Fourteenth Amendment—are reproduced below.

U.S. Constitution, Article I, Section 10, Clause 1 (1789)

No State shall enter into any Treaty, Alliance, or Confederation; grant Letters of Marque and Reprisal; coin Money; emit Bills of Credit; make any Thing but gold and silver Coin a Tender in Payment of Debts; pass any Bill of Attainder, ex post facto Law, or Law impairing the Obligation of Contracts, or grant any Title of Nobility.

Fifth Amendment (1791)

No person shall be held to answer for a capital, or otherwise infamous crime, unless on a presentment or indictment of a Grand Jury, except in cases arising in the land or naval forces, or in the Militia, when in actual service in time of War or public danger; nor shall any person be subject for the same offence to be twice put in jeopardy of life or limb; nor shall be compelled in any criminal case to be a witness against himself, nor be deprived of life, liberty, or property, without due process of law; nor shall private property be taken for public use, without just compensation.

Fourteenth Amendment (1868)

Section 1. All persons born or naturalized in the United States, and subject to the jurisdiction thereof, are citizens of the United States and of the State wherein they reside. No State shall make or enforce any law which shall abridge the privileges or immunities of citizens of the United States; nor shall any State deprive any person of life, liberty, or property, without due process of law; nor deny to any person within its jurisdiction the equal protection of the laws.

Federalist No. 10

James Madison wrote this essay, published in 1787, in support of ratification of the proposed federal Constitution. Madison proposes that the structure of the new federal government will best ensure protection of minorities against majority factions in state and local governments, particularly with respect to property rights. Federalist No. 10 has been quoted frequently by legal scholars and the U.S. Supreme Court.

AMONG the numerous advantages promised by a well-constructed Union, none deserves to be more accurately developed than its tendency to break and control the violence of faction. Complaints are everywhere heard from our most considerate and virtuous citizens, equally the friends of public and private faith, and of public and personal liberty, that our governments are too unstable, that the public good is disregarded in the conflicts of rival parties, and that measures are too often decided, not according to the rules of justice and the rights of the minor party, but by the superior force of an interested and overbearing majority. However anxiously we may wish that these complaints had no foundation, the evidence, of known facts will not permit us to deny that they are in some degree true. It will be found, indeed, on a candid review of our situation, that some of the distresses under which we labor have been erroneously charged on the operation of our governments; but it will be found, at the same time, that other causes will not alone account for many of our heaviest misfortunes; and, particularly, for that prevailing and increasing distrust of public engagements, and alarm for private rights, which are echoed from one end of the continent to the other.

By a faction, I understand a number of citizens, whether amounting to a majority or a minority of the whole, who are united and actuated by some common impulse of passion, or of interest, adverse to the rights of other citizens, or to the permanent and aggregate interests of the community.

The diversity in the faculties of men, from which the rights of property originate, is not less an insuperable obstacle to a uniformity of interests. The protection of these faculties is the first object of government. From the protection of different and unequal faculties of acquiring property, the possession of different degrees and kinds of property immediately results; and from the influence of these on the sentiments and views of the respective proprietors, ensues a division of the society into different interests and parties.

The most common and durable source of factions has been the various and unequal distribution of property. Those who hold and those who are without property have ever formed distinct interests in society.

Those who are creditors, and those who are debtors, fall under a like discrimination. A landed interest, a manufacturing interest, a mercantile interest, a moneyed interest, with many lesser interests, grow up of necessity in civilized nations, and divide them into different classes, actuated by different sentiments and views. The regulation of these various and interfering interests forms the principal task of modern legislation, and involves the spirit of party and faction in the necessary and ordinary operations of the government.

No man is allowed to be a judge in his own cause, because his interest would certainly bias his judgment, and, not improbably, corrupt his integrity. With equal, nay with greater reason, a body of men are unfit to be both judges and parties at the same time; yet what are many of the most important acts of legislation, but so many judicial determinations, not indeed concerning the rights of single persons, but concerning the rights of large bodies of citizens? And what are the different classes of legislators but advocates and parties to the causes which they determine? Is a law proposed concerning private debts? It is a question to which the creditors are parties on one side and the debtors on the other. Justice ought to hold the balance between them. Yet the parties are, and must be, themselves the judges; and the most numerous party, or, in other words, the most powerful faction must be expected to prevail. Shall domestic manufactures be encouraged, and in what degree, by restrictions on foreign manufactures? are questions which would be differently decided by the landed and the manufacturing classes, and probably by neither with a sole regard to justice and the public good. The apportionment of taxes on the various descriptions of property is an act which seems to require the most exact impartiality; yet there is, perhaps, no legislative act in which greater opportunity and temptation are given to a predominant party to trample on the rules of justice. Every shilling with which they overburden the inferior number, is a shilling saved to their own pockets.

It is in vain to say that enlightened statesmen will be able to adjust these clashing interests, and render them all subservient to the public good. Enlightened statesmen will not always be at the helm. Nor, in many cases, can such an adjustment be made at all without taking into view indirect and remote considerations, which will rarely prevail over the immediate interest which one party may find in disregarding the rights of another or the good of the whole.

The inference to which we are brought is, that the *causes* of faction cannot be removed, and that relief is only to be sought in the means of controlling its *effects.*

From this view of the subject it may be concluded that a pure democracy, by which I mean a society consisting of a small number of citizens, who assemble and administer the government in person, can admit of no cure for the mischiefs of faction. A common passion or interest will, in almost every case, be felt by a majority of the whole; a communication and concert result from the form of government itself; and there is nothing to check the inducements to sacrifice the weaker party or an obnoxious individual. Hence it is that such democracies have ever been spectacles of turbulence and contention; have ever been found incompatible with personal security or the rights of property; and have in general been as short in their lives as they have been violent in their deaths. Theoretic politicians, who have patronized this species of government, have erroneously supposed that by reducing mankind to a perfect equality in their political rights, they would, at the same time, be perfectly equalized and assimilated in their possessions, their opinions, and their passions.

A republic, by which I mean a government in which the scheme of representation takes place, opens a different prospect, and promises the cure for which we are seeking. The two great points of difference between a democracy and a republic are: first, the delegation of the government, in the latter, to a small number of citizens elected by the rest; secondly, the greater number of citizens, and greater sphere of country, over which the latter may be extended. The question resulting is, whether small or extensive republics are more favorable to the election of proper guardians of the public weal.

The greater number of citizens and extent of territory which may be brought within the compass of republican than of democratic government is this circumstance principally which renders factious combinations less to be dreaded in the former than in the latter. The smaller the society, the fewer probably will be the distinct parties and interests composing it; the fewer the distinct parties and interests, the more frequently will a majority be found of the same party; and the smaller the number of individuals composing a majority, and the smaller the compass within which they are placed, the more easily will they concert and execute their plans of oppression. Extend the sphere, and you take in a greater variety of parties and interests; you make it less probable that a majority of the whole will have a common motive to invade the rights of other citizens; or if such a common motive exists, it will be more difficult for all who feel it to discover their own strength, and to act in unison with each other.

Hence, it clearly appears, that the same advantage which a republic has over a democracy, in controlling the effects of faction, is enjoyed by a large over a small republic,—is enjoyed by the Union over the States composing it. The influence of factious leaders may kindle a flame within their particular States, but will be unable to spread a general conflagration through the other States. A rage for paper money, for an abolition of debts, for an equal division of property, or for any other improper or wicked project, will be less apt to pervade the whole body of the Union than a particular member of it; in the same proportion as such a malady is more likely to taint a particular county or district, than an entire State.

FLETCHER V. PECK, 10 U.S. 87 (1810)

Fletcher v. Peck *was the first decision by the U.S. Supreme Court to address in detail the significance of the federal Contracts Clause with respect to state legislation affecting property rights. In 1795, the Georgia legislature sold more than 40 million acres of land, for about a penny an acre, to several land companies that had bribed members of the legislature. A number of Georgia legislators were major stockholders in the companies. Public outcry following the sale resulted in election of a new legislature, which promptly rescinded the prior sale. The state refunded the money paid for the land, but some of the land had already been sold by the companies to other persons, a large number of whom lived in other states. One such purchaser brought suit in federal court, claiming that the Georgia legislature could not rescind the deal with respect to innocent purchasers of the land because of the federal Contracts Clause. The Supreme Court struck down the Georgia legislature's attempt to rescind its original land grant. A separate opinion by Justice William Johnson agrees with the result, but not on the basis of the Contracts Clause.*

Marshall, Ch. J.

If the legislature of Georgia was not bound to submit its pretensions to those tribunals which are established for the security of property, and to decide on human rights, if it might claim to itself the power of judging in its own case, yet there are certain great principles of justice, whose authority is universally acknowledged, that ought not to be entirely disregarded.

If a suit be brought to set aside a conveyance obtained by fraud, and the fraud be clearly proved, the conveyance will be set aside, as between the parties; but the rights of third persons, who are purchasers without notice, for a valuable consideration, cannot be disregarded. Titles, which, according to every legal test, are perfect, are acquired with that confidence which is inspired by the opinion that the purchaser is safe. If there be any concealed defect, arising from the conduct of those who had held the property long before he acquired it, of which he had no notice, that concealed defect cannot be set up against him. He has paid his money for a title good at law, he is innocent, whatever may be the guilt of others, and equity will not subject him to the penalties attached to that guilt. All titles would be insecure, and the intercourse between man and man would be very seriously obstructed, if this principle be overturned.

If the legislature felt itself absolved from those rules of property which are common to all the citizens of the United States, and from those principles of equity which are acknowledged in all our courts, its act is to be supported by its power alone, and the same power may devest any other individual of his lands, if it shall be the will of the legislature so to exert it.

It is not intended to speak with disrespect of the legislature of Georgia, or of its acts. Far from it. The question is a general question, and is treated as one. For although such powerful objections to a legislative grant, as are alleged against this, may not again exist, yet the principle, on which alone this rescinding act is to be supported, may be applied to every case to which it shall be the will of any legislature to apply it. The principle is this; that a legislature may, by its own act, devest the vested estate of any man whatever, for reasons which shall, by itself, be deemed sufficient.

In this case the legislature may have had ample proof that the original grant was obtained by practices which can never be too much reprobated, and which would have justified its abrogation so far as respected those to whom crime was imputable. But the grant, when issued, conveyed an estate in fee-simple to the grantee, clothed with all the solemnities which law can bestow. This estate was transferrable; and those who purchased parts of it were not stained by that guilt which infected the original transaction.

Is the power of the legislature competent to the annihilation of such title, and to a resumption of the property thus held? The principle asserted is, that one legislature is competent to repeal any act which a former legislature was competent to pass; and that one legislature cannot abridge the powers of a succeeding legislature.

The correctness of this principle, so far as respects general legislation, can never be controverted. But, if an act be done under a law, a succeeding legislature cannot undo it. The past cannot be recalled by the most absolute power. Conveyances have been made, those conveyances have vested legal estate, and, if those estates may be seized by the sovereign authority, still, that they originally vested is a fact, and cannot cease to be a fact.

When, then, a law is in its nature a contract, when absolute rights have vested under that contract, a repeal of the law cannot devest those rights; and the act of annulling them, if legitimate, is rendered so by a power applicable to the case of every individual in the community.

It may well be doubted whether the nature of society and of government does not prescribe some limits to the legislative power; and, if any be prescribed, where are they to be found, if the property of an individual, fairly and honestly acquired, may be seized without compensation.

It is the peculiar province of the legislature to prescribe general rules for the government of society; the application of those rules to individuals in society would seem to be the duty of other departments. How far the power of giving the law may involve every other power, in cases where the constitution is silent, never has been, and perhaps never can be, definitely stated.

The validity of this rescinding act, then, might well be doubted, were Georgia a single sovereign power. But Georgia cannot be viewed as a single, unconnected, sovereign power, on whose legislature no other restrictions are imposed than may be found in its own constitution. She is a part of a large empire; she is a member of the American union; and that union has a constitution the supremacy of which all acknowledge, and which imposes limits to the legislatures of the several states, which none claim a right to pass. The constitution of the United States declares that no state shall pass any bill of attainder, ex post facto law, or law impairing the obligation of contracts.

If, under a fair construction of the constitution, grants are comprehended under the term contracts, is a grant from the state excluded from the operation of the provision? Is the clause to be considered as inhibiting the state from impairing the obligation of contracts between two individuals, but as excluding from that inhibition contracts made with itself?

The words themselves contain no such distinction. They are general, and are applicable to contracts of every description. If contracts made with the state are to be exempted from their operation, the exception must arise from the character of the contracting party, not from the words which are employed.

Whatever respect might have been felt for the state sovereignties, it is not to be disguised that the framers of the constitution viewed, with some apprehension, the violent acts which might grow out of the feelings of the moment; and that the people of the United States, in adopting that instrument, have manifested a determination to shield themselves and their property from the effects of those sudden and strong passions to which men are exposed. The restrictions on the legislative power of the states are obviously founded in this sentiment; and the constitution of the United States contains what may be deemed a bill of rights for the people of each state.

It is, then, the unanimous opinion of the court, that, in this case, the estate having passed into the hands of a purchaser for a valuable consideration, without notice, the state of Georgia was restrained, either by general principles which are common to our free institutions, or by the particular provisions of the constitution of the United States, from passing a law whereby the estate of the plaintiff in the premises so purchased could be constitutionally and legally impaired and rendered null and void.

Johnson, J.

In this case I entertain an opinion different from that which has been delivered by the court. I do not hesitate to declare that a state does not possess the power of revoking its own grants. But I do it on a general principle, on the reason and nature of things: a principle which will impose laws even on the deity.

When the legislature have once conveyed their interest or property in any subject to the individual, they have lost all control over it; have nothing to act upon; it has passed from them; is vested in the individual;

becomes intimately blended with his existence, as essentially so as the blood that circulates through his system. The government may indeed demand of him the one or the other, not because they are not his, but because whatever is his is his country's.

I have thrown out these ideas that I may have it distinctly understood that my opinion on this point is not founded on the provision in the constitution of the United States, relative to laws impairing the obligation of contracts. The states and the United States are continually legislating on the subject of contracts, prescribing the mode of authentication, the time within which suits shall be prosecuted for them, in many cases affecting existing contracts by the laws which they pass, and declaring them to cease or lose their effect for want of compliance, in the parties, with such statutory provisions. All these acts appear to be within the most correct limits of legislative powers, and most beneficially exercised, and certainly could not have been intended to be affected by this constitutional provision, yet where to draw the line, or how to define or limit the words, "obligation of contracts," will be found a subject of extreme difficulty.

To give it the general effect of a restriction of the state powers in favor of private rights, is certainly going very far beyond the obvious and necessary import of the words, and would operate to restrict the states in the exercise of that right which every community must exercise, of possessing itself of the property of the individual, when necessary for public uses; a right which a magnanimous and just government will never exercise without amply indemnifying the individual, and which perhaps amounts to nothing more than a power to oblige him to sell and convey, when the public necessities require it.

WYNEHAMER V. THE PEOPLE, 13 N.Y. 378 (1856)

This case, from the highest state court in New York, represents the highwater mark of the vested rights doctrine in the nineteenth century. Relying on the state constitution's due process clause, the court invalidated a state prohibition statute prohibiting the sale of alcoholic beverages. Wynehamer v. The People *is representative of judicial views of private property rights prior to the civil war, although the U.S. Supreme Court would later uphold a prohibition law from the state of Kansas on the* *grounds that it was a valid exercise of the state's police power (*Mugler v. Kansas, *123 U.S. 623 [1887]). It is noteworthy, among other things, for defining property subject to constitutional protection as any object that historically had been bought and sold—an ominous view for the constitutional protection of slavery.*

Comstock, J.

In determining the question, whether the "Act for the prevention of intemperance, pauperism and crime" was an exercise of power prohibited to the legislature, an accurate perception of the subject to which it relates is the first requisite. It is, then, I believe, universally admitted that when this law was passed intoxicating liquors, to be used as a beverage, were *property* in the most absolute and unqualified sense of the term; and, as such, as much entitled to the protection of the constitution as lands, houses or chattels of any description. From the earliest ages they have been produced and consumed as a beverage, and have constituted an article of great importance in the commerce of the world. In this country the right of property in them was never, so far as I know, for an instant questioned. In this state, they were bought and sold like property; they were seized and sold upon legal process, for the payment of debts; they were, like other goods, the subject of actions at law; and when the owner died, their value constituted a fund for the benefit of his creditors, or went to his children and kindred, according to law or the will of the deceased. They entered largely into the foreign and internal commerce of the state, and when subjected to the operation of this statute, many millions in value were invested in them. In short, I do not understand it to be denied that they were property in just as high a sense as any other possession which a citizen can acquire.

It may be said, it is true, that intoxicating drinks are a species of property which performs no beneficent part in the political, moral or social economy of the world. It may even be urged, and, I will admit, demonstrated with reasonable certainty, that the abuses to which it is liable are so great, that the people of this state can dispense with its very existence, not only without injury to their aggregate interests, but with absolute benefit. The same can be said, although, perhaps, upon less palpable grounds, of other descriptions of property. Intoxicating beverages are by no means the only article of admitted property and of lawful commerce in this state against which arguments of this sort may be directed. But if such arguments can be allowed to subvert the fundamental idea of property, then there is no private right entirely safe, because there is no limitation upon the absolute discretion of the legislature, and the guarantees of the constitution are a mere waste of words. The foundation of property is not in philosophic or scientific speculations, nor even in the suggestion of benevolence or philanthropy. It is a simple and intelligible proposition, admitting, in the nature of the case, of no qualification, that that is property which the law of the land recognizes as such. It is, in short, an institution of law, and not a result of speculations in science, in morals or economy.

These observations appear to me quite elementary, yet they seem to be necessary, in order to exclude the discussion of extraneous topics. They lead us directly to the conclusion that all property is alike in the characteristic of inviolability. If the legislature has no power to confiscate and destroy property in general, it has no such power over any particular species. There may be, and there doubtless are, reasons of great urgency for regulation the trade in intoxicating drinks, as well as in other articles of commerce. In establishing such regulations merely, the legislature may proceed upon such views of policy, or economy or morals, as may be addressed to its discretion. The whole field of discussion is open, when the legislature, keeping within its acknowledged powers, seek to regulate and restrain a traffic, the general lawfulness of which is admitted; but when the simple question is, whether it can confiscate and *destroy* property lawfully acquired by the citizen in intoxicating liquors, then we are to remember that all property is equally sacred in the view of the constitution, and therefore that speculations as to its chemical or scientific qualities, or the mischief engendered by its abuse, have very little to do with the inquiry. Property, if protected by the constitution from such legislation as that we are now considering, is protected because *it is property* innocently acquired under existing laws, and not upon any theory which even so much as opens the question of its utility.

The act is one of fierce and intolerant proscription. It is unlawful to sell intoxicating liquors, to keep them for sale, or with intent to sell, and, with an exception of no importance to the question, it is to keep them at all. They are declared a public nuisance; and not only by that declaration, but by another express provision, all legal protection is withdrawn from them.

Chief Justice Marshall said, in *Fletcher v. Peck* (6 Cranch 135): "It may be doubted whether the nature of society and of government does not prescribe some limits to the legislative power; and if any be prescribed, where are they to be found, *if the property of an individual, fairly and honestly acquired, may be seized without compensation?*"

I am brought, therefore, to a more particular consideration of the limitations of power contained in the fundamental law: "No member of this state shall be disfranchised or deprived of any of the rights or privileges secured to any citizen thereof, unless by the law of the land or the judgment of his peers. No person shall be deprived of life, liberty or property, without due process of law; nor shall private property be taken for public use without just compensation." These provisions have been incorporated, in substance, into all our state constitutions. They are simple and comprehensive in themselves, and I do not perceive that they derive any additional force or meaning by tracing their origin to *Magna Charta* and the later fundamental statutes of Great Britain. In *Magna Charta*, they were wrested from the king as restraints upon the power of the crown. With us they are imposed by the people as restraints upon the power of the legislature.

I have not reached this result without an attentive examination of the arguments which have been urged in favor of an opposite conclusion. Prominent among these suggestions, our attention has been directed to a supposed analogy between the act under consideration and the license and excise laws of this and other states, the constitutionality of which is not questioned. I think the analogy does not exist. However difficult it may be to define, with accuracy and precision, the line of separation, there is a broad and perfectly intelligible distinction between what is plainly regulation on the one side, and what is plainly prohibition on the other.

The provision in the federal constitution, declaring that no state shall pass laws impairing the obligation of contracts, and the course of judicial decision under that provision, may be referred to as illustrating the distinction between legislation which is remedial merely, and that which is subversive of the rights intended to be saved. Under this provision the constitutionality of state laws has often been examined, and the difficulty of distinguishing between statutes which regulated the remedy and those which impaired or subverted the right has been great and acknowledged. But the distinction itself has been steadily maintained. Neither the federal nor the state courts have even shrunk from the inquiry; and laws which transcended the limits of regulation merely, and directly or indirectly invaded the right, have been uniformly adjudged to be void.

Statutes conferring upon municipal corporations power which, in their execution and ultimate result, inflict incidental or consequential injury upon the property of individuals—injury for which it is said the law affords no remedy—have been adjudged constitutional. In legislation of this kind it is also supposed some warrant can be found for the act under consideration. Here, again, the analogy fails. Laws of this character proscribe no species of property. They may injure it in their remote and accidental result, but they do not, like this act, say it shall not be allowed to exist at all, or strike directly at the qualities and attributes, without which it can have no legal existence. The constitutional requirement is, that no person shall be *deprived of his property,* and that private property shall not be taken for public use without just compensation. It is nowhere declared that, in the exercise of the admitted functions of government, private property may not receive remote and consequent injury without compensation.

It is scarcely necessary, perhaps, to observe, that in views which have been expressed, it is not intended to narrow the field of legislative discretion in regulating or controlling the traffic in intoxicating liquors. We only hold that, in all such legislation, the essential right of the citizen to his property must be preserved; a right which includes the power of disposition and sale, to be exercised under such restraints as a just regard both to the public good and private rights may suggest.

LOCHNER V. NEW YORK, 198 U.S. 45 (1905)

Lochner v. New York is the best-known example of the U.S. Supreme Court's use of the doctrine of substantive due process to invalidate state legislation regulating business operations. A New York statute limited employment in bakeries to 60 hours per week and 10 hours per day. The Court held that the legislation was an arbitrary interference with the freedom of contract guaranteed by the Fourteenth Amendment's Due Process Clause, which could not be sustained as a valid exercise of the state's police power to protect the public health, safety, morals, or general welfare. Four justices dissented (the dissent of Justice Oliver Wendell Holmes Jr. is excerpted below). In the New Deal era, substantive due process as a restriction on state economic regulation was repudiated by the Supreme Court. Since United States v. Carolene Products, *304 U.S. 144 (1938), federal courts review state economic legislation under a ratio-*

nal basis test, a lesser form of review than the strict scrutiny applied to laws affecting civil rights of minority groups and legislation interfering with political processes.

Mr. Justice PECKHAM delivered the opinion of the Court.

The statute necessarily interferes with the right of contract between the employer and employees, concerning the number of hours in which the latter may labor in the bakery of the employer. The general right to make a contract in relation to his business is part of the liberty of the individual protected by the 14th Amendment of the Federal Constitution. Under that provision no state can deprive any person of life, liberty, or property without due process of law. The right to purchase or to sell labor is part of the liberty protected by this amendment, unless there are circumstances which exclude the right. There are, however, certain powers, existing in the sovereignty of each state in the Union, somewhat vaguely termed police powers, the exact description and limitation of which have not been attempted by the courts. Those powers, broadly stated, and without, at present, any attempt at a more specific limitation, relate to the safety, health, morals, and general welfare of the public. Both property and liberty are held on such reasonable conditions as may be imposed by the governing power of the state in the exercise of those powers, and with such conditions the 14th Amendment was not designed to interfere.

The state, therefore, has power to prevent the individual from making certain kinds of contracts, and in regard to them the Federal Constitution offers no protection. If the contract be one which the state, in the legitimate exercise of its police power, has the right to prohibit, it is not prevented from prohibiting it by the 14th Amendment. Contracts in violation of a statute, either of the Federal or state government, or a contract to let one's property for immoral purposes, or to do any other unlawful act, could obtain no protection from the Federal Constitution, as coming under the liberty of person or of free contract. Therefore, when the state, by its legislature, in the assumed exercise of its police powers, has passed an act which seriously limits the right to labor or the right of contract in regard to their means of livelihood between persons who are sui juris (both employer and employee), it becomes of great importance to determine which shall prevail,—the right of the individual to labor for such time as he may choose, or the right of the state to prevent the individual from laboring, or from entering into any contract to labor, beyond a certain time prescribed by the state.

It must, of course, be conceded that there is a limit to the valid exercise of the police power by the state. There is no dispute concerning this general proposition. Otherwise the 14th Amendment would have no efficacy and the legislatures of the states would have unbounded power, and it would be enough to say that any piece of legislation was enacted to conserve the morals, the health, or the safety of the people; such legislation would be valid, no matter how absolutely without foundation the claim might be. The claim of the police power would be a mere pretext,—become another and delusive name for the supreme sovereignty of the state to be exercised free from constitutional restraint. This is not contended for. In every case that comes before this court, therefore, where legislation of this character is concerned, and where the protection of the Federal Constitution is sought, the question necessarily arises: Is this a fair, reasonable, and appropriate exercise of the police power of the state, or is it an unreasonable, unnecessary, and arbitrary interference with the right of the individual to his personal liberty, or to enter into those contracts in relation to labor which may seem to him appropriate or necessary for the support of himself and his family? Of course the liberty of contract relating to labor includes both parties to it. The one has as much right to purchase as the other to sell labor.

This is not a question of substituting the judgment of the court for that of the legislature. If the act be within the power of the state it is valid, although the judgment of the court might be totally opposed to the enactment of such a law. But the question would still remain: Is it within the police power of the state? and that question must be answered by the court.

The question whether this act is valid as a labor law, pure and simple, may be dismissed in a few words. There is no reasonable ground for interfering with the liberty of person or the right of free contract, by determining the hours of labor, in the occupation of a baker. There is no contention that bakers as a class are not equal in intelligence and capacity to men in other trades or manual occupations, or that they are not able to assert their rights and care for themselves without the protecting arm of the state, interfering with their independence of judgment and of action. They are in no sense wards of the state. Viewed in the light of a purely labor law, with no reference whatever to the question of health, we think that a law like the one before us involves neither the safety, the morals, nor the welfare, of the public, and that the interest of the public is not in the slightest degree affected by such an act. The law must be upheld, if at all, as a law pertaining to the health of the individual engaged in the occupation of a baker. It does not affect any other portion of the public than those who are engaged in that occupation. Clean and wholesome bread does not depend upon whether the baker works but ten hours per day or only sixty hours a week. The limitation of the hours of labor does not come within the police power on that ground.

It is a question of which of two powers or rights shall prevail,—the power of the state to legislate or the right of the individual to liberty of person and freedom of contract. The mere assertion that the subject relates, though but in a remote degree, to the public health, does not necessarily render the enactment valid. The act must have a more direct relation, as a means to an end, and the end itself must be appropriate and legitimate, before an act can be held to be valid which interferes with the general right of an individual to be free in his person and in his power to contract in relation to his own labor.

We think the limit of the police power has been reached and passed in this case. There is, in our judgment, no reasonable foundation for holding this to be necessary or appropriate as a health law to safeguard the public health, or the health of the individuals who are following the trade of a baker. If this statute be valid, and if, therefore, a proper case is made out in which to deny the right of an individual, sui juris, as employer or employee, to make contracts for the labor of the latter under the protection of the provisions of the Federal Constitution, there would seem to be no length to which legislation of this nature might not go.

This interference on the part of the legislatures of the several states with the ordinary trades and occupations of the people seems to be on the increase. It is impossible for us to shut our eyes to the fact that many of the laws of this character, while passed under what is claimed to be the police power for the purpose of protecting the public health or welfare, are, in reality, passed from other motives. We are justified in saying so when, from the character of the law and the subject upon which it legislates, it is apparent that the public health or welfare bears but the most remote relation to the law. The purpose of a statute must be determined from the natural and legal effect of the language employed; and whether it is or is not repugnant to the Constitution of the United States must be determined from the natural effect of such statutes when put into operation, and not from their proclaimed purpose.

Mr. Justice HOLMES, dissenting.

I regret sincerely that I am unable to agree with the judgment in this case, and that I think it my duty to express my dissent.

This case is decided upon an economic theory which a large part of the country does not entertain. If it were a question whether I agreed with that theory, I should desire to study it further and long before making up my mind. But I do not conceive that to be my duty, because I strongly believe that my agreement or disagreement has nothing to do with the right of a majority to embody their opinions in law. It is settled by various decisions of this court that state constitutions and state laws may regulate life in many ways which we as legislators might think as injudicious, or if you like as tyrannical, as this, and which, equally with this, interfere with the liberty to contract. Sunday laws and usury laws are ancient examples. A more modern one is the prohibition of lotteries. The liberty of the citizen to do as he likes so long as he does not interfere with the liberty of others to do the same, which has been a shibboleth for some well-known writers, is interfered with by school laws, by the Post office, by every state or municipal institution which takes his money for purposes thought desirable, whether he likes it or not. Some of these laws embody convictions or prejudices which judges are likely to share. Some may not. But a Constitution is not intended to embody a particular economic theory, whether of paternalism and the organic relation of the citizen to the state or of laissez faire. It is made for people of fundamentally differing views, and the accident of our finding certain opinions natural and familiar, or novel, and even shocking, ought not to conclude our judgment upon the question whether statutes embodying them conflict with the Constitution of the United States.

General propositions do not decide concrete cases. The decision will depend on a judgment or intuition more subtle than any articulate major premise. But I think that the proposition just stated, if it is accepted, will carry us far toward the end. Every opinion tends to become a law. I think that the word 'liberty,' in the 14th Amendment, is perverted when it is held to prevent the natural outcome of a dominant opinion, unless it can be said that a rational and fair man necessarily would admit that the statute proposed would infringe fundamental principles as they have been understood by the traditions of our people and our law. It does not need research to show that no such sweeping condemnation can be passed upon the statute before us. A reasonable man might think it a proper measure on the score of health. Men whom I certainly could not pronounce unreasonable would uphold it as a first installment of a general regulation of the hours of work. Whether in the latter aspect it would be open to the charge of inequality I think it unnecessary to discuss.

PENNSYLVANIA COAL V. MAHON, 260 U.S. 393 (1922)

Pennsylvania Coal is cited as the first U.S. Supreme Court decision to hold that the Takings Clause may require compensation for excessive regulatory measures, in addition to outright takings of property under a government's exercise of eminent domain. Pennsylvania landowners sued the Pennsylvania Coal Company to prevent it from mining under their property in such a way as to cause the surface of the land to collapse. The company owned deeds to the land conveying the surface to the owners but reserving the right to remove coal. The surface owners had agreed to waive all claims for damages due to mining of the subsurface coal. The surface owners claimed that a 1921 Pennsylvania statute, the Kohler Act, voided those parts of the deeds that permitted the company to damage surface structures. The Supreme Court invalidated the Kohler Act as an improper exercise of the state's police power because it effected a taking of preexisting property rights of the company. This case is best known for the statement that "if regulation goes too far it will be recognized as a taking." This case established no general rules for when a regulation goes "too far," and subsequent Supreme Court cases have continued this ad hoc inquiry in regulatory takings cases. A dissenting opinion by Justice Louis Brandeis is also excerpted below.

Mr. Justice HOLMES delivered the opinion of the Court.

The statute forbids the mining of anthracite coal in such a way as to cause the subsidence of, among other things, any structure used as a human habitation. As applied to this case the statute is admitted to destroy previously existing rights of property and contract. The question is whether the police power can be stretched so far.

Government could hardly go on if to some extent values incident to property could not be diminished without paying for every such change in the general law. As long recognized, some values are enjoyed under an implied limitation and must yield to the police power. But obviously the implied limitation must have its limits, or the contract and due process clauses are gone. One fact for consideration in determining such limits is the extent of the diminution. When it reaches a certain magnitude, in most if not in all cases there must be an exercise of eminent domain and compensation to sustain the act. So the question depends upon the particular facts. The greatest weight is given to the judgment of the legislature, but it always is open to interested parties to contend that the legislature has gone beyond its constitutional power.

It is our opinion that the act cannot be sustained as an exercise of the police power, so far as it affects the mining of coal under streets or cities in places where the right to mine such coal has been reserved.

The rights of the public in a street purchased or laid out by eminent domain are those that it has paid for. If in any case its representatives have been so short sighted as to acquire only surface rights without the right of support, we see no more authority for supplying the latter without compensation than there was for taking the right of way in the first place and refusing to pay for it because the public wanted it very much. The protection of private property in the Fifth Amendment presupposes that it is wanted for public use, but provides that it shall not be taken for such use without compensation. When this seemingly absolute protection is found to be qualified by the police power, the natural tendency of human nature is to extend the qualification more and more until at last private property disappears. But that cannot be accomplished in this way under the Constitution of the United States.

The general rule at least is, that while property may be regulated to a certain extent, if regulation goes too far it will be recognized as a taking. We are in danger of forgetting that a strong public desire to improve the public condition is not enough to warrant achieving the desire by a shorter cut than the constitutional way of paying for the change. As we already have said, this is a question of degree—and therefore cannot be disposed of by general propositions. But we regard this as going beyond any of the cases decided by this Court.

We assume, of course, that the statute was passed upon the conviction that an exigency existed that would warrant it, and we assume that an exigency exists that would warrant the exercise of eminent domain. But the question at bottom is upon whom the loss of the changes desired should fall. So far as private persons or communities have seen fit to take the risk of acquiring only surface rights, we cannot see that the fact that their risk has become a danger warrants the giving to them greater rights than they bought.

Mr. Justice BRANDEIS, dissenting.

Every restriction upon the use of property imposed in the exercise of the police power deprives the owner of some right theretofore enjoyed, and is, in that sense, an abridgment by the State of rights in property without making compensation. But restriction imposed to protect the public health, safety or morals from dangers threatened is not a taking. The restriction here in question is merely the prohibition of a noxious use. The property so restricted remains in the possession of its owner. The State does not appropriate it or make any use of it. The State merely prevents the owner from making a use which interferes with paramount rights of the public. Whenever the use prohibited ceases to be noxious,—as it may because of further change in local or social conditions,—the restriction will have to be removed and the owner will again be free to enjoy his property as heretofore.

It is said that one fact for consideration in determining whether the limits of the police power have been exceeded is the extent of the resulting diminution in value; and that here the restriction destroys existing rights of property and contract. But values are relative. If we are to consider the value of the coal kept in place by the restriction, we should compare it with the value of all other parts of the land. That is, with the value not of the coal alone, but with the value of the whole property.

And why should a sale of underground rights bar the State's power? For aught that appears the value of the coal kept in place by the restriction may be negligible as compared to the value of the whole property, or even as compared with that part of it which is represented by the coal remaining in place and which may be extracted despite the statute. Ordinarily a police regulation, general in operation, will not be held void as to a particular property, although proof is offered that owing to conditions peculiar to the restriction could not reasonably be applied. But even if the particular facts are to govern, the statute should, in my opinion, be upheld in this case.

Village of Euclid v. Ambler Realty Co., 272 U.S. 365 (1926)

The U.S. Supreme Court first considered the constitutionality of comprehensive zoning plans in this 1926 decision. The Ambler Realty Company brought suit challenging the village of Euclid's zoning ordinance as it affected the company's unimproved land. The company contended that the ordinance reduced the value of its property, that it deprived owners of liberty and property without due process, and that it constituted a taking of property without compensation. Rejecting these claims, the U.S. Supreme Court evinced wide latitude for police powers in its review of the zoning plan, ruling that the federal Constitution's property provisions were not violated. Three justices dissented.

Mr. Justice SUTHERLAND delivered the opinion of the Court.

The village of Euclid is an Ohio municipal corporation. Appellee is the owner of a tract of land containing 68 acres, situated in the westerly end of the village. On November 13, 1922, an ordinance was adopted by the village council, establishing a comprehensive zoning plan for regulating and restricting the location of trades, industries, apartment houses, two-family houses, single family houses, etc., the lot area to be built upon, the size and height of buildings, etc.

The ordinance is assailed on the grounds that it is in derogation of section 1 of the Fourteenth Amendment to the federal Constitution in that it deprives appellee of liberty and property without due process of law and denies it the equal protection of the law, and that it offends against certain provisions of the Constitution of the state of Ohio. The prayer of the bill is for an injunction restraining the enforcement of the ordinance and all attempts to impose or maintain as to appellee's property any of the restrictions, limitations or conditions.

Before proceeding to a consideration of the case, it is necessary to determine the scope of the inquiry. The bill alleges that the tract of land in question is vacant and has been held for years for the purpose of selling and developing it for industrial uses, for which it is especially adapted, being immediately in the path of progressive industrial development; that for such uses it has a market value of about $10,000 per acre, but if the use be limited to residential purposes the market value is not in excess of $2,500 per acre; that the first 200 feet of the parcel back from Euclid avenue, if unrestricted in respect of use, has a value of $150 per front foot, but if limited to residential uses, and ordinary mercantile business be excluded therefrom, its value is not in excess of $50 per front foot.

It is specifically averred that the ordinance attempts to restrict and control the lawful uses of appellee's land, so as to confiscate and destroy a great part of its value; that it is being enforced in accordance with its terms; that prospective buyers of land for industrial, commercial, and residential uses in the metropolitan district of Cleveland are deterred from buying any part of this land because of the existence of the ordinance and the necessity thereby entailed of conducting burdensome and expensive litigation in order to vindicate the right to use the land for lawful and legitimate purposes; that the ordinance constitutes a cloud upon the land, reduces and destroys its value, and has the effect of diverting the normal industrial, commercial, and residential development thereof to other and less favorable locations.

It is not necessary to set forth the provisions of the Ohio Constitution which are thought to be infringed. The question is the same under both Constitutions, namely, as stated by appellee: Is the ordinance invalid, in that it violates the constitutional protection 'to the right of property in the appellee by attempted regulations under the guise of the police power, which are unreasonable and confiscatory'?

Building zone laws are of modern origin. They began in this country about 25 years ago. Until recent years, urban life was comparatively simple; but, with the great increase and concentration of population, problems have developed, and constantly are developing, which require, and will continue to require, additional restrictions in respect of the use and occupation of private lands in urban communities. Regulations, the wisdom, necessity, and validity of which, as applied to existing conditions, are so apparent that they are now uniformly sustained, a century ago, or even half a century ago, probably would have been rejected as arbitrary and oppressive. Such regulations are sustained, under the complex conditions of our day, for reasons analogous to those which justify traffic regulations, which, before the advent of automobiles and rapid transit street railways, would have been condemned as fatally arbitrary and unreasonable. And in this there is no inconsistency, for, while the meaning of constitutional guaranties never varies, the scope of their application must expand or contract to meet the new and different conditions which are constantly coming within the field of their operation. In a changing world it is impossible that it should be otherwise. But although a degree of elasticity is thus imparted, not to the meaning, but to the application of constitutional principles, statutes and ordinances, which, after giving due weight to the new conditions, are found clearly not to conform to the Constitution, of course, must fall.

The ordinance now under review, and all similar laws and regulations, must find their justification in some aspect of the police power, asserted for the public welfare. The line which in this field separates the legitimate from the illegitimate assumption of power is not capable of precise delimitation. It varies with circumstances and conditions. A regulatory zoning ordinance, which would be clearly valid as applied to the great cities, might be clearly invalid as applied to rural communities. In solving doubts, the maxim 'sic utere tuo ut alienum non laedas,' which lies at the foundation of so much of the common low of nuisances, ordinarily will furnish a fairly helpful clue. And the law of nuisances, likewise, may be consulted, not for the purpose of controlling, but for the helpful aid of its analogies in the process of ascertaining the scope of, the power. Thus the question whether the power exists to forbid the erection of a building of a particular kind or for a particular use, like the question whether a particular thing is a nuisance, is to be determined, not by an abstract consideration of the building or of the thing considered apart, but by considering it in connection with the circumstances and the locality. A nuisance may be merely a right thing in the wrong place, like a pig in the parlor instead of the barnyard. If the validity of the legislative classification for zoning purposes be fairly debatable, the legislative judgment must be allowed to control.

There is no serious difference of opinion in respect of the validity of laws and regulations fixing the height of buildings within reasonable limits, the character of materials and methods of construction, and the adjoining area which must be left open, in order to minimize the danger of fire or collapse, the evils of overcrowding and the like, and excluding from residential sections offensive trades, industries and structures likely to create nuisances.

Here, however, the exclusion is in general terms of all industrial establishments, and it may thereby happen that not only offensive or dangerous industries will be excluded, but those which are neither offensive nor dangerous will share the same fate. But this is no more than happens in respect of many practice-forbidding laws which this court has upheld, although drawn in general terms so as to include individual cases that may turn out to be innocuous in themselves. The inclusion of a reasonable margin, to insure effective enforcement, will not put upon a law, otherwise valid, the stamp of invalidity. Such laws may also find their justification in the fact that, in some fields, the bad fades into the good by such insensible degrees that the two are not capable of being readily distinguished and separated in terms of legislation. In the light of these considerations, we are not prepared to say that the end in view was not sufficient to justify the general rule of the ordinance, although some industries of an innocent character might fall within the proscribed class. It cannot be said that the ordinance in this respect passes the bounds of reason and assumes the character of a merely arbitrary fiat. Moreover, the restrictive provisions of the ordinance in this particular may be sustained upon the principles applicable to the broader exclusion from residential districts of all business and trade structures, presently to be discussed.

The matter of zoning has received much attention at the hands of commissions and experts, and the results of their investigations have been set forth in comprehensive reports. These reports which bear every evidence of painstaking consideration, concur in the view that the segregation of residential, business and industrial buildings will make it easier to provide fire apparatus suitable for the character and intensity of the development in each section; that it will increase the safety and security of home life, greatly tend to prevent street accidents, especially to children, by reducing the traffic and resulting confusion in residential sections, decrease noise and other conditions which produce or intensify nervous disorders, preserve a more favorable environment in which to rear children, etc. With particular reference to apartment houses, it is pointed out that the development of detached house sections is greatly retarded by the coming of apartment houses, which has sometimes resulted in destroying the entire section for private house purposes; that in such sections very often the apartment house is a mere parasite, constructed in order to take advantage of the open spaces and attractive surroundings created by the residential character of the district. Moreover, the coming of one apartment house is followed by others, interfering by their height and bulk with the free circulation of air and monopolizing the rays of the sun which otherwise would fall upon the smaller homes, and bringing, as their necessary accompaniments, the disturbing noises incident to increased traffic and business, and the occupation, by means of moving and parked automobiles, of larger portions of the streets, thus detracting from their safety and depriving children of the privilege of quiet and open spaces for play, enjoyed by those in more favored localities—until, finally, the residential character of the neighborhood and its desirability as a place of detached residences are utterly destroyed. Under these circumstances, apartment houses, which in a different environment would be not only entirely unobjectionable but highly desirable, come very near to being nuisances.

If these reasons, thus summarized, do not demonstrate the wisdom or sound policy in all respects of those restrictions which we have indicated as pertinent to the inquiry, at least, the reasons are sufficiently cogent to preclude us from saying, as it must be said before the ordinance can be declared unconstitutional, that such provisions are clearly arbitrary and unreasonable, having no substantial relation to the public health, safety, morals, or general welfare.

It is true that when, if ever, the provisions set forth in the ordinance in tedious and minute detail, come to be concretely applied to particular premises, including those of the appellee, or to particular conditions, or to be considered in connection with specific complaints, some of them, or even many of them, may be found to be clearly arbitrary and unreasonable. But where the equitable remedy of injunction is sought, as it is here, not upon the ground of a present infringement or denial of a specific right, or of a particular injury in process of actual execution, but upon the broad ground that the mere existence and threatened enforcement of the ordinance, by materially and adversely affecting values and curtailing the opportunities of the market, constitute a present and irreparable injury, the court will not scrutinize its provisions, sentence by sentence, to ascertain by a process of piecemeal dissection whether there may be, here and there, provisions of a minor character, or relating to matters of administration, or not shown to contribute to the injury complained of, which, if attacked separately, might not withstand the test of constitutionality. In respect of such provisions, of which specific complaint is not made, it cannot be said that the landowner has suffered or is threatened with an injury which entitles him to challenge their constitutionality.

Under these circumstances, therefore, it is enough for us to determine, as we do, that the ordinance in its general scope and dominant features, so far as its provisions are here involved, is a valid exercise of authority, leaving other provisions to be dealt with as cases arise directly involving them.

And this is in accordance with the traditional policy of this court. In the realm of constitutional law, especially, this court has perceived the embarrassment which is likely to result from an attempt to formulate rules or decide questions beyond the necessities of the immediate issue. It has preferred to follow the method of a gradual approach to the general by a systematically guarded application and extension of constitutional principles to particular cases as they arise, rather than by out of hand attempts to establish general rules to which future cases must be fitted. This process applies with peculiar force to the solution of questions arising under the due process clause of the Constitution as applied to the exercise of the flexible powers of police, with which we are here concerned.

PENN CENTRAL TRANSPORTATION CO. V. CITY OF NEW YORK, 438 U.S. 104 (1978)

Penn Central *is significant for its holding that regulatory takings are determined by a balancing test. Penn Central challenged the constitutionality of a New York historic preservation law. The New York City Landmarks Preservation Commission refused to grant Penn Central permission to build a 53-story office building on top of Grand Central Station because the commission designated the property as a landmark. The Supreme Court held that this application of New York's landmark preservation act did not constitute a taking. Three justices dissented. However, the Court indicated that land-use restrictions on real property may constitute a taking if not reasonably related to a substantial public purpose, or if they have an unduly harsh impact on an owner's use of property, components of a balancing test still used in most regulatory takings cases.*

Mr. Justice BRENNAN delivered the opinion of the Court.

The question presented is whether a city may, as part of a comprehensive program to preserve historic landmarks and historic districts, place restrictions on the development of individual historic landmarks—in addition to those imposed by applicable zoning ordinances—without effecting a "taking" requiring the payment of "just compensation." Specifically, we must decide whether the application of New York City's Landmarks Preservation Law to the parcel of land occupied by Grand Central Terminal has "taken" its owners' property in violation of the Fifth and Fourteenth Amendments.

Over the past 50 years, all 50 States and over 500 municipalities have enacted laws to encourage or require the preservation of buildings and areas with historic or aesthetic importance. These nationwide legislative efforts have been precipitated by two concerns. The first is recognition that, in recent years, large numbers of historic structures, landmarks, and areas have been destroyed without adequate consideration of either the values represented therein or the possibility of preserving the destroyed properties for use in economically productive ways. The second is a widely shared belief that structures with special historic, cultural, or architectural significance enhance the quality of life for all. Not only do these buildings and their workmanship represent the lessons of the past and embody precious features of our heritage, they serve as examples of quality for today. Historic conservation is but one aspect of the much larger problem, basically an environmental one, of enhancing—or perhaps developing for the first time—the quality of life for people.

New York City, responding to similar concerns and acting pursuant to a New York State enabling Act, adopted its Landmarks Preservation Law in 1965. The city acted from the conviction that "the standing of [New York City] as a world-wide tourist center and world capital of business, culture and government" would be threatened if legislation were not enacted to protect historic landmarks and neighborhoods from precipitate decisions to destroy or fundamentally alter their character. The city believed that comprehensive measures to safeguard desirable features of the existing urban fabric would benefit its citizens in a variety of ways: *e.g.,* fostering "civic pride in the beauty and noble accomplishments of the past"; protecting and enhancing "the city's attractions to tourists and visitors"; "support[ing] and stimul[ating] business and industry"; "strengthen[ing] the economy of the city"; and promoting "the use of historic districts, landmarks, interior landmarks and scenic landmarks for the education, pleasure and welfare of the people of the city."

The New York City law is typical of many urban landmark laws in that its primary method of achieving its goals is not by acquisitions of historic properties, but rather by involving public entities in land-use decisions affecting these properties and providing services, standards, controls, and incentives that will encourage preservation by private owners and users. While the law does place special restrictions on landmark properties as a necessary feature to the attainment of its larger objectives, the major theme of the law is to ensure the owners of any such properties both a "reasonable return" on their investments and maximum latitude to use their parcels for purposes not inconsistent with the preservation goals. Thus far, 31 historic districts and over 400 individual landmarks have been finally designated, and the process is a continuing one.

This case involves the application of New York City's Landmarks Preservation Law to Grand Central Terminal (Terminal). The Terminal, which is owned by the Penn Central Transportation Co. and its affiliates (Penn Central), is one of New York City's most famous buildings. The Terminal itself is an eight-story structure which Penn Central uses as a railroad station and in which it rents space not needed for railroad purposes to a variety of commercial interests. On January 22, 1968, appellant Penn Central, to increase its income, entered into a renewable 50-year lease and sublease agreement with appellant UGP Properties, Inc. (UGP), a wholly owned subsidiary of Union General Properties, Ltd., a United Kingdom corporation. Under the terms of the agreement, UGP was to construct a multistory office building above the Terminal. UGP promised to pay Penn Central $1 million annually during construction and at least $3 million annually thereafter.

Appellants claim that the application of the Landmarks Preservation Law to prohibit the proposed structure had "taken" their property without just compensation in violation of the Fifth and Fourteenth Amendments and arbitrarily deprived them of their property without due process of law in violation of the Fourteenth Amendment.

Before considering appellants' specific contentions, it will be useful to review the factors that have shaped the jurisprudence of the Fifth Amendment injunction "nor shall private property be taken for public use, without just compensation." The question of what constitutes a "taking" for purposes of the Fifth Amendment has proved to be a problem of considerable difficulty. While this Court has recognized that the "Fifth Amendment's guarantee ... [is] designed to bar Government from forcing some people alone to bear public burdens which, in all fairness and justice, should be borne by the public as a whole," this Court, quite simply, has been unable to develop any "set formula" for determining when "justice and fairness" require that economic injuries caused by public action be compensated by the government, rather than remain disproportionately concentrated on a few persons. Indeed, we have frequently observed that whether a particular restriction will be rendered invalid by the government's failure to pay for any losses proximately caused by it depends largely "upon the particular circumstances [in that] case."

In engaging in these essentially ad hoc, factual inquiries, the Court's decisions have identified several factors that have particular significance. The economic impact of the regulation on the claimant and, particularly, the extent to which the regulation has interfered with distinct investment-backed expectations are, of course, relevant considerations. So, too, is the character of the governmental action. A "taking" may more readily be found when the interference with property can be characterized as a physical invasion by government than when interference arises from some public program adjusting the benefits and burdens of economic life to promote the common good.

"Government hardly could go on if to some extent values incident to property could not be diminished without paying for every such change in the general law," *Pennsylvania Coal Co. v. Mahon*, 260 U.S. 393 (1922), and this Court has accordingly recognized, in a wide variety of contexts, that government may execute laws or programs that adversely affect recognized economic values. Exercises of the taxing power are one obvious example. A second are the decisions in which this Court has dismissed "taking" challenges on the ground that, while the challenged government action caused economic harm, it did not interfere with interests that were sufficiently bound up with the reasonable expectations of the claimant to constitute "property" for Fifth Amendment purposes.

More importantly for the present case, in instances in which a state tribunal reasonably concluded that "the health, safety, morals, or general welfare" would be promoted by prohibiting particular contemplated uses of land, this Court has upheld land-use regulations that destroyed or adversely affected recognized real property interests. Zoning laws are, of course, the classic example, which have been viewed as permissible governmental action even when prohibiting the most beneficial use of the property.

Zoning laws generally do not affect existing uses of real property, but "taking" challenges have also been held to be without merit in a wide variety of situations when the challenged governmental actions prohibited a beneficial use to which individual parcels had previously been devoted and thus caused substantial individualized harm. In *Miller v. Schoene*,

276 U.S. 272 (1928), a state entomologist, acting pursuant to a state statute, ordered the claimants to cut down a large number of ornamental red cedar trees because they produced cedar rust fatal to apple trees cultivated nearby. Although the statute provided for recovery of any expense incurred in removing the cedars, and permitted claimants to use the felled trees, it did not provide compensation for the value of the standing trees or for the resulting decrease in market value of the properties as a whole. A unanimous Court held that this latter omission did not render the statute invalid. The Court held that the State might properly make "a choice between the preservation of one class of property and that of the other" and since the apple industry was important in the State involved, concluded that the State had not exceeded "its constitutional powers by deciding upon the destruction of one class of property [without compensation] in order to save another which, in the judgment of the legislature, is of greater value to the public."

Pennsylvania Coal Co. v. Mahon is the leading case for the proposition that a state statute that substantially furthers important public policies may so frustrate distinct investment-backed expectations as to amount to a "taking." There the claimant had sold the surface rights to particular parcels of property, but expressly reserved the right to remove the coal thereunder. A Pennsylvania statute, enacted after the transactions, forbade any mining of coal that caused the subsidence of any house, unless the house was the property of the owner of the underlying coal and was more than 150 feet from the improved property of another. Because the statute made it commercially impracticable to mine the coal, and thus had nearly the same effect as the complete destruction of rights claimant had reserved from the owners of the surface land, the Court held that the statute was invalid as effecting a "taking" without just compensation.

In contending that the New York City law has "taken" their property in violation of the Fifth and Fourteenth Amendments, appellants make a series of arguments, which, while tailored to the facts of this case, essentially urge that any substantial restriction imposed pursuant to a landmark law must be accompanied by just compensation if it is to be constitutional. They first observe that the airspace above the Terminal is a valuable property. They urge that the Landmarks Law has deprived them of any gainful use of their "air rights" above the Terminal and that, irrespective of the value of the remainder of their parcel, the city has "taken" their right to this superadjacent airspace, thus entitling them to "just compensation" measured by the fair market value of these air rights. Secondly, appellants, focusing on the character and impact of the New York City law, argue that it effects a "taking" because its operation has significantly diminished the value of the Terminal site. We now must consider whether the interference with appellants' property is of such a magnitude that "there must be an exercise of eminent domain and compensation to sustain [it]."

The New York City law does not interfere in any way with the present uses of the Terminal. Its designation as a landmark not only permits but contemplates that appellants may continue to use the property precisely as it has been used for the past 65 years: as a railroad terminal containing office space and concessions. So the law does not interfere with what must be regarded as Penn Central's primary expectation concerning the use of the parcel. More importantly, on this record, we must regard the New York City law as permitting Penn Central not only to profit from the Terminal but also to obtain a "reasonable return" on its investment.

Appellants, moreover, exaggerate the effect of the law on their ability to make use of the air rights above the Terminal in two respects. First, it simply cannot be maintained, on this record, that appellants have been prohibited from occupying *any* portion of the airspace above the Terminal. While the Commission's actions in denying applications to construct an office building in excess of 50 stories above the Terminal may indicate that it will refuse to issue a certificate of appropriateness for any comparably sized structure, nothing the Commission has said or done suggests an intention to prohibit *any* construction above the Terminal. Since appellants have not sought approval for the construction of a smaller structure, we do not know that appellants will be denied any use of any portion of the airspace above the Terminal.

Second, to the extent appellants have been denied the right to build above the Terminal, it is not literally accurate to say that they have been denied *all* use of even those pre-existing air rights. Their ability to use these rights has not been abrogated; they are made transferable to at least eight parcels in the vicinity of the Terminal, one or two of which have been found suitable for the construction of new office buildings. Although appellants and others have argued that New York City's transferable development-rights program is far from ideal, the New York courts here supportably found that, at least in the case of the Terminal, the rights afforded are valuable. While these rights may well not have constituted "just compensation" if a "taking" had occurred, the rights nevertheless undoubtedly mitigate whatever financial burdens the law has imposed on appellants and, for that reason, are to be taken into account in considering the impact of regulation.

On this record, we conclude that the application of New York City's Landmarks Law has not effected a "taking" of appellants' property. The restrictions imposed are substantially related to the promotion of the general welfare and not only permit reasonable beneficial use of the landmark site but also afford appellants opportunities further to enhance not only the Terminal site proper but also other properties.

PruneYard Shopping Center v. Robins, 447 U.S. 74 (1980)

In 1980, the U.S. Supreme Court held that state constitutional provisions, which permit individuals to exercise free speech and petition rights on the property of a privately owned shopping center to which the public is invited, did not violate the shopping center owner's property rights under the Fifth and Fourteenth Amendments. Four justices wrote separate opinions. This case represents the view that other constitutional rights may trump the traditional right of private property owners to exclude others from their property. Heart of Atlanta Motel v. United States, *379 U.S. 241 (1964), previously held that a landowner who decides to rent to tenants can be compelled to accept tenants over the owner's racial preference, thus upholding Title II of the Civil Rights Act of 1964.*

Mr. Justice REHNQUIST delivered the opinion of the Court.

We postponed jurisdiction of this appeal from the Supreme Court of California to decide the important federal constitutional questions it presented. Those are whether state constitutional provisions, which permit individuals to exercise free speech and petition rights on the property of a privately owned shopping center to which the public is invited, violate the shopping center owner's property rights under the Fifth and Fourteenth Amendments or his free speech rights under the First and Fourteenth Amendments.

Appellant PruneYard is a privately owned shopping center in the city of Campbell, Cal. It covers approximately 21 acres—5 devoted to parking and 16 occupied by walkways, plazas, sidewalks, and buildings that contain more than 65 specialty shops, 10 restaurants, and a movie theater. The PruneYard is open to the public for the purpose of encouraging the patronizing of its commercial establishments. It has a policy not to permit any visitor or tenant to engage in any publicly expressive activity, including the circulation of petitions, that is not directly related to its commercial purposes. This policy has been strictly enforced in a nondiscriminatory fashion.

Appellees are high school students who sought to solicit support for their opposition to a United Nations resolution against "Zionism." On a Saturday afternoon they set up a card table in a corner of PruneYard's central courtyard. They distributed pamphlets and asked passers by to sign petitions, which were to be sent to the President and Members of Congress. Their activity was peaceful and orderly and so far as the record indicates was not objected to by PruneYard's patrons.

Soon after appellees had begun soliciting signatures, a security guard informed them that they would have to leave because their activity violated PruneYard regulations. The guard suggested that they move to the public sidewalk at the PruneYard's perimeter. Appellees immediately left the premises and later filed this lawsuit. They sought to enjoin appellants from denying them access to the PruneYard for the purpose of circulating their petitions.

Appellants contend that a right to exclude others underlies the Fifth Amendment guarantee against the taking of property without just compensation and the Fourteenth Amendment guarantee against the deprivation of property without due process of law.

It is true that one of the essential sticks in the bundle of property rights is the right to exclude others. And here there has literally been a "taking" of that right to the extent that the California Supreme Court has interpreted the State Constitution to entitle its citizens to exercise free expression and petition rights on shopping center property. But it is well established that "not every destruction or injury to property by governmental action has been held to be a 'taking' in the constitutional sense." Rather, the determination whether a state law unlawfully infringes a landowner's property in violation of the Taking Clause requires an examination of whether the restriction on private property "forc[es] some people alone to bear public burdens which, in all fairness and justice, should be borne by the public as a whole." This examination entails inquiry into such factors as the character of the governmental action, its economic impact, and its interference with reasonable investment-backed expectations. When "regulation goes too far it will be recognized as a taking." *Pennsylvania Coal Co. v. Mahon,* 260 U.S. 393 (1922).

Here the requirement that appellants permit appellees to exercise state-protected rights of free expression and petition on shopping center property clearly does not amount to an unconstitutional infringement of appellants' property rights under the Taking Clause. There is nothing to suggest that preventing appellants from prohibiting this sort of activity will unreasonably impair the value or use of their property as a shopping center. The PruneYard is a large commercial complex that covers several city blocks, contains numerous separate business establishments, and is open to the public at large. The decision of the California Supreme Court makes it clear that the PruneYard may restrict expressive activity by adopting time, place, and manner regulations that will minimize any interference with its commercial functions. Appellees were orderly, and they limited their activity to the common areas of the shopping center. In these circumstances, the fact that they may have "physically invaded" appellants' property cannot be viewed as determinative.

This case is quite different from *Kaiser Aetna v. United States.* Kaiser Aetna was a case in which the owners of a private pond had invested substantial amounts of money in dredging the pond, developing it into an exclusive marina, and building a surrounding marina community. The marina was open only to fee-paying members, and the fees were paid in part to "maintain the privacy and security of the pond." The Federal Government sought to compel free public use of the private marina on the ground that the marina became subject to the federal navigational servitude because the owners had dredged a channel connecting it to "navigable water."

The Government's attempt to create a public right of access to the improved pond interfered with Kaiser Aetna's "reasonable investment backed expectations." We held that it went "so far beyond ordinary regulation or improvement for navigation as to amount to a taking...." Nor as a general proposition is the United States, as opposed to the several States, possessed of residual authority that enables it to define "property" in the first instance. A State is, of course, bound by the Just Compensation Clause of the Fifth Amendment, *Chicago, B. & Q. R.*

Co. v. Chicago, 166 U.S. 226 (1897), but here appellants have failed to demonstrate that the "right to exclude others" is so essential to the use or economic value of their property that the state-authorized limitation of it amounted to a "taking."

There is also little merit to appellants' argument that they have been denied their property without due process of law. In *Nebbia v. New York,* 291 U.S. 502 (1934), this Court stated:

"[N]either property rights nor contract rights are absolute ... Equally fundamental with the private right is that of the public to regulate it in the common interest.... [T]he guaranty of due process, as has often been held, demands only that the law shall not be unreasonable, arbitrary or capricious, and that the means selected shall have a real and substantial relation to the objective sought to be attained." Appellants have failed to provide sufficient justification for concluding that this test is not satisfied by the State's asserted interest in promoting more expansive rights of free speech and petition than conferred by the Federal Constitution.

We conclude that neither appellants' federally recognized property rights nor their First Amendment rights have been infringed by the California Supreme Court's decision recognizing a right of appellees to exercise state-protected rights of expression and petition on appellants' property. The judgment of the Supreme Court of California is therefore affirmed.

HAWAII HOUSING AUTHORITY V. MIDKIFF, 467 U.S. 229 (1984)

The "public use" requirement for governmental power to take private property is considered in this 1984 U.S. Supreme Court decision. The Hawaii legislature enacted the Land Reform Act of 1967, which transferred title in real property from lessors to lessees in order to reduce the concentration of landownership. The act redistributed land from large landowners to be resold to leaseholders by the state's housing authority, with compensation. The act was challenged as an unconstitutional exercise of governmental authority because the purpose of the taking was to benefit the new leaseholders rather than the public. The Supreme Court held that the act did not violate the public use requirement of the Fifth Amendment for taking of private property, holding that the mere fact that property taken outright by eminent domain is transferred in the first instance to private beneficiaries does not mean that the taking has only a private purpose. The decision indicates wide latitude for state and local government to determine what constitutes a public use. No justices dissented.

Justice O'CONNOR delivered the opinion of the Court.

The Fifth Amendment of the United States Constitution provides, in pertinent part, that "private property [shall not] be taken for public use, without just compensation." These cases present the question whether the Public Use Clause of that Amendment, made applicable to the States through the Fourteenth Amendment, prohibits the State of Hawaii from taking, with just compensation, title in real property from lessors and transferring it to lessees in order to reduce the concentration of ownership of fees simple in the State. We conclude that it does not.

The legislature concluded that concentrated land ownership was responsible for skewing the State's residential fee simple market, inflating land prices, and injuring the public tranquility and welfare. To redress these problems, the legislature decided to compel the large landowners to break up their estates. The legislature considered requiring large landowners to sell lands which they were leasing to homeowners. However, the landowners strongly resisted this scheme, pointing out the significant federal tax liabilities they would incur. Indeed, the landowners claimed that the federal tax laws were the primary reason they previously had chosen to lease, and not sell, their lands. Therefore, to accommodate the needs of both lessors and lessees, the Hawaii Legislature enacted the Land Reform Act of 1967 (Act), which created a mechanism for condemning residential tracts and for transferring ownership of the condemned fees simple to existing lessees. By condemning the land in question, the Hawaii Legislature intended to make the land sales involuntary, thereby making the federal tax consequences less severe while still facilitating the redistribution of fees simple.

The starting point for our analysis of the Act's constitutionality is the Court's decision in *Berman v. Parker,* 348 U.S. 26 (1954). In Berman, the Court held constitutional the District of Columbia Redevelopment Act of 1945. That Act provided both for the comprehensive use of the eminent domain power to redevelop slum areas and for the possible sale or lease of the condemned lands to private interests. In discussing whether the takings authorized by that Act were for a "public use," the Court stated: "We deal, in other words, with what traditionally has been known as the police power. An attempt to define its reach or trace its outer limits is fruitless, for each case must turn on its own facts. The definition is essentially the product of legislative determinations addressed to the purposes of government, purposes neither abstractly nor historically capable of complete definition. Subject to specific constitutional limitations, when the legislature has spoken, the public interest has been declared in terms well-nigh conclusive. In such cases the legislature, not the judiciary, is the main guardian of the public needs to be served by social legislation, whether it be Congress legislating concerning the District of Columbia . . . or the States legislating concerning local affairs. . . . This principle admits of no exception merely because the power of eminent domain is involved. . . ."

The Court explicitly recognized the breadth of the principle it was announcing, noting: "Once the object is within the authority of Congress, the right to realize it through the exercise of eminent domain is clear. For the power of eminent domain is merely the means to the end. . . . Once the object is within the authority of Congress, the means by which it will be attained is also for Congress to determine. Here one of the means chosen is the use of private enterprise for redevelopment of the area. Appellants argue that this makes the project a taking from one businessman for the benefit of another businessman. But the means of executing the project are for Congress and Congress alone to determine, once the public purpose has been established." The "public use" requirement is thus coterminous with the scope of a sovereign's police powers.

There is, of course, a role for courts to play in reviewing a legislature's judgment of what constitutes a public use, even when the eminent domain power is equated with the police power. But the Court in Berman made clear that it is "an extremely narrow" one. The Court has made clear that it will not substitute its judgment for a legislature's judgment as to what constitutes a public use "unless the use be palpably without reasonable foundation."

To be sure, the Court's cases have repeatedly stated that "one person's property may not be taken for the benefit of another private person without a justifying public purpose, even though compensation be paid." Thus, in *Missouri Pacific R. Co. v. Nebraska*, 164 U.S. 403 (1896), where the "order in question was not, and was not claimed to be, ... a taking of private property for a public use under the right of eminent domain," the Court invalidated a compensated taking of property for lack of a justifying public purpose. But where the exercise of the eminent domain power is rationally related to a conceivable public purpose, the Court has never held a compensated taking to be proscribed by the Public Use Clause.

On this basis, we have no trouble concluding that the Hawaii Act is constitutional. The people of Hawaii have attempted, much as the settlers of the original 13 Colonies did, to reduce the perceived social and economic evils of a land oligopoly traceable to their monarchs. The land oligopoly has, according to the Hawaii Legislature, created artificial deterrents to the normal functioning of the State's residential land market and forced thousands of individual homeowners to lease, rather than buy, the land underneath their homes. Regulating oligopoly and the evils associated with it is a classic exercise of a State's police powers. We cannot disapprove of Hawaii's exercise of this power.

Nor can we condemn as irrational the Act's approach to correcting the land oligopoly problem. The Act presumes that when a sufficiently large number of persons declare that they are willing but unable to buy lots at fair prices the land market is malfunctioning. When such a malfunction is signaled, the Act authorizes HHA to condemn lots in the relevant tract. The Act limits the number of lots any one tenant can purchase and authorizes HHA to use public funds to ensure that the market dilution goals will be achieved. This is a comprehensive and rational approach to identifying and correcting market failure.

Of course, this Act, like any other, may not be successful in achieving its intended goals. But "whether in fact the provision will accomplish its objectives is not the question: the [constitutional requirement] is satisfied if ... the ... [state] Legislature rationally could have believed that the [Act] would promote its objective." When the legislature's purpose is legitimate and its means are not irrational, our cases make clear that empirical debates over the wisdom of takings—no less than debates over the wisdom of other kinds of socioeconomic legislation—are not to be carried out in the federal courts. Redistribution of fees simple to correct deficiencies in the market determined by the state legislature to be attributable to land oligopoly is a rational exercise of the eminent domain power. Therefore, the Hawaii statute must pass the scrutiny of the Public Use Clause.

The mere fact that property taken outright by eminent domain is transferred in the first instance to private beneficiaries does not condemn that taking as having only a private purpose. The Court long ago rejected any literal requirement that condemned property be put into use for the general public. "It is not essential that the entire community, nor even any considerable portion, . . . directly enjoy or participate in any improvement in order [for it] to constitute a public use." As the unique way titles were held in Hawaii skewed the land market, exercise of the power of eminent domain was justified. The Act advances its purposes without the State's taking actual possession of the land. In such cases, government does not itself have to use property to legitimate the taking; it is only the taking's purpose, and not its mechanics, that must pass scrutiny under the Public Use Clause.

Similarly, the fact that a state legislature, and not the Congress, made the public use determination does not mean that judicial deference is less appropriate. Judicial deference is required because, in our system of government, legislatures are better able to assess what public purposes should be advanced by an exercise of the taking power. State legislatures are as capable as Congress of making such determinations within their respective spheres of authority. Thus, if a legislature, state or federal, determines there are substantial reasons for an exercise of the taking power, courts must defer to its determination that the taking will serve a public use.

The State of Hawaii has never denied that the Constitution forbids even a compensated taking of property when executed for no reason other than to confer a private benefit on a particular private party. A purely private taking could not withstand the scrutiny of the public use requirement; it would serve no legitimate purpose of government and would thus be void. But no purely private taking is involved in these cases. The Hawaii Legislature enacted its Land Reform Act not to benefit a particular class of identifiable individuals but to attack certain perceived evils of concentrated property ownership in Hawaii—a legitimate public purpose. Use of the condemnation power to achieve this purpose is not irrational. Since we assume for purposes of these appeals that the weighty demand of just compensation has been met, the requirements of the Fifth and Fourteenth Amendments have been satisfied.

NOLLAN V. CALIFORNIA COASTAL COMMISSION, 483 U.S. 825 (1987)

In 1987, the U.S. Supreme Court decided several cases on the subject of regulatory takings. In the case excerpted here, the Court, for the first time since the 1920s, struck down a land-use regulation as an unconstitutional taking. Property owners in California sued the California Coastal Commission because it conditioned a permit to rebuild a beach house upon the owner's grant of public access to the beach. The Supreme Court held that the commission could not condition the permit in this way without paying compensation. Four justices dissented.

Justice SCALIA delivered the opinion of the Court.

James and Marilyn Nollan appeal from a decision of the California Court of Appeal ruling that the California Coastal Commission could condition its grant of permission to rebuild their house on their transfer to the public of an easement across their beachfront property.

The Nollans own a beachfront lot in Ventura County, California. A quarter-mile north of their property is Faria County Park, an oceanside public park with a public beach and recreation area. Another public beach area, known locally as "the Cove," lies 1,800 feet south of their lot. A concrete seawall approximately eight feet high separates the beach portion of the Nollans' property from the rest of the lot. The historic mean high tide line determines the lot's oceanside boundary.

The Nollans originally leased their property with an option to buy. The building on the lot was a small bungalow, totaling 504 square feet, which for a time they rented to summer vacationers. After years of rental use, however, the building had fallen into disrepair, and could no longer be rented out.

The Nollans' option to purchase was conditioned on their promise to demolish the bungalow and replace it. In order to do so, they were required to obtain a coastal development permit from the California Coastal Commission. On February 25, 1982, they submitted a permit application to the Commission in which they proposed to demolish the existing structure and replace it with a three-bedroom house in keeping with the rest of the neighborhood.

The Nollans were informed that their application had been placed on the administrative calendar, and that the Commission staff had recommended that the permit be granted subject to the condition that they allow the public an easement to pass across a portion of their property bounded by the mean high tide line on one side, and their seawall on the other side. This would make it easier for the public to get to Faria County Park and the Cove. The Nollans protested imposition of the condition, but the Commission overruled their objections and granted the permit subject to their recordation of a deed restriction granting the easement.

Had California simply required the Nollans to make an easement across their beachfront available to the public on a permanent basis in order to increase public access to the beach, rather than conditioning their permit to rebuild their house on their agreeing to do so, we have no doubt there would have been a taking. To say that the appropriation of a public easement across a landowner's premises does not constitute the taking of a property interest but rather "a mere restriction on its use," is to use words in a manner that deprives them of all their ordinary meaning. Indeed, one of the principal uses of the eminent domain power is to assure that the government be able to require conveyance of just such interests, so long as it pays for them. Perhaps because the point is so obvious, we have never been confronted with a controversy that required us to rule upon it, but our cases' analysis of the effect of other governmental action leads to the same conclusion. We have repeatedly held that, as to property reserved by its owner for private use, "the right to exclude [others is] 'one of the most essential sticks in the bundle of rights that are commonly characterized as property.'" In Loretto we observed that where governmental action results in "[a] permanent physical occupation" of the property, by the government itself or by others, "our cases uniformly have found a taking to the extent of the occupation, without regard to whether the action achieves an important public benefit or has only minimal economic impact on the owner." We think a "permanent physical occupation" has occurred, for purposes of that rule, where individuals are given a permanent and continuous right to pass to and fro, so that the real property may continuously be traversed, even though no particular individual is permitted to station himself permanently upon the premises.

Given, then, that requiring uncompensated conveyance of the easement outright would violate the Fourteenth Amendment, the question becomes whether requiring it to be conveyed as a condition for issuing a land-use permit alters the outcome. We have long recognized that land-use regulation does not effect a taking if it "substantially advance[s] legitimate state interests" and does not "den[y] an owner economically viable use of his land," Our cases have not elaborated on the standards for determining what constitutes a "legitimate state interest" or what type of connection between the regulation and the state interest satisfies the requirement that the former "substantially advance" the latter. They have made clear, however, that a broad range of governmental purposes and regulations satisfies these requirements. The Commission argues that among these permissible purposes are protecting the public's ability to see the beach, assisting the public in overcoming the "psychological barrier" to using the beach created by a developed shorefront, and preventing congestion on the public beaches. We assume, without deciding, that this is so—in which case the Commission unquestionably would be able to deny the Nollans their permit outright if their new house (alone, or by reason of the cumulative impact produced in conjunction with other construction) would substantially impede these purposes, unless the denial would interfere so drastically with the Nollans' use of their property as to constitute a taking.

The Commission argues that a permit condition that serves the same legitimate police-power purpose as a refusal to issue the permit should not be found to be a taking if the refusal to issue the permit would not constitute a taking. We agree. Thus, if the Commission attached to the permit some condition that would have protected the public's ability to see the beach notwithstanding construction of the new house—for example, a height limitation, a width restriction, or a ban on fences—so long as the Commission could have exercised its police power (as we have assumed it could) to forbid construction of the house altogether, imposition of the condition would also be constitutional. Moreover (and here we come closer to the facts of the present case), the condition would be constitutional even if it consisted of the requirement that the Nollans provide a viewing spot on their property for passers by with whose sighting of the ocean their new house would interfere. Although such a requirement, constituting a permanent grant of continuous access to the property, would have to be considered a taking if it were not attached to a development permit, the Commission's assumed power to forbid construction of the house in order to protect the public's view of the beach must surely include the power to condition construction upon some concession by the owner, even a concession of property rights, that serves the same end. If a prohibition designed to accomplish that purpose would be a legitimate exercise of the police power rather than a taking, it would be strange to conclude that providing the owner an alternative to that prohibition which accomplishes the same purpose is not.

Justice Brennan argues that imposition of the access requirement is not irrational. In his version of the Commission's argument, the reason for the requirement is that in its absence, a person looking toward the beach from the road will see a street of residential structures including the Nollans' new home and conclude that there is no public beach nearby. If, however, that person sees people passing and re-passing along the dry sand behind the Nollans' home, he will realize that there is a public beach somewhere in the vicinity. The Commission's action, however, was based on the opposite factual finding that the wall of houses completely blocked the view of the beach and that a person looking from the road would not be able to see it at all.

Even if the Commission had made the finding that Justice Brennan proposes, however, it is not certain that it would suffice. We do not share Justice Brennan's confidence that the Commission "should have little difficulty in the future in utilizing its expertise to demonstrate a specific connection between provisions for access and burdens on access," that will avoid the effect of today's decision. We view the Fifth Amendment's Property Clause to be more than a pleading requirement, and compliance with it to be more than an exercise in cleverness and imagination. As indicated earlier, our cases describe the condition for abridgement of property rights through the police power as a "substantial advanc[ing]" of a legitimate state interest. We are inclined to be particularly careful about the adjective where the actual conveyance of property is made a condition to the lifting of a land-use restriction, since in that context there is heightened risk that the purpose is avoidance of the compensation requirement, rather than the stated police-power objective.

California is free to advance its "comprehensive program," if it wishes, by using its power of eminent domain for this "public purpose," but if it wants an easement across the Nollans' property, it must pay for it.

YEE V. CITY OF ESCONDIDO, 503 U.S. 519 (1992)

The U.S. Supreme Court has long recognized the authority of local governments to enact rent control ordinances. In this 1992 decision, the Supreme Court ruled against mobile home park owners who claimed that a rent control ordinance amounted to physical occupation of their property, entitling them to compensation under the Takings Clause. The Supreme Court held that, although the Fifth Amendment's Takings Clause generally requires just compensation where the government authorizes a physical occupation of property, this rent control ordinance did not amount to physical taking of the park owners' property. The Court, however, did not consider whether the ordinance constituted a regulatory taking.

Justice O'CONNOR delivered the opinion of the Court.

The Takings Clause of the Fifth Amendment provides: "[N]or shall private property be taken for public use, without just compensation." Most of our cases interpreting the Clause fall within two distinct classes. Where the government authorizes a physical occupation of property (or actually takes title), the Takings Clause generally requires compensation. But where the government merely regulates the use of property, compensation is required only if considerations such as the purpose of the regulation or the extent to which it deprives the owner of the economic use of the property suggest that the regulation has unfairly singled out the property owner to bear a burden that should be borne by the public as a whole. The first category of cases requires courts to apply a clear rule; the second necessarily entails complex factual assessments of the purposes and economic effects of government actions.

Petitioners own mobile home parks in Escondido, California. They contend that a local rent control ordinance, when viewed against the backdrop of California's Mobilehome Residency Law, amounts to a physical occupation of their property, entitling them to compensation.

In 1978, California enacted its Mobilehome Residency Law. The legislature found "that, because of the high cost of moving mobile homes, the potential for damage resulting therefrom, the requirements relating to the installation of mobile homes, and the cost of landscaping or lot preparation, it is necessary that the owners of mobile homes occupied within mobile home parks be provided with the unique protection from actual or constructive eviction afforded by the provisions of this chapter."

The Mobilehome Residency Law limits the bases upon which a park owner may terminate a mobile home owner's tenancy. These include the nonpayment of rent, the mobile home owner's violation of law or park rules, and the park owner's desire to change the use of his land. While a rental agreement is in effect, however, the park owner generally may not require the removal of a mobile home when it is sold. The park owner may neither charge a transfer fee for the sale, nor disapprove of the purchaser, provided that the purchaser has the ability to pay the rent. The Mobilehome Residency Law contains a number of other detailed provisions, but none limit the rent the park owner may charge.

Petitioners John and Irene Yee own the Friendly Hills and Sunset Terrace Mobile Home Parks, both of which are located in the city of Escondido. A few months after the adoption of Escondido's rent control ordinance, they filed suit in San Diego County Superior Court. According to the complaint, "[t]he rent control law has had the effect of depriving the plaintiffs of all use and occupancy of [their] real property and granting to the tenants of mobile homes presently in The Park, as well as the successors in interest of such tenants, the right to physically permanently occupy and use the real property of Plaintiff." The Yees requested damages of $6 million, a declaration that the rent control ordinance is unconstitutional, and an injunction barring the ordinance's enforcement.

Petitioners do not claim that the ordinary rent control statutes regulating housing throughout the country violate the Takings Clause. Instead, their argument is predicated on the unusual economic relationship between park owners and mobile home owners. Park owners may no longer set rents or decide who their tenants will be. As a result, according to petitioners, any reduction in the rent for a mobile home pad causes a corresponding increase in the value of a mobile home, because the mobile home owner now owns, in addition to a mobile home, the right to occupy a pad at a rent below the value that would be set by the free market. Because under the California Mobilehome Residency Law the park owner cannot evict a mobile home owner or easily convert the property to other uses, the argument goes, the mobile home owner is effectively a perpetual tenant of the park, and the increase in the mobile home's value thus represents the right to occupy a pad at below-market rent indefinitely. And because the Mobilehome Residency Law permits the mobile home owner to sell the mobile home in place, the mobile home owner can receive a premium from the purchaser corresponding to this increase in value. The amount of this premium is not limited by the Mobilehome Residency Law or the Escondido ordinance. As a result, petitioners conclude, the rent control ordinance has transferred a discrete interest in land—the right to occupy the land indefinitely at a submarket rent—from the park owner to the mobile home owner. Petitioners contend that what has been transferred from park owner to mobile home owner is no less than a right of physical occupation of the park owner's land.

This argument, while perhaps within the scope of our regulatory taking cases, cannot be squared easily with our cases on physical takings. The government effects a physical taking only where it *requires* the landowner to submit to the physical occupation of his land. "This element of required acquiescence is at the heart of the concept of occupation." Thus whether the government floods a landowner's property, or does no more than require the landowner to suffer the installation of a cable, the Takings Clause requires compensation if the government authorizes a compelled physical invasion of property.

But the Escondido rent control ordinance, even when considered in conjunction with the California Mobilehome Residency Law, authorizes no such thing. Petitioners voluntarily rented their land to mobile home owners. At least on the face of the regulatory scheme, neither the city nor the State compels petitioners, once they have rented their property to tenants, to continue doing so. To the contrary, the Mobilehome Residency Law provides that a park owner who wishes to change the use of his land may evict his tenants, albeit with 6 or 12 months notice. Put bluntly, no government has required any physical invasion of petitioners' property. Petitioners' tenants were invited by petitioners, not forced upon them by the government. While the "right to exclude" is doubtless, as petitioners assert, "one of the most essential sticks in the bundle of rights that are commonly characterized as property," we do not find that right to have been taken from petitioners on the mere face of the Escondido ordinance.

Petitioners suggest that the statutory procedure for changing the use of a mobile home park is in practice "a kind of gauntlet," in that they are not in fact free to change the use of their land. Because petitioners do not claim to have run that gauntlet, however, this case provides no occasion to consider how the procedure has been applied to petitioners' property, and we accordingly confine ourselves to the face of the statute. A different case would be presented were the statute, on its face or as applied, to compel a landowner over objection to rent his property or to refrain in perpetuity from terminating a tenancy.

On their face, the state and local laws at issue here merely regulate petitioners' *use* of their land by regulating the relationship between landlord and tenant. This Court has consistently affirmed that States have broad power to regulate housing conditions in general and the landlord–tenant relationship in particular without paying compensation for all economic injuries that such regulation entails. When a landowner decides to rent his land to tenants, the government may place ceilings on the rents the landowner can charge, or require the landowner to accept tenants he does not like, without automatically having to pay compensation. Such forms of regulation are analyzed by engaging in the "essentially ad hoc, factual inquiries" necessary to determine whether a regulatory taking has occurred. In the words of Justice Holmes, "while property may be regulated to a certain extent, if regulation goes too far it will be recognized as a taking."

Petitioners emphasize that the ordinance transfers wealth from park owners to incumbent mobile home owners. Other forms of land use regulation, however, can also be said to transfer wealth from the one who is regulated to another. Ordinary rent control often transfers wealth from landlords to tenants by reducing the landlords' income and the tenants' monthly payments, although it does not cause a one-time transfer of value as occurs with mobile homes. Traditional zoning regulations can transfer wealth from those whose activities are prohibited to their neighbors; when a property owner is barred from mining coal on his land, for example, the value of his property may decline but the value of his neighbor's property may rise. The mobile home owner's ability to sell the mobile home at a premium may make this wealth transfer more *visible* than in the ordinary case, but the existence of the transfer in itself does not convert regulation into physical invasion.

Petitioners also rely heavily on their allegation that the ordinance benefits incumbent mobile home owners without benefitting future mobile home owners, who will be forced to purchase mobile homes at premiums. Mobile homes, like motor vehicles, ordinarily decline in value with age. But the effect of the rent control ordinance, coupled with the restrictions on the park owner's freedom to reject new tenants, is to increase significantly the value of the mobile home. This increased value normally benefits only the tenant in possession at the time the rent control is imposed. Petitioners are correct in citing the existence of this premium as a difference between the alleged effect of the Escondido ordinance and that of an ordinary apartment rent control statute. Most apartment tenants do not sell anything to their successors (and are often prohibited from charging "key money"), so a typical rent control statute will transfer wealth from the landlord to the incumbent tenant and all future tenants. By contrast, petitioners contend that the Escondido ordinance transfers wealth only to the incumbent mobile home owner. This effect might have some bearing on whether the ordinance causes a *regulatory* taking, as it may shed some light on whether there is a sufficient nexus between the effect of the ordinance and the objectives it is supposed to advance. But it has nothing to do with whether the ordinance causes a *physical* taking. Whether the ordinance benefits only current mobile home owners or all mobile home owners, it does not require petitioners to submit to the physical occupation of their land.

The same may be said of petitioners' contention that the ordinance amounts to compelled physical occupation because it deprives petitioners of the ability to choose their incoming tenants. Again, this effect may be relevant to a regulatory taking argument, as it may be one factor a reviewing court would wish to consider in determining whether the ordinance unjustly imposes a burden on petitioners that should "be compensated by the government, rather than remain[ing] disproportionately concentrated on a few persons." But it does not convert regulation into the unwanted physical occupation of land. Because they voluntarily open their property to occupation by others, petitioners cannot assert a *per se* right to compensation based on their inability to exclude particular individuals.

The Escondido rent control ordinance, even considered against the backdrop of California's Mobilehome Residency Law, does not authorize an unwanted physical occupation of petitioners' property. It is a regulation of petitioners' *use* of their property, and thus does not amount to a *per se* taking. Because the Escondido rent control ordinance does not compel a landowner to suffer the physical occupation of his property, it does not effect a *per se* taking under *Loretto v. Teleprompter Manhatten CATV Corp.*, 458 U.S. 419 (1982). The judgment of the Court of Appeal is accordingly affirmed.

LUCAS V. SOUTH CAROLINA COASTAL COUNCIL, 505 U.S. 1003 (1992)

The regulatory takings doctrine was sharply strengthened in this 1992 U.S. Supreme Court decision. An owner of beachfront property chal-

lenged the application of the South Carolina Beachfront Management Act to his property as an unconstitutional taking without just compensation. The act prohibited beachfront construction to prevent erosion and to preserve the public value of the beach. In 1986, Lucas bought two residential lots on a South Carolina barrier island, intending to build single-family homes. At the time of his purchase, the lots were not subject to the Beachfront Management Act. The 1988 legislation prevented the landowner from constructing any permanent structure on his land. The Supreme Court held that because "all economically beneficial or productive use of the land" had been denied to Lucas, the act constituted a taking notwithstanding the public interest advanced to justify it. Two justices dissented; the justices wrote a total of five separate opinions in addition to the opinion for the court excerpted below. This opinion is noteworthy because it linked the question of whether a taking had occurred to historic property rights reflected in the common law.

Justice SCALIA delivered the opinion of the Court.

In 1986, petitioner David H. Lucas paid $975,000 for two residential lots on the Isle of Palms in Charleston County, South Carolina, on which he intended to build single-family homes. In 1988, however, the South Carolina Legislature enacted the Beachfront Management Act, which had the direct effect of barring petitioner from erecting any permanent habitable structures on his two parcels. A state trial court found that this prohibition rendered Lucas's parcels "valueless." This case requires us to decide whether the Act's dramatic effect on the economic value of Lucas's lots accomplished a taking of private property under the Fifth and Fourteenth Amendments requiring the payment of "just compensation."

In the late 1970's, Lucas and others began extensive residential development of the Isle of Palms, a barrier island situated eastward of the city of Charleston. Toward the close of the development cycle for one residential subdivision known as "Beachwood East," Lucas in 1986 purchased the two lots at issue in this litigation for his own account. No portion of the lots, which were located approximately 300 feet from the beach, qualified as a "critical area" under the 1977 Act; accordingly, at the time Lucas acquired these parcels, he was not legally obliged to obtain a permit from the Council in advance of any development activity. His intention with respect to the lots was to do what the owners of the immediately adjacent parcels had already done: erect single-family residences. He commissioned architectural drawings for this purpose.

The Beachfront Management Act brought Lucas's plans to an abrupt end. Under that 1988 legislation, the Council was directed to establish a "baseline" connecting the landward-most "point[s] of erosion ... during the past forty years" in the region of the Isle of Palms that includes Lucas's lots.

Prior to Justice Holmes's exposition in *Pennsylvania Coal Co. v. Mahon,* 260 U.S. 393 (1922), it was generally thought that the Takings Clause reached only a "direct appropriation" of property, or the functional equivalent of a "practical ouster of [the owner's] possession." Justice Holmes recognized in *Mahon,* however, that if the protection against physical appropriations of private property was to be meaningfully enforced, the government's power to redefine the range of interests included in the ownership of property was necessarily constrained by constitutional limits. If, instead, the uses of private property were subject to unbridled, uncompensated qualification under the police power, "the natural tendency of human nature [would be] to extend the qualification more and more until at last private property disappeared." These considerations gave birth in that case to the oft-cited maxim that, "while property may be regulated to a certain extent, if regulation goes too far it will be recognized as a taking."

Nevertheless, our decision in *Mahon* offered little insight into when, and under what circumstances, a given regulation would be seen as going "too far" for purposes of the Fifth Amendment. In 70-odd years of succeeding "regulatory takings" jurisprudence, we have generally eschewed any "set formula" for determining how far is too far, preferring to "engage in ... essentially ad hoc, factual inquiries." *Penn Central Transportation Co. v. New York City,* 438 U.S. 104 (1978). We have, however, described at least two discrete categories of regulatory action as compensable without case-specific inquiry into the public interest advanced in support of the restraint. The first encompasses regulations that compel the property owner to suffer a physical "invasion" of his property. In general (at least with regard to permanent invasions), no matter how minute the intrusion, and no matter how weighty the public purpose behind it, we have required compensation.

The second situation in which we have found categorical treatment appropriate is where regulation denies all economically beneficial or productive use of land. As we have said on numerous occasions, the

Fifth Amendment is violated when land-use regulation "does not substantially advance legitimate state interests *or denies an owner economically viable use of his land.*"

We have never set forth the justification for this rule. Perhaps it is simply, as Justice Brennan suggested, that total deprivation of beneficial use is, from the landowner's point of view, the equivalent of a physical appropriation. Surely, at least, in the extraordinary circumstance when *no* productive or economically beneficial use of land is permitted, it is less realistic to indulge our usual assumption that the legislature is simply "adjusting the benefits and burdens of economic life" in a manner that secures an "average reciprocity of advantage" to everyone concerned. And the *functional* basis for permitting the government, by regulation, to affect property values without compensation—that "Government hardly could go on if to some extent values incident to property could not be diminished without paying for every such change in the general law,"—does not apply to the relatively rare situations where the government has deprived a landowner of all economically beneficial uses.

On the other side of the balance, affirmatively supporting a compensation requirement, is the fact that regulations that leave the owner of land without economically beneficial or productive options for its use—typically, as here, by requiring land to be left substantially in its natural state—carry with them a heightened risk that private property is being pressed into some form of public service under the guise of mitigating serious public harm. As Justice Brennan explained: "From the government's point of view, the benefits flowing to the public from preservation of open space through regulation may be equally great as from creating a wildlife refuge through formal condemnation or increasing electricity production through a dam project that floods private property." The many statutes on the books, both state and federal, that provide for the use of eminent domain to impose servitudes on private scenic lands preventing developmental uses, or to acquire such lands altogether, suggest the practical equivalence in this setting of negative regulation and appropriation.

We think, in short, that there are good reasons for our frequently expressed belief that when the owner of real property has been called upon to sacrifice *all* economically beneficial uses in the name of the common good, that is, to leave his property economically idle, he has suffered a taking.

It is correct that many of our prior opinions have suggested that "harmful or noxious uses" of property may be proscribed by government regulation without the requirement of compensation. For a number of reasons, however, we think the South Carolina Supreme Court was too quick to conclude that that principle decides the present case. The "harmful or noxious uses" principle was the Court's early attempt to describe in theoretical terms why government may, consistent with the Takings Clause, affect property values by regulation without incurring an obligation to compensate—a reality we nowadays acknowledge explicitly with respect to the full scope of the State's police power. We made this very point in *Penn Central Transportation Co.*, where, in the course of sustaining New York City's landmarks preservation program against a takings challenge, we rejected the petitioner's suggestion that *Mugler* and the cases following it were premised on, and thus limited by, some objective conception of "noxiousness." "Harmful or noxious use" analysis was simply the progenitor of our more contemporary statements that "land-use regulation does not effect a taking if it 'substantially advance[s] legitimate state interests'. . . ."

The transition from our early focus on control of "noxious" uses to our contemporary understanding of the broad realm within which government may regulate without compensation was an easy one, since the distinction between "harm-preventing" and "benefit-conferring" regulation is often in the eye of the beholder. It is quite possible, for example, to describe in *either* fashion the ecological, economic, and esthetic concerns that inspired the South Carolina Legislature in the present case. One could say that imposing a servitude on Lucas's land is necessary in order to prevent his use of it from "harming" South Carolina's ecological resources; or, instead, in order to achieve the "benefits" of an ecological preserve. Whether one or the other of the competing characterizations will come to one's lips in a particular case depends primarily upon one's evaluation of the worth of competing uses of real estate. A given restraint will be seen as mitigating "harm" to the adjacent parcels or securing a "benefit" for them, depending upon the observer's evaluation of the relative importance of the use that the restraint favors. Whether Lucas's construction of single-family residences on his parcels should be described as bringing "harm" to South Carolina's adjacent ecological resources thus depends principally upon whether the describer believes that the State's use interest in nurturing those resources is so important that *any* competing adjacent use must yield.

When it is understood that "prevention of harmful use" was merely our early formulation of the police power justification necessary to sustain (without compensation) *any* regulatory diminution in value; and that the distinction between regulation that "prevents harmful use" and that which "confers benefits" is difficult, if not impossible, to discern on an objective, value-free basis; it becomes self-evident that noxious-use logic cannot serve as a touchstone to distinguish regulatory "takings"—which require compensation—from regulatory deprivations that do not require compensation. *A fortiori* the legislature's recitation of a noxious-use justification cannot be the basis for departing from our categorical rule that total regulatory takings must be compensated. If it were, departure would virtually always be allowed. The South Carolina Supreme Court's approach would essentially nullify *Mahon*'s affirmation of limits to the noncompensable exercise of the police power. Our cases provide no support for this: None of them that employed the logic of "harmful use" prevention to sustain a regulation involved an allegation that the regulation wholly eliminated the value of the claimant's land.

Where the State seeks to sustain regulation that deprives land of all economically beneficial use, we think it may resist compensation only if the logically antecedent inquiry into the nature of the owner's estate shows that the proscribed use interests were not part of his title to begin with. This accords, we think, with our "takings" jurisprudence, which has traditionally been guided by the understandings of our citizens regarding the content of, and the State's power over, the "bundle of rights" that they acquire when they obtain title to property. It seems to us that the property owner necessarily expects the uses of his property to be restricted, from time to time, by various measures newly enacted by the State in legitimate exercise of its police powers; "[a]s long recognized, some values are enjoyed under an implied limitation and must yield to the police power." *Pennsylvania Coal Co. v. Mahon*, 260 U.S., at 413. And in the case of personal property, by reason of the State's traditionally high degree of control over commercial dealings, he ought to be aware of the possibility that new regulation might even render his property economically worthless (at least if the property's only economically productive use is sale or manufacture for sale). In the case of land, however, we think the notion pressed by the Council that title is somehow held subject to the "implied limitation" that the State may subsequently eliminate all economically valuable use is inconsistent with the historical compact recorded in the Takings Clause that has become part of our constitutional culture.

Where "permanent physical occupation" of land is concerned, we have refused to allow the government to decree it anew (without compensation), no matter how weighty the asserted "public interests" involved,—though we assuredly *would* permit the government to assert a permanent easement that was a pre-existing limitation upon the landowner's title. We believe similar treatment must be accorded confiscatory regulations, *i.e.*, regulations that prohibit all economically beneficial use of land: Any limitation so severe cannot be newly legislated or decreed (without compensation), but must inhere in the title itself, in the restrictions that background principles of the State's law of property and nuisance already place upon land ownership. A law or decree with such an effect must, in other words, do no more than duplicate the result that could have been achieved in the courts—by adjacent landowners (or other uniquely affected persons) under the State's law of private nuisance, or by the State under its complementary power to abate nuisances that affect the public generally, or otherwise.

On this analysis, the owner of a lake-bed, for example, would not be entitled to compensation when he is denied the requisite permit to engage in a land filling operation that would have the effect of flooding others' land. Nor the corporate owner of a nuclear generating plant, when it is directed to remove all improvements from its land upon discovery that the plant sits astride an earthquake fault. Such regulatory action may well have the effect of eliminating the land's only economically productive use, but it does not proscribe a productive use that was previously permissible under relevant property and nuisance principles. The use of these properties for what are now expressly prohibited purposes was *always* unlawful, and (subject to other constitutional limitations) it was open to the State at any point to make the implication of those background principles of nuisance and property law explicit. In light of our traditional resort to "existing rules or understandings that stem from an independent source such as state law" to define the range of interests that qualify for protection as "property" under the Fifth and Fourteenth Amendments, this recognition that the Takings Clause does not require compensation when an owner is barred from putting land to a use that is proscribed by those "existing rules or understandings" is surely unexceptional. When, however, a regulation that declares "off-limits" all economically productive or beneficial uses of land goes beyond what the relevant background principles would dictate, compensation must be paid to sustain it.

The "total taking" inquiry we require today will ordinarily entail (as the application of state nuisance law ordinarily entails) analysis of, among other things, the degree of harm to public lands and resources, or adjacent private property, posed by the claimant's proposed activities, the social value of the claimant's activities and their suitability to the locality in question, and the relative ease with which the alleged harm can be avoided through measures taken by the claimant and the government (or adjacent private landowners) alike. The fact that a particular use has long been engaged in by similarly situated owners ordinarily imports a lack of any common-law prohibition (though changed circumstances or new knowledge may make what was previously permissible no longer so. So also does the fact that other landowners, similarly situated, are permitted to continue the use denied to the claimant.

TAHOE-SIERRA PRESERVATION COUNCIL V. TAHOE REGIONAL PLANNING AGENCY, 535 U.S. 302 (2002)

Property rights groups who had been encouraged by the U.S. Supreme Court's decisions in Nollan *and* Lucas *were disappointed with this 2002 decision. The Court ruled 6–3 against a group of property owners claiming that a temporary moratorium of nearly three years on development effected an unconstitutional regulatory taking of property. The Court held that temporary prohibitions on development do not constitute a per se taking, and thus the question whether the Takings Clause requires compensation is to be decided by applying the factors of* Penn Central, *not by applying any categorical rule. Three justices dissented.*

Justice STEVENS delivered the opinion of the Court.

The question presented is whether a moratorium on development imposed during the process of devising a comprehensive land-use plan constitutes a *per se* taking of property requiring compensation under the Takings Clause of the United States Constitution.

In the 1960's, when the problems associated with the burgeoning development began to receive significant attention, jurisdiction over the Basin, which occupies 501 square miles, was shared by the States of California and Nevada, five counties, several municipalities, and the Forest Service of the Federal Government. In 1968, the legislatures of the two States adopted the Tahoe Regional Planning Compact. The compact set goals for the protection and preservation of the lake and created TRPA as the agency assigned "to coordinate and regulate development in the Basin and to conserve its natural resources."

Pursuant to the compact, in 1972 TRPA adopted a Land Use Ordinance that divided the land in the Basin into seven "land capability districts," based largely on steepness but also taking into consideration other factors affecting runoff. Each district was assigned a "land coverage coefficient—a recommended limit on the percentage of such land that could be covered by impervious surface." Unfortunately, the 1972 ordinance allowed numerous exceptions and did not significantly limit the construction of new residential housing. California became so dissatisfied with TRPA that it withdrew its financial support and unilaterally imposed stricter regulations on the part of the Basin located in California. Eventually the two States, with the approval of Congress and the President, adopted an extensive amendment to the compact that became effective on December 19, 1980.

The 1980 Tahoe Regional Planning Compact (Compact) redefined the structure, functions, and voting procedures of TRPA, and directed it to develop regional "environmental threshold carrying capacities"—a term that embraced "standards for air quality, water quality, soil conservation, vegetation preservation and noise." Accordingly, for the period prior to the adoption of the final plan ("or until May 1, 1983, whichever is earlier"), the Compact itself prohibited the development of new subdivisions, condominiums, and apartment buildings, and also prohibited each city and county in the Basin from granting any more permits in 1981, 1982, or 1983 than had been granted in 1978.

Petitioners contend that the mere enactment of a temporary regulation that, while in effect, denies a property owner all viable economic use of her property gives rise to an unqualified constitutional obligation to compensate her for the value of its use during that period. Hence, they "face an uphill battle," that is made especially steep by their desire for a categorical rule requiring compensation whenever the government imposes such a moratorium on development. Under their proposed rule, there is no need to evaluate the landowners' investment-backed expectations, the actual impact of the regulation on any individual, the importance of the public interest served by the regulation, or the reasons for imposing the temporary restriction. For petitioners, it is enough that a regulation imposes a temporary deprivation—no matter how brief—of all economically viable use to trigger a *per se* rule that a taking has occurred. Petitioners assert that our opinions in *First English* and *Lucas* have already endorsed their view, and that it is a logical application of the principle that the Takings Clause was "designed to bar Government from forcing some people alone to bear burdens which, in all fairness and justice, should be borne by the public as a whole."

In our view the answer to the abstract question whether a temporary moratorium effects a taking is neither "yes, always" nor "no, never"; the answer depends upon the particular circumstances of the case. Resisting "[t]he temptation to adopt what amount to *per se* rules in either direction," we conclude that the circumstances in this case are best analyzed within the Penn Central framework.

The text of the Fifth Amendment itself provides a basis for drawing a distinction between physical takings and regulatory takings. Its plain language requires the payment of compensation whenever the government acquires private property for a public purpose, whether the acquisition is the result of a condemnation proceeding or a physical appropriation. But the Constitution contains no comparable reference to regulations that prohibit a property owner from making certain uses of her private property. Our jurisprudence involving condemnations and physical takings is as old as the Republic and, for the most part, involves the straightforward application of *per se* rules. Our regulatory takings jurisprudence, in contrast, is of more recent vintage and is characterized by "essentially ad hoc, factual inquiries," *Penn Central,* 438 U.S., at 124, designed to allow "careful examination and weighing of all the relevant circumstances."

When the government physically takes possession of an interest in property for some public purpose, it has a categorical duty to compensate the former owner, regardless of whether the interest that is taken constitutes an entire parcel or merely a part thereof. Thus, compensation is mandated when a leasehold is taken and the government occupies the property for its own purposes, even though that use is temporary. Similarly, when the government appropriates part of a rooftop in order to provide cable TV access for apartment tenants, or when its planes use private airspace to approach a government airport, it is required to pay for that share no matter how small. But a government regulation that merely prohibits landlords from evicting tenants unwilling to pay a higher rent, that bans certain private uses of a portion of an owner's property, or that forbids the private use of certain airspace, does not constitute a categorical taking. The first category of cases requires courts to apply a clear rule; the second necessarily entails complex factual assessments of the purposes and economic effects of government actions.

This longstanding distinction between acquisitions of property for public use, on the one hand, and regulations prohibiting private uses, on the other, makes it inappropriate to treat cases involving physical takings as controlling precedents for the evaluation of a claim that there has been a "regulatory taking," and vice versa. For the same reason that we do not ask whether a physical appropriation advances a substantial government interest or whether it deprives the owner of all economically valuable use, we do not apply our precedent from the physical takings context to regulatory takings claims. Land-use regulations are ubiquitous and most of them impact property values in some tangential way—often in completely unanticipated ways. Treating them all as *per se* takings would transform government regulation into a luxury few governments could afford. By contrast, physical appropriations are relatively rare, easily identified, and usually represent a greater affront to individual property rights. "This case does not present the 'classi[c] taking' in which the government directly appropriates private property for its own use," instead the interference with property rights "arises from some public program adjusting the benefits and burdens of economic life to promote the common good."

Perhaps recognizing this fundamental distinction, petitioners wisely do not place all their emphasis on analogies to physical takings cases. Instead, they rely principally on our decision in *Lucas v. South Carolina Coastal Council,* 505 U.S. 1003 (1992)—a regulatory takings case that, nevertheless, applied a categorical rule—to argue that the Penn Central framework is inapplicable here.

We have generally eschewed any set formula for determining how far is too far, choosing instead to engage in "essentially ad hoc, factual inquiries." *Lucas,* 505 U.S., at 1015. Indeed, we still resist the temptation to adopt *per se* rules in our cases involving partial regulatory takings, preferring to examine "a number of factors" rather than a simple "mathematically precise" formula. Justice Brennan's opinion for the Court in *Penn Central* did, however, make it clear that even though multiple factors are relevant in the analysis of regulatory takings claims, in such cases we must focus on "the parcel as a whole:" "Taking jurisprudence does not divide a single parcel into discrete segments and attempt to determine whether rights in a particular segment have been entirely abrogated. In deciding whether a particular governmental action has effected a taking, this Court focuses rather both on the character of the action and on the nature and extent of the interference with rights in the parcel as a whole—here, the city tax block designated as the landmark site."

Certainly, our holding that the permanent "obliteration of the value" of a fee simple estate constitutes a categorical taking does not answer the question whether a regulation prohibiting any economic use of land for a 32-month period has the same legal effect. Petitioners seek to bring this case under the rule announced in *Lucas* by arguing that we can effectively sever a 32-month segment from the remainder of each landowner's fee simple estate, and then ask whether that segment has been taken in its entirety by the moratoria. Of course, defining the property interest taken in terms of the very regulation being challenged is circular. With property so divided, every delay would become a total ban; the moratorium and the normal permit process alike would constitute categorical takings. Petitioners' "conceptual severance" argument is unavailing because it ignores *Penn Central*'s admonition that in regulatory takings cases we must focus on "the parcel as a whole. We have consistently rejected such an approach to the 'denominator' question."

An interest in real property is defined by the metes and bounds that describe its geographic dimensions and the term of years that describes the temporal aspect of the owner's interest. Both dimensions must be considered if the interest is to be viewed in its entirety. Hence, a permanent deprivation of the owner's use of the entire area is a taking of "the parcel as a whole," whereas a temporary restriction that merely causes a diminution in value is not. Logically, a fee simple estate cannot be rendered valueless by a temporary prohibition on economic use, because the property will recover value as soon as the prohibition is lifted.

Neither *Lucas*, nor *First English*, nor any of our other regulatory takings cases compels us to accept petitioners' categorical submission. In fact, these cases make clear that the categorical rule in *Lucas* was carved out for the "extraordinary case" in which a regulation permanently deprives property of all value; the default rule remains that, in the regulatory taking context, we require a more fact specific inquiry. Nevertheless, we will consider whether the interest in protecting individual property owners from bearing public burdens which, in all fairness and justice, should be borne by the public as a whole, justifies creating a new rule for these circumstances.

Considerations of "fairness and justice" arguably could support the conclusion that TRPA's moratoria were takings of petitioners' property based on any of seven different theories. First, even though we have not previously done so, we might now announce a categorical rule that, in the interest of fairness and justice, compensation is required whenever government temporarily deprives an owner of all economically viable use of her property. Second, we could craft a narrower rule that would cover all temporary land-use restrictions except those normal delays in obtaining building permits, changes in zoning ordinances, variances, and the like. Third, we could adopt a rule like the one suggested by an *amicus* supporting petitioners that would "allow a short fixed period for deliberations to take place without compensation—say maximum one year—after which the just compensation requirements" would "kick in." Fourth, with the benefit of hindsight, we might characterize the successive actions of TRPA as a "series of rolling moratoria" that were the functional equivalent of a permanent taking. Fifth, were it not for the findings of the District Court that TRPA acted diligently and in good faith, we might have concluded that the agency was stalling in order to avoid promulgating the environmental threshold carrying capacities and regional plan mandated by the 1980 Compact. Sixth, apart from the District Court's finding that TRPA's actions represented a proportional response to a serious risk of harm to the lake, petitioners might have argued that the moratoria did not substantially advance a legitimate state interest. Finally, if petitioners had challenged the application of the moratoria to their individual parcels, instead of making a facial challenge, some of them might have prevailed under a *Penn Central* analysis.

As the case comes to us, however, none of the last four theories is available. The "rolling moratoria" theory was presented in the petition for certiorari, but our order granting review did not encompass that issue. Recovery under a *Penn Central* analysis is also foreclosed both because petitioners expressly disavowed that theory, and because they did not appeal from the District Court's conclusion that the evidence would not support it. Nonetheless, each of the three *per se* theories is fairly encompassed within the question that we decided to answer.

With respect to these theories, the ultimate constitutional question is whether the concepts of "fairness and justice" that underlie the Takings Clause will be better served by one of these categorical rules or by a *Penn Central* inquiry into all of the relevant circumstances in particular cases. From that perspective, the extreme categorical rule that any deprivation of all economic use, no matter how brief, constitutes a compensable taking surely cannot be sustained. Petitioners' broad submission would apply to numerous normal delays in obtaining building permits, changes in zoning ordinances, variances, and the like, as well as to orders temporarily prohibiting access to crime scenes, businesses that violate health codes, fire-damaged buildings, or other areas that we cannot now foresee. Such a rule would undoubtedly require changes in numerous practices that have long been considered permissible exercises of the police power. As Justice Holmes warned, "[g]overnment hardly could go on if to some extent values incident to property could not be diminished without paying for every such change in the general law." A rule that required compensation for every delay in the use of property would render routine government processes prohibitively expensive or encourage hasty decisionmaking. Such an important change in the law should be the product of legislative rulemaking rather than adjudication.

More importantly, for reasons set out at some length by Justice O'Connor in her concurring opinion in *Palazzolo v. Rhode Island*, 533 U.S., at 636 (2001), we are persuaded that the better approach to claims that a regulation has effected a temporary taking "requires careful examination and weighing of all the relevant circumstances." In that opinion, Justice O'Connor specifically considered the role that the "temporal relationship between regulatory enactment and title acquisition" should play in the analysis of a takings claim. We have no occasion to address that particular issue in this case, because it involves a different temporal relationship—the distinction between a temporary restriction and one that is permanent. In rejecting petitioners' *per se* rule, we do not hold that the temporary nature of a land-use restriction precludes finding that it effects a taking; we simply recognize that it should not be given exclusive significance one way or the other.

A narrower rule that excluded the normal delays associated with processing permits, or that covered only delays of more than a year, would certainly have a less severe impact on prevailing practices, but it would still impose serious financial constraints on the planning process. Unlike the "extraordinary circumstance" in which the government deprives a property owner of all economic use, *Lucas,* 505 U.S., at 1017, moratoria like Ordinance 81–5 and Resolution 83–21 are used widely among land-use planners to preserve the status quo while formulating a more permanent development strategy. In fact, the consensus in the planning community appears to be that moratoria, or "interim development controls" as they are often called, are an essential tool of successful development. Yet even the weak version of petitioners' categorical rule would treat these interim measures as takings regardless of the good faith of the planners, the reasonable expectations of the landowners, or the actual impact of the moratorium on property values.

The interest in facilitating informed decisionmaking by regulatory agencies counsels against adopting a *per se* rule that would impose such severe costs on their deliberations. Otherwise, the financial constraints of compensating property owners during a moratorium may force officials to rush through the planning process or to abandon the practice altogether. To the extent that communities are forced to abandon using moratoria, landowners will have incentives to develop their property quickly before a comprehensive plan can be enacted, thereby fostering inefficient and ill-conceived growth.

Moreover, with a temporary ban on development there is a lesser risk that individual landowners will be "singled out" to bear a special burden that should be shared by the public as a whole. At least with a moratorium there is a clear reciprocity of advantage because it protects the interests of all affected landowners against immediate construction that might be inconsistent with the provisions of the plan that is ultimately adopted. In fact, there is reason to believe property values often will continue to increase despite a moratorium. Such an increase makes sense in this context because property values throughout the Basin can be expected to reflect the added assurance that Lake Tahoe will remain in its pristine state. Since in some cases a 1-year moratorium may not impose a burden at all, we should not adopt a rule that assumes moratoria always force individuals to bear a special burden that should be shared by the public as a whole.

Private Property Protection Act of 1995 (Bill Proposed in the U.S. House of Representatives)

In 1995 and 1996, both houses of Congress considered property protection legislation as part of the Republican Party's Contract with America. Various proposals in the Senate were not passed. The House of Representatives passed property legislation (H.R. 925), but the bill was not enacted into law. The bill would have created a statutory right to compensation when federal actions under certain federal programs reduce the value of private property by more than a specified percentage. The House bill is reproduced below, followed by an excerpt from the report of the Judiciary Committee accompanying the bill.

Section 1. Short Title.

This Act may be cited as the "Private Property Protection Act of 1995."

Sec. 2. Right to Compensation.

(a) In General.—The Federal Government shall compensate an owner of property whose use of that property has been limited by an agency action that diminishes the fair market value of that property by 10 percent or more. The amount of the compensation shall equal the diminution in value of the property that resulted from the agency action.

(b) Duration of Limitation on Use.—Property with respect to which compensation has been paid under this Act shall not thereafter be used contrary to the limitation imposed by the agency action, even if that action is later rescinded or otherwise vitiated. However, if that action is later rescinded or otherwise vitiated, and the owner elects to refund the amount of the compensation, adjusted for inflation, to the Treasury of the United States, the property may be so used.

Sec. 3. Effect of State Law.

No compensation shall be made under this Act if the use limited by Federal agency action is proscribed under the law of the State in which the property is located (other than a proscription required by a Federal law, either directly or as a condition for assistance). If a use is a nuisance as defined by the law of a State or is prohibited under a local zoning ordinance, that use is proscribed for the purposes of this subsection.

Sec. 4. Exceptions.

(a) Prevention of Hazard to Health and Safety or Damage to Specific Property.—No compensation shall be made under this Act with respect to an agency action the purpose of which is to prevent an identifiable-
   (1) hazard to public health or safety; or
   (2) damage to specific property other than the property whose use is limited.
   (b) Navigational Servitude.—No compensation shall be made under this Act with respect to an agency action pursuant to the Federal navigational servitude.

Sec. 5. Procedure.

(a) Request of Owner.—An owner seeking compensation under this Act shall make a written request for compensation to the agency whose agency action resulted in the limitation. No such request may be made later than 180 days after the owner receives actual notice of that agency action.
   (b) Negotiations.—The agency may bargain with that owner to establish the amount of the compensation. If the agency and the owner agree to such an amount, the agency shall promptly pay the owner the amount agreed upon.
   (c) Choice of Remedies.—If, not later than 180 days after the written request is made, the parties do not come to an agreement, the owner may choose to take the issue to binding arbitration or seek compensation in a civil action.
   (d) Arbitration.—The procedures that govern the arbitration shall, as nearly as practicable, be those established under title 9, United States Code, for arbitration proceedings to which that title applies. An award made in such arbitration shall include a reasonable attorney's fee and appraisal fees. The agency shall promptly pay any award made to the owner.

(e) Civil Action.—An owner who does not choose arbitration, or who does not receive prompt payment when required by this section, may obtain appropriate relief in a civil action against the agency. An owner who prevails in a civil action under this section shall be entitled to, and the agency shall be liable for, a reasonable attorney's fee and appraisal fees. The court shall award interest on the amount of any compensation from the time of the limitation.

(f) Source of Payments.—Any payment made under this section to an owner, and any judgment obtained by an owner in a civil action under this section shall, notwithstanding any other provision of law, be made from the annual appropriation of the agency whose action occasioned the payment or judgment. If the agency action resulted from a requirement imposed by another agency, then the agency making the payment or satisfying the judgment may seek partial or complete reimbursement from the appropriated funds of the other agency. For this purpose the head of the agency concerned may transfer or reprogram any appropriated funds available to the agency. If insufficient funds exist for the payment or to satisfy the judgment, it shall be the duty of the head of the agency to seek the appropriation of such funds for the next fiscal year.

Sec. 6. Definitions.

For the purposes of this Act—

(1) the term "property" means land and includes the right to use or receive water;

(2) a use of property is limited by an agency action if a particular legal right to use that property no longer exists because of the action;

(3) the term "agency action" has the meaning given that term in section 551 of title 5, United States Code, but also includes the making of a grant to a public authority conditioned upon an action by the recipient that would constitute a limitation if done directly by the agency;

(4) the term "agency" has the meaning given that term in section 551 of title 5, United States Code;

(5) the term "State" includes the District of Columbia, Puerto Rico, and any other territory or possession of the United States; and

(6) the term "law of the State" includes the law of a political subdivision of a State.

Purpose and Summary

The purpose of H.R. 925, the "Private Property Rights Protection Act of 1995," is to ensure that private property owners are compensated when the use of their property is limited by overreaching Federal regulations. H.R. 925 requires the Federal government to compensate an owner of property when a limitation placed on the use of that owner's property by a Federal agency action causes the fair market value of the property to be reduced by ten percent or more.

The Act expressly prohibits compensation for any agency action that limits the use of an owner's property if the action is undertaken to prevent an identifiable hazard to public health or safety or to prevent identifiable damage to any other specific property. No compensation is allowed under the Act if the use which has been limited by Federal agency action is also prohibited under the law of the State where the property is located or would be considered a nuisance under State law. However, the Federal government is required to compensate an owner of property for State action if the State action is required by Federal law or is imposed as a condition for Federal assistance.

H.R. 925 establishes a procedural mechanism for compensation. If the owner and the agency are unable to come to an agreement regarding compensation for the diminution in the value of the property, the owner may seek compensation through binding arbitration or a civil action and can obtain reasonable attorney's fees and appraisal fees.

Background and Need for Legislation

The concept of private property is generally recognized as a "bundle" of rights including the right to possess property and exclude others from that property, the right to freely use property in one's possession unless that use will cause harm to others or constitute a public nuisance, and the right to transfer the property. *Presbytery of Seattle v. King County*, 114 Wash. 2d 320, 787 P. 2d 907, 1990.

The Takings Clause in the Bill of Rights limits government encroachment on private property rights. The clause is included in the Fifth Amendment to the United States Constitution and states, "*** [N]or shall private property be taken for public use, without just compensation." The Takings Clause prohibits the government from taking private property, unless the property is taken for public use, and the owner receives compensation equal to the value of the property.

In *Pennsylvania Coal Co. v. Mahon,* 260 U.S. 393, 415 (1922), the Supreme Court recognized that regulation of property could be considered a taking if it "goes too far." Unfortunately, there are no bright lines to guide the courts in determining whether a government regulation "goes too far." Courts must engage in ad hoc factual inquiry on a case-by-case basis to determine whether a compensable taking has occurred as a result of regulation.

Both proponents and opponents of property rights legislation seem to agree that Takings Clause jurisprudence is complicated and unclear. During the February 10, 1995 hearing before the Subcommittee on the Constitution, J. Peter Byrne, a Georgetown Law School professor who opposes property rights legislation, testified that current takings law is "confused" and called the regulatory takings doctrine "nuanced and fact-specific."

This "nuanced and fact-specific" doctrine leaves both government officials and property owners confused and uncertain regarding the extent to which regulations can limit the use of private property without compensation being required. In fact, Chief Judge Loren Smith of the Court of Federal Claims recently voiced his concern over the inadequacy of the law of takings in addressing the impact of regulations on private property rights. In *Bowles v. United States,* he stated:

> This case presents in sharp relief the difficulty that current takings law forces upon both the federal government and the private citizen. The government here had little guidance from the law as to whether its action was a taking in advance of a long and expensive course of litigation. The citizen likewise had little more precedential guidance than faith in the justice of his cause to sustain a long and costly suit in several courts. There must be a better way to balance legitimate public goals with fundamental individual rights. Courts, however, cannot produce comprehensive solutions. They can only interpret the rather precise language of the fifth amendment to our Constitution in very specific factual circumstances.*** Judicial decisions are far less sensitive to societal problems than the law and policy made by the political branches of our great constitutional system. At best courts sketch the

outlines of individual rights, they cannot hope to fill in the portrait of wise and just social and economic policy." 31 Fed.Cl. 37 (1994).

The burden of the uncertainty of takings law falls most heavily on small property owners who are intimidated by the power of bureaucrats. Takings litigation is a long and expensive process which only the most well-financed and dedicated property owner can endure. Small property owners do not have the time or money to bring a lawsuit against the Federal government.

H.R. 925 establishes clear guidance for property owners and government officials as to when agency actions go too far and infringe on property rights. The Act will force agencies to recognize that when they limit the use of an owner's property, there are costs imposed on that owner. Agencies will have to weigh the benefits and costs of their actions carefully, paying close attention to the impact of those actions on individuals and the general public. Agencies will also be more accountable to Congress, and therefore, be more likely to carry out the true intent of the statutes they are charged with enforcing rather than continually extending their bureaucratic reach.

Supreme Court Justice Joseph Story stated that, "One of the fundamental objects of every good government must be the due administration of justice; and how vain it would be to speak of such an administration, when all property is subject to the will or caprice of the legislature and the rulers." "Commentaries on the Constitution of the United States," 2nd ed., vol. II (Boston, 1851), 534–535. H.R. 925 will help to ensure that property is not subjected "to the will or caprice of" Federal agencies.

State Property Rights Legislation

In the 1990s, a number of state legislatures enacted some form of property rights legislation. Some of these acts require state government agencies to evaluate the potential impact of a proposed regulation on private property prior to promulgation of the regulation. A few states have enacted compensation statutes that require compensation when government action causes a diminution in property value above a stated percentage. Two examples of state statutes designed to address regulatory takings—from Florida and Texas—are provided below.

Florida Private Property Rights Protection Act (1995)

Florida Statutes sec. 70.001 (1995)

70.001. Private property rights protection

(1) This act may be cited as the "Bert J. Harris, Jr., Private Property Rights Protection Act." The Legislature recognizes that some laws, regulations, and ordinances of the state and political entities in the state, as applied, may inordinately burden, restrict, or limit private property rights without amounting to a taking under the State Constitution or the United States Constitution. The Legislature determines that there is an important state interest in protecting the interests of private property owners from such inordinate burdens. Therefore, it is the intent of the Legislature that, as a separate and distinct cause of action from the law of takings, the Legislature herein provides for relief, or payment of compensation, when a new law, rule, regulation, or ordinance of the state or a political entity in the state, as applied, unfairly affects real property.

(2) When a specific action of a governmental entity has inordinately burdened an existing use of real property or a vested right to a specific use of real property, the property owner of that real property is entitled to relief, which may include compensation for the actual loss to the fair market value of the real property caused by the action of government, as provided in this section.

(3) For purposes of this section:

(a) The existence of a "vested right" is to be determined by applying the principles of equitable estoppel or substantive due process under the common law or by applying the statutory law of this state.

(b) The term "existing use" means an actual, present use or activity on the real property, including periods of inactivity which are normally associated with, or are incidental to, the nature or type of use or activity or such reasonably foreseeable, nonspeculative land uses which are suitable for the subject real property and compatible with adjacent land uses and which have created an existing fair market value in the property greater than the fair market value of the actual, present use or activity on the real property.

(c) The term "governmental entity" includes an agency of the state, a regional or a local government created by the State Constitution or by general or special act, any county or municipality, or any other entity that independently exercises governmental authority. The term does not include the United States or any of its agencies, or an agency of the state, a regional or a local government created by the State Constitution or by general or special act, any county or municipality, or any other entity that independently exercises governmental authority, when exercising the powers of the United States or any of its agencies through a formal delegation of federal authority.

(d) The term "action of a governmental entity" means a specific action of a governmental entity which affects real property, including action on an application or permit.

(e) The terms "inordinate burden" or "inordinately burdened" mean that an action of one or more governmental entities has directly restricted or limited the use of real property such that the property owner is permanently unable to attain the reasonable, investment-backed expectation for the existing use of the real property or a vested right to a specific use of the real property with respect to the real property as a whole, or that the property owner is left with existing or vested uses that are unreasonable such that the property owner bears permanently a disproportionate share of a burden imposed for the good of the public, which in fairness should be borne by the public at large. The terms "inordinate burden" or "inordinately burdened" do not include temporary impacts to real property; impacts to real property occasioned by governmental abatement, prohibition, prevention, or remediation of a public nuisance at common law or a noxious use of private property; or impacts to real property caused by an action of a governmental entity taken to grant relief to a property owner under this section.

(f) The term "property owner" means the person who holds legal title to the real property at issue. The term does not include a governmental entity.

(g) The term "real property" means land and includes any appurtenances and improvements to the land, including any other relevant real property in which the property owner had a relevant interest.

(4)(a) Not less than 180 days prior to filing an action under this section against a governmental entity, a property owner who seeks compensation under this section must present the claim in writing to the head of the governmental entity. The property owner must submit, along with the claim, a bona fide, valid appraisal that supports the claim and demonstrates the loss in fair market value to the real property. If the action of government is the culmination of a process that involves more than one governmental entity, or if a complete resolution of all relevant issues, in the view of the property owner or in the view of a governmental entity to whom a claim is presented, requires the active participation of more than one governmental entity, the property owner shall present the claim as provided in this section to each of the governmental entities.

(5)(a) During the 180-day-notice period, unless a settlement offer is accepted by the property owner, each of the governmental entities provided notice pursuant to paragraph (4)(a) shall issue a written ripeness decision identifying the allowable uses to which the subject property may be put. The failure of the governmental entity to issue a written ripeness decision during the 180-day-notice period shall be deemed to ripen the prior action of the governmental entity, and shall operate as a ripeness decision that has been rejected by the property owner. The ripeness decision, as a matter of law, constitutes the last prerequisite to judicial review, and the matter shall be deemed ripe or final for the purposes of the judicial proceeding created by this section, notwithstanding the availability of other administrative remedies.

(b) If the property owner rejects the settlement offer and the ripeness decision of the governmental entity or entities, the property owner may file a claim for compensation in the circuit court, a copy of which shall be served contemporaneously on the head of each of the governmental entities that made a settlement offer and a ripeness decision that was rejected by the property owner. Actions under this section shall be brought only in the county where the real property is located.

(6)(a) The circuit court shall determine whether an existing use of the real property or a vested right to a specific use of the real property existed and, if so, whether, considering the settlement offer and ripeness decision, the governmental entity or entities have inordinately burdened the real property. If the actions of more than one governmental entity, considering any settlement offers and ripeness decisions, are responsible for the action that imposed the inordinate burden on the real property of the property owner, the court shall determine the percentage of responsibility each such governmental entity bears with respect to the inordinate burden.

(b) Following its determination of the percentage of responsibility of each governmental entity, and following the resolution of any interlocutory appeal, the court shall impanel a jury to determine the total amount of compensation to the property owner for the loss in value due to the inordinate burden to the real property. The award of compensation shall be determined by calculating the difference in the fair market value of the real property, as it existed at the time of the governmental action at issue, as though the owner had the ability to attain the reasonable investment-backed expectation or was not left with uses that are unreasonable, whichever the case may be, and the fair market value of the real property, as it existed at the time of the governmental action at issue, as inordinately burdened, considering the settlement offer together with the ripeness decision, of the governmental entity or entities. In determining the award of compensation, consideration may not be given to business damages relative to any development, activity, or use that the action of the governmental entity or entities, considering the settlement offer together with the ripeness decision has restricted, limited, or prohibited.

(9) This section provides a cause of action for governmental actions that may not rise to the level of a taking under the State Constitution or the United States Constitution. This section may not necessarily be construed under the case law regarding takings if the governmental action does not rise to the level of a taking. The provisions of this section are cumulative, and do not abrogate any other remedy lawfully available, including any remedy lawfully available for governmental actions that rise to the level of a taking.

Texas Private Real Property Rights Preservation Act (1995)

10 Texas Government Code § 2007

§ 2007.002. Definitions

(5) "Taking" means:

(A) a governmental action that affects private real property, in whole or in part or temporarily or permanently, in a manner that requires the governmental entity to compensate the private real property owner as provided by the Fifth and Fourteenth Amendments to the United States Constitution or Section 17 or 19, Article I, Texas Constitution; or

(B) a governmental action that:

(i) affects an owner's private real property that is the subject of the governmental action, in whole or in part or temporarily or permanently, in a manner that restricts or limits the owner's right to the property that would otherwise exist in the absence of the governmental action; and

(ii) is the producing cause of a reduction of at least 25 percent in the market value of the affected private real property, determined by comparing the market value of the property as if the governmental action is not in effect and the market value of the property determined as if the governmental action is in effect.

§ 2007.003. Applicability

(a) This chapter applies only to the following governmental actions:

(1) the adoption or issuance of an ordinance, rule, regulatory requirement, resolution, policy, guideline, or similar measure;

(2) an action that imposes a physical invasion or requires a dedication or exaction of private real property;

(3) an action by a municipality that has effect in the extraterritorial jurisdiction of the municipality, excluding annexation, and that enacts or enforces an ordinance, rule, regulation, or plan that does not impose identical requirements or restrictions in the entire extraterritorial jurisdiction of the municipality; and

(4) enforcement of a governmental action listed in Subdivisions (1) through (3), whether the enforcement of the governmental action is accomplished through the use of permitting, citations, orders, judicial or quasi-judicial proceedings, or other similar means.

§ 2007.021. Suit Against Political Subdivision

(a) A private real property owner may bring suit under this subchapter to determine whether the governmental action of a political subdivision results in a taking under this chapter. A suit under this subchapter must be filed in a district court in the county in which the private real property owner's affected property is located. If the affected private real property is located in more than one county, the private real property owner may file suit in any county in which the affected property is located.

(b) A suit under this subchapter must be filed not later than the 180th day after the date the private real property owner knew or should have known that the governmental action restricted or limited the owner's right in the private real property.

§ 2007.023. Entitlement to Invalidation of Governmental Action

(a) Whether a governmental action results in a taking is a question of fact.

(b) If the trier of fact in a suit or contested case filed under this subchapter finds that the governmental action is a taking under this chapter, the private real property owner is only entitled to, and the governmental entity is only liable for, invalidation of the governmental action or the part of the governmental action resulting in the taking.

§ 2007.043. Takings Impact Assessment

(a) A governmental entity shall prepare a written takings impact assessment of a proposed governmental action described in Section 2007.003(a)(1) through (3) that complies with the evaluation guidelines developed by the attorney general under Section 2007.041 before the governmental entity provides the public notice required under Section 2007.042.

(b) The takings impact assessment must:

(1) describe the specific purpose of the proposed action and identify:

(A) whether and how the proposed action substantially advances its stated purpose; and

(B) the burdens imposed on private real property and the benefits to society resulting from the proposed use of private real property.

(2) determine whether engaging in the proposed governmental action will constitute a taking; and

(3) describe reasonable alternative actions that could accomplish the specified purpose and compare, evaluate, and explain:

(A) how an alternative action would further the specified purpose; and

(B) whether an alternative action would constitute a taking.

(c) A takings impact assessment prepared under this section is public information.

Chronology

1215	Magna Carta. American colonists viewed this ancient British charter as a guarantee that all British subjects possessed the right to no taxation without representation, along with the due process principle that "no freeman shall be taken, imprisoned, disseised [dispossessed of property] . . . except by the lawful judgment of his peers and by the law of the land."
1689	The English Declaration of Rights. American colonists claimed entitlement to this list of thirteen "undoubted Rights and Liberties" of the English people, including parliamentary approval prior to any taxation, freedom from excessive fines or bail, and the right to a jury trial before forfeiture of property.
1763	Stamp Act (British Parliament). Together with other measures, this act imposed taxes on the colonists, leading to the charge that the property rights of colonists were violated because they were not represented in Parliament.
1765	Quartering Act (British Parliament). Forced American colonists to house British soldiers upon demand.
1765	Publication of William Blackstone's *Commentaries on the Laws of England,* widely available in the American colonies, defines property rights of British subjects.

1776	Declaration of Independence (Continental Congress). Newly formed states enact constitutions that recognize a variety of "inalienable" natural rights, including "due process" clauses providing generally that no person should be "deprived of life, liberty, or property, without due process of law."
1781	Conclusion of Revolutionary War.
1781	Articles of Confederation, first national constitution for the United States.
1786–1787	Shays's Rebellion. Armed rebellion in Massachusetts protesting state fiscal policies and foreclosures against property to satisfy debts.
1787	Northwest Ordinance (Confederation Congress). Enacted to govern American territories later to become states. The Northwest Ordinance protected contract and due process property rights, instituted a "just compensation" clause for government takings of property, and banned slavery.
1787–1789	States ratify U.S. Constitution.
1791	Bill of Rights added to the U.S. Constitution, including the Fifth Amendment's Due Process and Takings Clauses.
1808	National ban on importation of slaves.
1810	*Fletcher v. Peck:* U.S. Supreme Court holds that the Contracts Clause prevents states from rescinding previously issued land grants.
1820	Missouri Compromise bans slavery in certain federal territories.
1833	*Barron v. Baltimore:* U.S. Supreme Court holds that the Fifth Amendment's Takings Clause does not apply to state and local governments.
1850	Kentucky Constitution, similar to views in other slave states, is amended to include: "The right of the owner of a slave, to such slave, and its increase, is the

same, and as inviolable as the right of the owner of any property whatever."

1857 *Dred Scott v. Sandford:* U.S. Supreme Court declares the Missouri Compromise to be invalid because slaves were property protected by the Constitution, and therefore Congress had no power to prohibit slavery in the federal territories.

1861 U.S. Civil War begins.

1865 Civil War ends; Thirteenth Amendment, abolishing slavery without compensation to slave owners, is ratified.

1868 Fourteenth Amendment ratified.

1871 *Pumpelly v. Green Bay Co.:* U.S. Supreme Court holds that a federal government must compensate landowners when a physical invasion caused by the government prevents the owner's use of the land.

1873 *Slaughterhouse Cases:* The Supreme Court's first major interpretation of the Fourteenth Amendment holds that the amendment does not alter state authority over property rights of state citizens.

1877 *Munn v. Illinois:* U.S. Supreme Court upholds rate regulation of grain elevators as a legitimate exercise of state police power, against the claim that the fixed rate deprived owners of property without due process of law. A dissenting opinion by Justice Stephen Field argued that the statute was unconstitutional and set forth a rationale for that conclusion that later courts would adopt as "substantive due process."

1887 *Mugler v. Kansas:* U.S. Supreme Court upholds Kansas prohibition statute as a valid exercise of state police power. A dissenting opinion by Justice Stephen Field viewed the measure to violate property rights under the Due Process Clause.

1892	*Illinois Central Railroad v. Illinois:* U.S. Supreme Court recognizes "public trust" doctrine, holding that a state may revoke previous grants for land under navigable waters.
1897	*Allgeyer v. Louisiana:* U.S. Supreme Court holds that the Fourteenth Amendment protects freedom of contract against state infringement.
1897	*Chicago, B. & Q. R.R. v. City of Chicago:* U.S. Supreme Court holds that the Fourteenth Amendment's Due Process Clause prevents uncompensated state government takings of private property; this case marks the beginning of the application of the Takings Clause of the Fifth Amendment to state and local governmental actions.
1905	*Lochner v. New York:* The best-known instance of the Supreme Court's substantive due process doctrine. This case invalidated a New York law regulating the working hours of bakers.
1910	Congress enacts the predecessor to 28 USC 1498, permitting suit against the federal government for its unauthorized use of patented inventions and processes.
1922	*Pennsylvania Coal Co. v. Mahon:* Chief Justice Oliver Wendell Holmes Jr. interprets the Takings Clause, for the first time, to include regulatory takings.
1926	*Village of Euclid v. Ambler Realty Co.:* The U.S. Supreme Court sustains a comprehensive city zoning ordinance against claims that the plan violates private property rights.
1937	U.S. Supreme Court decision in *West Coast Hotel Co. v. Parrish* (1937) is termed the "constitutional revolution of 1937," reversing the Court's previous stance on substantive due process.

1938	*United States v. Carolene Products:* Establishes rational basis review of economic regulations and a higher level of scrutiny for laws that affect minorities and the political process.
1978	*Penn Central Transportation v. New York:* U.S. Supreme Court upholds a historic preservation law against a claim that the prohibition on building above Grand Central Station was an uncompensated taking.
1987	U.S. Supreme Court expresses a renewed interest in the Takings Clause in a series of cases including *Nollan v. California Coastal Commission* and *First English Evangelical Lutheran Church v. County of Los Angeles.*
1988	President Ronald Reagan issues an executive order requiring all federal agencies to undertake a takings impact analysis before implementing a regulation to review the potential effects of their actions on property owners.
1990s	Approximately twenty states enact some form of property rights legislation, including assessment requirements prior to government regulation of property (modeled upon President Ronald Reagan's 1988 executive order) and compensation statutes requiring that payment be made when a state regulation reduces the value of property by a stated percentage.
1992	*Lucas v. South Carolina Coastal Council:* U.S. Supreme Court recognizes a categorical rule that requires compensation under the Takings Clause when a property regulation deprives an owner of "all economically beneficial or productive use of land."
2001	*Palazzolo v. Coastal Resources Management Council:* U.S. Supreme Court states that the categorical taking rule in *Lucas v. South Carolina Coastal Council* (1992) may also apply to property owners who pur-

chase land already subject to a prior building restriction.

2002 *Newman v. Sathyavaglswaran:* The Ninth U.S. Circuit Court of Appeals recognizes a property interest in the next of kin in the bodily integrity of deceased relatives; presumed-consent statutes authorizing removal of corneas for transplantation to others requires due process protections for this property right.

2002 *Tahoe-Sierra Preservation Council v. Tahoe Regional Planning Agency:* U.S. Supreme Court holds that no compensation is required for a three-year development moratorium affecting hundreds of property owners. The temporary ban on development was imposed in order to assess the environmental impact of construction.

TABLE OF CASES

This table provides the full citation for the court opinions referenced in this book. The legal citation form includes an abbreviated reference style to identify the particular court. A brief guide to this abbreviation style is below:

U.S.	U.S. Supreme Court
F.2d or F.3d	U.S. Courts of Appeals
Fed. Cl.	U.S. Court of Federal Claims (renamed in 1992)
Ct. Cl.	U.S. Court of Claims

State supreme courts are identified with the state's abbreviation in parentheses. Page numbers on which cases can be found in the text are listed after the year for each citation.

Adair v. United States, 208 U.S. 161 (1908), 85
Adkins v. Children's Hospital, 261 U.S. 525 (1923), 84
Agins v. City of Tiburon, 447 U.S. 255 (1980), 100, 115, 183
Allgeyer v. Louisiana, 165 U.S. 578 (1897), 68, 185
Amalgamated Food Employees Union v. Logan Valley Plaza, Inc., 391 U.S. 308 (1968), 91
Amerace Esna Corp. v. United States, 462 F.2d 1377 (Ct. Cl. 1972), 146
Argent v. United States, 124 F.3d 1277 (Fed. Cir. 1997), 112
Barron v. City of Baltimore, 32 U.S. 243 (1833), 47, 69, 186
Bennis v. Michigan, 516 U.S. 442 (1996), 128

Buchanan v. Warley, 256 U.S. 60 (1917), 99
Calder v. Bull, 3 U.S. 386 (1798), 59, 108, 187
Calero-Toledo v. Pearson Yacht Leasing Co., 416 U.S. 663 (1974), 127
Caplin & Drysdale v. United States, 491 U.S. 617 (1989), 128
Chicago, B. & Q. R.R. v. City of Chicago, 166 U.S. 226 (1897), 69, 187
Consolidated Fruit-Jar Co. v. Wright, 94 U.S. 92 (1876), 142
Coppage v. Kansas, 236 U.S. 1 (1915), 85
Dartmouth College v. Woodward, 17 U.S. 518 (1819), 14, 58, 190
DeGraffenried v. United States, 29 Fed. Cl. 384 (Fed. Cl. 1993), 142
Diamond v. Chakrabarty, 447 U.S. 303 (1980), 165
Dolan v. City of Tigard, 512 U.S. 374 (1994), 105, 122, 191
Dred Scott v. Sandford, 60 U.S. 393 (1856), 64, 192
Eastern Enterprises v. Apfel, 524 U.S. 498 (1998), 108, 193
Eldred v. Ashcroft, 123 S.Ct. 769 (2003), 141
Festo Corp. v. Shoketsu Kinzoku Kogyo Kabushiki Co., 535 U.S. 722 (2002), 143
First English Evangelical Lutheran Church v. County of Los Angeles, 482 U.S. 304 (1987), 123, 196
Fletcher v. Peck, 10 U.S. 87 (1810), 14, 56, 222
Florida v. Powell, 497 So.2d 1188 (FL 1986), 160
Florida Prepaid v. College Savings Bank, 527 U.S. 627 (1999), 142, 150
Franco-American Charolaise, Ltd. v. Okla. Water Res. Bd., 855 P.2d 568 (OK 1990), 174
Gardner v. Village of Newburgh, 2 Johns. Ch. 162 (Ch. Ct. NY 1816), 33, 197
Georgia Lions Eye Bank, Inc. v. Lavant, 335 S.E.2d 127 (GA 1985), 161
Gibbons v. Ogden, 22 U.S. 1 (1824), 48, 197
Hadacheck v. Sebastian, 239 U.S. 394 (1915), 96
Hage v. United States, 35 Fed. Cl. 147 (Fed. Cl. 1996), 71

Hawaii Housing Authority v. Midkiff, 467 U.S. 229 (1984), 108, 198, 252
Heart of Atlanta Motel, Inc. v. United States, 379 U.S. 241 (1964), 90, 198
Hepburn v. Griswold, 75 U.S. 603 (1870), 202
Holden v. Hardy, 169 U.S. 366 (1898), 84
Home Building and Loan Association v. Blaisdell, 290 U.S. 238 (1934), 88
Hudgens v. NLRB, 424 U.S. 507 (1976), 91
Hudson County Water Co. v. McCarter, 209 U.S. 349 (1908), 175
Hughes v. Washington, 389 U.S. 290 (1967), 125
Illinois Central Railroad v. Illinois, 146 U.S. 387 (1892), 102, 211
International News Service v. Associated Press, 248 U.S. 215 (1918), 138
Ives v. South Buffalo Rwy. Co., 201 N.Y. 271 (NY 1911), 83
James v. Campbell, 104 U.S. 356 (1882), 145
J.E.M. Ag Supply, Inc. v. Pioneer Hi-Bred International, Inc., 534 U.S. 124 (2001), 165
Johnson v. M'Intosh, 21 U.S. 543 (1823), 54, 201
Just v. Marinette County, 201 N.W.2d 761 (WI 1972), 101, 169
Keystone Bituminous Coal Association v. DeBenedictis, 480 U.S. 470 (1987), 114
Kohl v. United States, 91 U.S. 367 (1875), 45
Kyllo v. United States, 533 U.S. 27 (2001), 13
Legal Tender Cases, 79 U.S. 457 (1871), 67, 202
Lindsay v. Commissioners, 2 Bay 38 (SC 1796), 56
Lochner v. New York, 198 U.S. 45 (1905), 77, 82, 230
Loretto v. Teleprompter Manhattan CATV Corp., 458 U.S. 419 (1982), 111, 138, 203
Lowell v. Lewis, 15 F. Cas. 1018 (C.C.D. MA 1817), 165
Lucas v. South Carolina Coastal Council, 505 U.S. 1003 (1992), 92, 117, 265
Martin v. Struthers, 319 U.S. 141 (1943), 91
Miller v. Schoene, 276 U.S. 272 (1928), 114

Moore v. Regents of Univ. of California, 51 Cal.3d 120 (CA 1990, 157
Morehead v. New York, 97 U.S. 702 (1936), 85
Mugler v. Kansas, 123 U.S. 623 (1887), 60, 81, 93, 113, 114, 204
Muller v. Oregon, 208 U.S. 412 (1908), 84
Munn v. Illinois, 94 U.S. 113 (1877), 80, 92
Nectow v. City of Cambridge, 277 U.S. 183 (1928), 99
New York Cent. R.R. Co. v. White, 243 U.S. 188 (1917), 83
Newman v. Sathyavaglswaran, 287 F.3d 786 (9th Cir. 2002), 161
Noble State Bank v. Haskell, 219 U.S. 104 (1911), 85
Nollan v. California Coastal Commission, 483 U.S. 825 (1987), 121, 205, 257
Ogden v. Saunders, 25 U.S. 213 (1827), 60
Palazzolo v. Rhode Island, 533 U.S. 606 (2001), 119, 208
Pallin v. Singer, 1996 WL 274407 (Dist. VT 1996), 144
Penn Central Transp. Co. v. City of New York, 438 U.S. 104 (1978), 103, 116, 209, 243
Pennsylvania Coal Co. v. Mahon, 260 U.S. 393 (1922), 77, 92, 235
Petit v. Minnesota, 177 U.S. 164 (1900), 84
Phillips v. Washington Legal Foundation, 524 U.S. 156 (1998), xxi, 137
Plessy v. Ferguson, 163 U.S. 537 (1896), 99
Poletown Neighborhood Council v. City of Detroit, 304 N.W.2d 455 (MI 1981), 109
Pollock v. Farmers' Loan & Trust Co., 157 U.S. 429 (1895), 10
Powell v. Pennsylvania, 127 U.S. 678 (1888), 93
PruneYard Shopping Center v. Robins, 447 U.S. 74 (1980), 91, 210, 249
Pumpelly v. Green Bay Co., 80 U.S. 166 (1871), 67, 93, 211
Queenside Hills Realty v. Saxl, 328 U.S. 80 (1946), 115
Roe v. Wade, 410 U.S. 113 (1973), 164
Ruckelshaus v. Monsanto Corp., 467 U.S. 986 (1984), 152
San Diego Gas & Electric Co. v. City of San Diego, 450 U.S. 621 (1981), 201

Santa Clara County v. Southern Pacific Railroad Co., 118 U.S. 394 (1886)
Slaughterhouse Cases, 83 U.S. 36 (1873), 80, 213
State v. Powell, 497 So.2d 1188 (FL 1986), 160
Stevens v. City of Cannon Beach, 510 U.S. 1207 (1994), 125
Tahoe-Sierra Preservation Council, Inc., v. Tahoe Regional Planning Agency, 535 U.S. 302 (2002), 1, 123, 213, 272
Tektronix, Inc. v. United States, 552 F.2d 343 (Ct.Cl. 1977), 147
Tennessee Valley Authority v. Hill, 437 U.S. 153 (1978), 102
United States v. Caltex, Inc., 344 U.S. 149 (1952), 89
United States v. Carolene Products Co., 304 U.S. 144 (1938), 87, 89
United States v. Causby, 328 U.S. 256 (1946), 112
United States v. Fifty Acres of Land, 469 U.S. 24 (1984), 109
United States v. General Motors Corp., 323 U.S. 373 (1945), 138
United States v. James Daniel Good Real Properties, 510 U.S. 43 (1993), 127
United States v. Riverside Bayview Homes, Inc., 474 U.S. 121 (1985), 106
Vanhorne's Lessee v. Dorrance, 2 U.S. 304 (1795), 32, 45, 47
Village of Belle Terre v. Boraas, 416 U.S. 1 (1974), 100
Village of Euclid v. Ambler Realty Co., 272 U.S. 365 (1926), 97, 214
West Coast Hotel Co. v. Parrish, 300 U.S. 379 (1937), 87, 214, 237
Worcester v. Georgia, 31 U.S. 515 (1832), 55
Wynehamer v. People, 13 N.Y. 378 (NY 1856), 58, 226
Yee v. City of Escondido, 503 U.S. 519 (1992), 112, 260

BIBLIOGRAPHY

The literature on constitutional protection of property rights is voluminous and comprises a wide range of views by economists, political scientists, lawyers, philosophers, and historians. The works cited at the conclusion of each chapter in this book represent only a small portion of this scholarship. This bibliographic essay provides an overview of some of the more important and useful books on this subject.

HISTORICAL DEVELOPMENT

James W. Ely Jr.'s magisterial book, *The Guardian of Every Other Right: A Constitutional History of Property Rights* (Oxford Press, 2d ed., 1998), systematically relates the historical development of constitutional property rights in the United States. No other single book to date provides historical context for contemporary property rights disputes over the broad range of U.S. history. Professor Ely has also assembled in book form a collection of the most important scholarly articles on the development of constitutional property rights. This six-volume series, **"Property Rights in American History"** (Garland Publishing, 1997), includes *Property Rights in the Colonial Era and Early Republic* (volume 1); *Property Rights in the Age of Enterprise* (volume 2); *Reform and Regulation of Property Rights* (volume 3); *The Contract Clause in American History* (volume 4); *Contemporary Property Rights Issues* (volume 5); and *Main Themes in the Debate Over Property Rights* (volume 6).

For an excellent analysis of the origins of the U.S. Constitution's property clauses, as well as other rights protected by the Constitution, see Jack Rakove's book, *Declaring Rights* (Bedford Books, 1998).

William J. Novak's book, *The People's Welfare: Law and Regulation in Nineteenth-Century America* (University of North Carolina Press, 1996), explores the reach of the police power and governments' regulatory role in the nineteenth century. Although Novak concludes that property rights were protected in the formative years of the United States, property rights were not absolute. Novak argues that private property was heavily regulated, and there was no clear separation of the "market" from government. In this book, Novak attempts to show that the historical record reveals a strong tradition of public rights.

Bernard H. Siegan's *Property Rights: From Magna Carta to the Fourteenth Amendment* (Transaction Publishers, 2001), considers in detail the English view of property rights preceding U.S. independence and the adoption of the federal and state constitutions. His subsequent review of property rights in the United States ends in 1868 with the ratification of the Fourteenth Amendment, because Siegan's purpose is to explore in greater detail property rights cases decided by state courts in the first 100 years after independence. Siegan concludes that more recent U.S. Supreme Court decisions on constitutional property rights are consistent with the historical traditions exemplified by these early state courts.

Richard Epstein, another prolific scholar in the area of constitutional property rights, has also assembled a series of books collecting important scholarly articles on this subject, largely from a historical perspective. This five-volume series, **"Liberty, Property, and the Law"** (Garland Publishing, 2000), includes *Classical Foundations of Liberty and Property* (volume 1); *Modern Understandings of Liberty and Property* (volume 2); *Private and Common Property* (volume 3); *Contract – Freedom and Restraint* (volume 4); and *Constitutional Protection of Private Property and Freedom of Contract* (volume 5). Epstein's book *Takings: Private Property and the Power of Eminent Domain* (Cambridge University Press, 1985) argues that property rights deserve greater protection than the U.S. Supreme Court has yet recognized. Epstein maintains that compensation is required for all government restrictions on private property that could not be obtained by individuals bringing common law nuisance actions, a position that is fairly controversial and that relies upon historical interpretation to determine the scope of contemporary limits on government regulatory authority.

Other scholars who have considered the historical development of constitutional property rights include Jennifer Nedelsky and Ellen Frankel Paul. Nedelsky's *Private Property and the Limits of American Constitutionalism* (University of Chicago Press, 1990) explores competing visions of property rights and how constitutional structures were thought to protect those rights in the founding era. Paul's *Property Rights and Eminent Domain* (Transaction Books, 1987) is concerned primarily with environmental land-use regulations, which she views to constitute greater encroachments on private property rights than historical views of the Constitution's property clauses would allow. Paul and Howard Dickman coedited *Liberty, Property, and the Foundations of the American Constitution* (State University of New York Press, 1989), a very useful collection of essays by various authors concerning views in the founding period about economic rights. Two other volumes in the "SUNY Series in the Constitution and Economic Rights," coedited by Paul and Dickman, include *Liberty, Property, and Government: Constitutional Interpretation Before the New Deal* (State University of New York Press, 1989) and *Liberty, Property, and the Future of Constitutional Development* (State University of New York Press, 1990).

Contemporary Takings Law: Regulatory Takings

The relatively recent development of regulatory takings is a difficult and often highly technical subject. Steven J. Eagle has published a comprehensive treatise, *Regulatory Takings* (Michie, 1996). This treatise categorizes and discusses numerous state and federal cases, including an annual supplement that includes newly decided constitutional property cases. Among other topics, Eagle provides an exhaustive discussion of court cases involving zoning practices and environmental regulations.

The subject of constitutional property rights in a regulatory state lends itself to wide-ranging views on the appropriate scope of governmental power. Recent books that examine land-use regulations from various perspectives include Dennis J. Coyle, *Property Rights and the Constitution: Shaping Society Through Land Use Regulation* (State University of New York Press, 1993); William A. Fischel, *Regulatory Takings: Law, Economics, and Politics* (Harvard University Press, 1995); and Bernard H. Siegan, *Property and Freedom: The Constitution, the Courts, and Land-Use Regulation* (Transaction Publishers, 1997). A particularly insightful consideration of regulatory takings for environmental issues is found in Robert Meltz, Dwight H. Merriam, and Richard M. Frank, *The Takings Issue: Constitutional Limits on Land Use Control and Environmental Regulation* (Island Press, 1999).

City planners, government attorneys, and environmental advocates will find useful a recent book prepared by the Community Rights Counsel and the California Community Land Use Project. This book, *Takings Litigation Handbook: Defending Takings Challenges to Land Use Regulations*

(American Legal Publishing, 2000), by Douglas T. Kendall, Timothy J. Dowling, and Andrew W. Schwartz, discusses the litigation framework in property rights cases and provides a cogent review of the regulatory takings doctrine.

Property Rights in Other Contexts

Many aspects of property law are not "constitutional" in the sense that courts use property rules established by legislatures and by the common law to resolve property disputes between private persons. Nonetheless, the background principles of property law are often important to determine the extent of property interests that may be considered constitutional. Joseph William Singer's *Introduction to Property* (New York: Aspen Law and Business, 2001) provides an overview of common law property rights and limitations on those rights (nuisance, adverse possession, and so on), as well as an excellent summary of regulatory takings and public land-use planning.

Four other books present provocative essays on the nature of property rights generally, including the underlying philosophical constructs that determine the boundaries of private property rights. Nicholas Mercuro and Warren J. Samuels, eds., *The Fundamental Interrelationships Between Government and Property* (JAI Press, 1999), is part of a series (**"The Economics of Legal Relationships"**) and focuses primarily upon economic analyses of property issues. *Perspectives on Property Law* (Little, Brown, 2d ed., 1995), edited by Robert C. Ellickson, Carol M. Rose, and Bruce A. Ackerman, provides a diverse selection of readings on the debate over private property, property rights that arise outside the legal system, and land use and the environment. Carol Rose's *Property and Persuasion: Essays on the History, Theory, and Rhetoric of Ownership* (Westview Press, 1994) includes essays on the development of public property doctrines and a classical theory of property, which contends that property rights originate in the efforts of individuals to maximize their aggregate welfare. Finally, Margaret Jane Radin's *Reinterpreting Property* (University of Chicago Press, 1993) collects a series of articles written by Radin over a twelve-year period, in which she develops her personality theory of property, including essays titled "Residential Rent Control" and "Government Interests and Takings: Cultural Commitments of Property and the Role of Political Theory."

In Chapter 4 of this book, we considered the extent to which components of the human body may be considered property and, as such, may form a constitutionally protected property interest. An interesting and thorough book, David Price's *Legal and Ethical Aspects of Organ Transplantation* (Cambridge University Press, 2000), provides a useful overview of these issues.

ARTICLES

Many scholars have made important contributions in articles rather than books. The review of books in this essay is not meant to discount the significance of these contributions; I urge the reader to consult the end-of-chapter Further Reading sections for specific references. Articles by Joseph Sax, Carol Rose, and Frank Michelman have been particularly important in furthering debate about the scope of constitutional protection for private property, by those who agree with them and those who do not.

OTHER REFERENCE WORKS

An extensive bibliography of constitutional property rights scholarship prior to 1980 is available in Kermit L. Hall's five-volume compilation, *A Comprehensive Bibliography of American Constitutional and Legal History, 1896–1979* (Kraus International Publications, 1984). A two-volume treatise by Melvin I. Urofsky (another author in this "America's Freedoms" series) and Paul Finkelman, *A March of Liberty: A Constitutional History of the United States* (Oxford University Press, 2002) also contains an excellent bibliography of sources. Finally, a useful general reference work is *The Oxford Companion to the Supreme Court of the United States* (Oxford University Press, 1992), edited by Kermit L. Hall, James W. Ely Jr., Joel B. Grossman, and William Wiecek. This book provides a comprehensive guide to the U.S. Supreme Court's history, including biographical entries on individual Supreme Court justices, summaries of important cases, and essays on legal doctrines and the history and current operation of the Supreme Court.

Index

Adams, John, 37–38
Administrative agencies, federal, 141, 153–154, 156, 166, 172
  in New Deal era, 86
Adverse possession, doctrine of, 50, 183
Agricultural Adjustment Act, 86
Airports, 112
Alcoholic beverages. *See* Prohibition of alcohol
Alien land laws, 11, 184
Amendments. *See* Bill of Rights; Eleventh Amendment; Fifth Amendment; First Amendment; Fourteenth Amendment; Fourth Amendment; Seventh Amendment; Third Amendment; Thirteenth Amendment
American Medical Association, 157
Americans with Disabilities Act, 91
Ancient lights, doctrine of, 49
Anti-Federalists, as critics of the Constitution, 13, 42, 195
Articles of Confederation, 35, 36, 43, 185
Atomic Energy Act, 144

Bankruptcy clause, 40
Bankruptcy law, 40, 60

Bill of Rights, 42–48, 186
Biotechnology, 139, 155. *See also* Human body; Property, intellectual; Quasi-property
Bituminous Coal Conservation Act, 86
Blackstone, William, 19, 20, 23–25, 31, 38, 186–187
Blue laws, 84
Brandeis, Louis, 96
Brennen, William, 208
Brutus, 13
Bush, George W., 155, 163

California, Supreme Court of, 110, 157
Chase, Samuel, 59, 108, 187
Cherokee Indians
  and Supreme Court cases, 54–55
  and Trail of Tears, 55
Child labor, 77, 81
Citizenship, xxi, 9, 11, 145, 184
Civil rights, 87–90, 99
Civil Rights Act of 1964, 90–91, 188, 198–199
Civil War, 14
Clean Air Act, 101, 146, 172
Clean Water Act, 101, 172
Clinton, William, 163
Cloning. *See* Human body; Property, in living things

Colonial America
  economic development in, 26, 27
  Magna Carta as influence on, 7, 21
  right of eminent domain in, 25–26
Commentaries on the Laws of England, 24, 186–187. *See also* Blackstone, William
Commerce
  congressional power over, 188
  as defined by Court, 188, 197
  foreign. *See* Foreign commerce
  interstate.
  See also Interstate commerce
Commerce clause
  judicial interpretations of, 90–91, 188, 197
  in New Deal era, 86, 90–91
Common law, of states, 71, 75, 118–119, 126, 188–189. *See also* English common law
Compensation principle
  and eminent domain, 65–67, 70, 109–111
  and intellectual property, 145–146
  in state constitutions, 29–32
Comprehensive Environmental Reclamation and Control Liability Act (CERCLA), 101
Condemnation. *See* Eminent domain
Confiscation of property, 11, 26, 33, 56, 126–128
Congress
  and regulation of economy, 86–89, 214–215
  taxation authority of, 10, 40
Constitution, Confederate, 64–65
Constitution, U.S.
  development of, 14, 20, 35–42
  opponents of, 13, 42, 195
  property rights in, 7–8, 39–40, 43, 46
  ratification of, 36–43
  See also Bill of Rights; Commerce clause; Contract clause; Eleventh Amendment; Fifth Amendment; First Amendment; Fourteenth Amendment; Fourth Amendment; Seventh Amendment; Third Amendment; Thirteenth Amendment
Constitutional revolution of 1937, 87–88, 189, 214–215
Constitutions, state, 7, 15, 19, 29–32, 44, 52, 104, 110–111, 129
Contracts clause, 14, 39, 185, 218
  declining importance of, 68, 76, 88
  judicial interpretations of, 56–58, 60, 88, 189–190
  See also Liberty of contract doctrine
Copyright protection, 140–141, 199. *See also* Property, intellectual
Copyright Term Extension Act of 1988, 141
Corneal tissue. *See* Human body; Presumed consent statutes
Corporations, 15, 190
Court of Appeals for the Federal Circuit, 112
Court of Claims, U.S., 142, 148
Creditors. *See* Debtor-relief laws
Cuba, 4–5, 7

Dartmouth College, and corporate charters, 58, 190
Davis, Jefferson, 64

Debtor-relief laws, 34, 191
  judicial review of, 60
Debts, owed to British merchants, 36
Declaration of Independence, 27, 29
  property rights under, 28
Declaration of Rights, English, 22, 34, 194
Department of Agriculture, U.S., 141
Depression, Great, 86
Discovery, doctrine of, 54
Due process
  economic, 136, 185
  procedural, 78–79, 192–193
  substantive, 77, 80, 83–84, 87, 90, 93, 193, 230
Due process clause
  of Fifth Amendment, 43, 93, 106, 126
  of Fourteenth Amendment, 106, 126
  in state constitutions, 43, 44, 58

Economic due process. *See* Due process, substantive; Liberty of contract doctrine
Economic rights. *See* Property rights
Eleventh amendment, 150
Ely, James W., xxiii, 305
Emancipation Proclamation, 63
Embryo. *See* Human body
Emergency Price Control Act, 89
Eminent domain, right of
  and compensation principle, xxii, 8–9, 45–46, 106–110, 146, 193
  and police power, 108
  state use of, 9, 65–67, 94, 107–109, 151, 194
Endangered Species Act, 101, 102

England, colonists' disagreements with, 22, 24, 27–28, 34
English common law, 23, 24, 28, 49–50, 53–54, 145, 189. *See also* Blackstone, William
Environmental laws, 101–103, 169–170, 171–173
Environmental Protection Agency, U.S., 153–154, 172
Epstein, Richard A., 118, 167
Ex post facto clause, 40, 187, 194–195
Export regulations, federal, 148

Fair market value, 107, 109–110, 146
Federal Torts Claims Act, 150
Federalism, constitutional principle of, 14, 77. *See also* Federalists
The Federalist Papers, 6, 35–37, 39, 40, 45, 52, 195, 218
Federalists, as proponents of the Constitution, 35, 51, 195
Fee simple, 9, 196
Field, Stephen J., 10, 81
Fifth Amendment, 19, 21, 218
  as applicable to States, 14–15, 21, 47–48, 69–70, 93
  and compensation requirement, 43–44, 65–67, 70, 109–111
  due process clause of, 6, 127, 142
  takings clause of, 6, 69, 89, 142, 144
First Amendment, 91–92, 210, 249
Florida, Supreme Court of, 160–162
  legislation, 286
Food and Drug Administration, U.S., 156, 166
Foreign commerce, power to regulate, 35, 36, 40
Forfeiture. *See* Confiscation

Fourteenth Amendment, 14, 169, 218
  due process clause of, 6, 67–68, 79, 99, 150–151
  equal protection clause of, 144
  and incorporation, 15, 67–69, 186–188
  and liberty of contract doctrine, 68
  privileges or immunities clause of, 218
Fourth Amendment, 12–13
Freedom of contract. *See* Liberty of contract
Friedman, Milton, 178
Fugitive slave clause, 64

General Motors Corp., 109, 138
Georgia
  legislature, 56, 110, 214, 222
  statutes, 53, 164
  Supreme Court of, 160–162
  water allocation in, 175
  Yazoo land fraud, 54, 56–57, 214, 222
Germany, land claims in the former East Germany, 6
Gholson, James, 62
Government regulation
  and growth of administrative state, 81–84, 86–87
  and property rights, 76, 92–96, 212
  See also Interstate commerce
Grain elevators, regulation of, 80–81, 205
Grand Central Station, New York, 103–104

Hamilton, Alexander, 35, 36, 39–40, 52
Harlan, John, 60

Hart, John, 27
Hawaii land reform statute, 108–109, 252–253
Historic preservation, 103–105, 209, 243
Holmes, Oliver Wendell, Jr., 85, 94–95, 116, 129, 138, 168, 175, 199
Human body, property rights in, 15–17, 139, 155–162, 163–165. *See also* Quasi-property

Income tax, 10
Incorporation, doctrine of. *See* Fourteenth amendment, incorporation
Inheritance law, 11, 51
Intangible property. *See* Property, intangible
Intellectual property. *See* Property, intellectual
Intellectual property clause, 40, 140
Interstate commerce
  constitutional provisions protecting, 40
  federal regulation of, 188, 197
  See also Commerce clause
Inventions Secrecy Act, 147–149, 200
Inverse condemnation, 92, 200–201. *See also* Regulatory takings
Investment-backed expectations, 104, 116, 119

Jay, John, 35
Jefferson, Thomas, 27, 28
Johnson, William, 57
Judicial takings, 125–126
Jury, trial by, 13, 29, 46–47. *See also* Seventh Amendment
Just compensation. *See* Compensation principle

Kansas
  labor statutes, 85
  prohibition, 60, 81, 204–205
Kent, James, 33
Kohler Act, 94, 235

Labor unions, 85–86
Laissez-faire constitutionalism, 79, 81–83
  attacks on, 83–85
  demise of, 87–88
Lake Tahoe, construction moratorium, 1–2, 123–124
Land patent, 53–55, 201
Land use, regulation of, 26–27, 48, 50–52, 96–99, 100–101
Landownership. *See* Land use, regulation of; Property ownership
"Law of the land" clauses, 24. *See also* Due Process; Magna Carta
Lee, Richard Henry, 13
Legal Tender Act, 202
Legislation, economic, 81–87
  judicial review of, 83–86
  See also Commerce clause; Contract clause; New Deal; Progressivism
Legislation, federal, 86–87, 90, 91, 144. *See also* Takings impact analysis
Legislation, state, 50–51, 285
  and eminent domain, 109–111
  and intellectual property, 151
  in New Deal era, 81–84
  and property rights, 60, 107, 128–129, 285
  See also Kohler Act; Presumed consent statutes
Liberty of contract doctrine, 78–79, 83, 202–203, 230
Lincoln, Abraham, 63, 168

Liquor. *See* Prohibition
Literary property. *See* Copyright; Property, intellectual
Lochner era, 82–83
Locke, John, 7, 22–25, 29, 34, 55, 142, 167, 203
Louisiana, slaughterhouse monopoly in, 80, 213
  property legislation, 128
Loyalist property, confiscation of, 33
Lucas, David, 266

Madison, James, 3, 6, 35, 37, 39–45, 52, 130, 135, 139, 177–178
Magna Carta
  and due process clause, 7, 21, 30–31, 43
  as influence on Constitutions, 7, 204
Marshall, John, 9, 48, 55–58, 188, 197–198, 214
Maryland Ironworks Act, 27
Massachusetts
  Body of Liberties (1641), 28
  Declaration of Rights (1780), 30, 31, 46
Mathews, George, 54
Medical methods, patents for, 143–144
Michigan, Supreme Court of, 109
Microsoft Corp., 141
Minimum wages. *See* Wages, minimum
Mining
  regulation of, 84
  sub-surface coal, 94–95
Minnesota, Constitution of, 111
Mississippi, property legislation, 128

Monopolies, 33, 140
  slaughterhouse, 80, 213
  steamboat, 197
Monsanto Corp., 153–154
Moore, John, 157
Mugler, Peter, 204–205

National Environmental Policy
  Act, 101
National Industrial Recovery Act,
  86
National Institutes of Health, U.S.,
  163
Native Americans, 9–10, 54–56,
  201. See also Cherokee Indians
Natural rights, philosophy of, 3, 7,
  28, 29, 34, 44, 166. See also
  Locke, John
Nedelsky, Jennifer, 37
New Deal
  legislation under, 86–87
  Supreme Court decisions during,
  87–89
New York
  constitution of, 33
  courts of, 58, 83, 174
Ninth U.S. Circuit Court of
  Appeals, 161–162
North American Free Trade
  Agreement (NAFTA), 6
Northwest Ordinance, 43, 44, 206
Novak, William, 51
Nuisance, doctrine of, 11, 33,
  48–49, 115, 118, 172, 206–207

O'Connor, Sandra Day, 108, 125
Offsetting benefits, doctrine of, 66,
  207
Oklahoma, Supreme Court of, 174
Oleomargarine, regulation of, 93
Oregon, constitutional property
  amendment, 129
Originalism, as method of
  constitutional interpretation,
  70

Paper money, issuance of, 34, 36, 39
Parcel-as-a-whole rule, 124–125,
  208
Patent law and patents, 139,
  140–142, 144–147, 148, 165,
  199
Patent Office, U.S., 148, 156,
  165–166
Patent Remedy Act of 1992, 150
Pennsylvania,
  colonial laws, 27
  Constitution, 32, 170
  Council of Safety, 33
  Declaration of Rights of 1776, 30,
  34, 46
  See also Kohler Act
Petition of Right, English (1628),
  21–22, 194
Police power
  and regulatory takings, 113–116
  of states, 10, 60, 65, 84, 94–96, 98,
  106, 114, 121, 209–210
Pound, Roscoe, 84
Powers, separation of, 7–8, 40–41
Presumed Consent Statutes,
  158–162
Prices, government regulation of, 89
Prior appropriation, doctrine of.
  See Water, access to
Private Property Protection Act,
  128–129, 280
Private property rights movement,
  128–129
Progressivism,
  and government regulation of
  economy, 81–82
  and laissez-faire
  constitutionalism, 82

Prohibition of alcohol, 10, 60, 81,
  93, 114, 204–205, 226
Property
  common, 158, 166, 170–171
  compensation for, 29–32, 65–67,
    70, 109–111
  confiscation of, 11, 33
  definitions of, xxi, 118, 136–140,
    161–162, 166, 168
  as dynamic concept, 3, 15, 17,
    136, 137–139, 166
  intangible, 140–142, 153
  intellectual, 140–144, 151, 155,
    199
  in living things, 15, 17, 155–156,
    162–166
  See also Historic preservation;
    Human Body; Quasi-property
Property ownership, 9, 10, 53–54,
  55, 136, 196. See also Land use;
  Property rights
Property rights
  in antebellum era, 48–52, 174
  colonial origins of, 7, 19, 21–22,
    24
  in conflict with other rights,
    90–92
  constitutional status of, 89, 105,
    128, 137, 174
  influence of Magna Carta on, 7,
    21, 30–31, 43
  in international law, 4–7, 141, 158
  legislation affecting, 50–52,
    58–59, 80–81, 235, 285
  Locke's theory of, 22–25
  movement in support of, 2,
    128–129, 285
  in New Deal era, 77, 86–89
  private property rights laws,
    128–129
  as protected by the Constitution,
    12–15, 35, 42, 76

  and the regulatory state, 81–82,
    83, 86–89
  restrictions on, 26–27, 48, 50–52,
    96–101, 147, 152
  under state constitutions, 48–52,
    58–59
  and wartime necessity, 89
  See also Regulatory takings
Public necessity, doctrine of, 49
Public trust, doctrine of, 102, 170,
  210–211
Public use
  as requirement of eminent
    domain, 108–109, 198,
    252–253

Quartering of soldiers, 13, 27. See
  also Third Amendment
Quasi-property, 5, 156, 158–159,
  164, 212

Racial discrimination, 89–91, 99
Railroads, 66, 92
Reagan, Ronald, 105, 128
Regulatory takings,
  deprivation of all economically
    viable use, 106, 113, 117–118,
    120, 124, 208, 265–266
  generally, 76, 92–96, 212
  and intellectual property, 143,
    152–155
  physical invasion distinguished,
    92–93, 106, 111–113, 203–204,
    211
  temporary takings, 122–125, 196,
    272
  unconstitutional conditions, 113,
    121–122, 205, 257
  See also Parcel-as-a-whole rule
Rehnquist, William, 105
Reich, Charles A., 1, 4, 138–
  139

Rent control, 112–113, 260–261
Revolution, American, 27, 34
Rhode Island, courts of, 120
Riparian rights. *See* Water, access to
Roberts, Owen, 87
Roosevelt, Franklin D., 10, 77, 86, 87
   Court-packing plan of, 87
Royalty, calculation of reasonable, 147

Sax, Joseph, 167
Scalia, Antonin, 92, 118, 125
Second Treatise on Government, 22–23, 203
Separation of powers, 7–8, 40–41
Seventh Amendment, 13, 46. *See also* Jury trials
Shays's Rebellion, 294
Shopping centers. *See* First Amendment
Sixth U.S. Circuit Court of Appeals, 161
Slaughterhouse business, monopolies in, 80, 213
Slave ownership
   in colonial era, 28, 61
   constitutional protection of, 15, 62–65, 137, 168, 192
   following Civil War, 63–64, 168–169
   state regulation of, 61–65
Snail darter case, 102
South Carolina,
   Beachfront property regulations, 117–119, 265–266
   Supreme Court of, 56, 117
Sovereign immunity, doctrine of. *See* Eleventh Amendment
Soviet Union, 4, 7
Spring guns, 119
Stamp Act (1763), 34

States
   prohibition of alcoholic beverages in, 58–60, 81, 204–205
   restrictions on power of, 39–40, 83, 119, 137
   See also Commerce clause; Constitutions, state; Contract clause; Due process clause, in state constitutions; Eminent domain, right of; Interstate commerce; Legislation, state; Police power
Stem cells. *See* Human body; Property, in living things
Stevens, John Paul, 2, 123–124
Stewart, Potter, 125
Story, Joseph, 165
Supreme Court (state-level). *See individual states*
Supreme Court, U.S.
   and commerce clause, 48, 90–91, 197–199
   and contracts clause, 14, 56–58, 60, 88, 190, 222
   in depression era, 83, 86–87
   and economic due process, 68, 82, 84–85, 185
   and eminent domain, 46, 47, 67, 108–109, 198, 252
   and the Fourteenth Amendment, 69, 80, 111, 114, 187–188, 213
   and intellectual property, 141, 142, 145, 150, 152–154, 165
   and liberty of contract doctrine, 202
   and Native American lands, 54–55, 201
   in New Deal era, 82–87, 89, 214
   and per se takings, 111, 117, 119, 203, 205, 265–266

as protector of property rights, 3, 12, 15, 59, 92
and slavery, 64, 192
and state regulation of private property, 21, 60–61, 77, 80–81, 92, 103, 106, 116, 125
and substantive due process, 68, 82, 84–85, 88–89, 230
and temporary takings, 2, 123–124, 196, 272
and unconstitutional conditions, 113, 121–122, 205, 257
and zoning laws, 96–100, 115, 121, 122, 183, 191, 214, 237
Sutherland, George, 85

Taft, William Howard, 85
Takings clause, of Fifth Amendment, 43, 44, 76, 93, 105, 130, 174, 193
Takings impact analysis, 105, 128, 285
Taney, Roger B., 64
Taverns, regulation of, 26
Taxation
  property rights as affected by, 10, 34–35
  without consent of governed, 27, 34, 40
  See also Income tax
Texas, property legislation, 128, 289
Third Amendment, 13
Thirteenth Amendment, 15, 169
Tolls, regulation of, 26
Trade secret, 152–155, 199–200
Trademark, 140, 199
Traitors, property of, 9, 33
Trespass, 53
Trial by jury, right to, 13, 29, 46–47

Unconstitutional conditions. *See* Regulatory takings

Uniform Anatomical Gift Act, 159, 160
United Nations
  Commission on Human Rights, 6
Universal Declaration of Human Rights, 5, 6, 7

Vermont, constitution of, 32
Vested rights, doctrine of, 14, 21, 56–58, 97, 213–214
Virginia
  abolition debates, 62–64
  Bill of Rights (1776), 30
  colonial charter, 22
  Declaration of Rights, 31–32, 46
  slavery in, 28, 62–63
Voting, qualifications for, 4, 38

Wages
  government regulation of, 214–215
  minimum, 84–85
Waite, Morrison, 80
Water, access to, 171–176, 197
Wetlands preservation. *See* Environmental laws
Wilson, James, 42
Wisconsin,
  Constitution of, 211
  Supreme Court of, 101
Women
  married women's property acts, 28
  maximum work hours for, 84
  minimum wage law for, 84–85
  right of dower, 50
Workers' compensation laws, 83
Working conditions, regulation of, 81–85
Working hours, laws affecting, 82–84

World War II, 10, 89
Writs of Assistance, 27

Yazoo land fraud, 54–56–57, 222

Zimbabwe, 5, 7
Zoning, 12, 50–51, 96–100, 120, 183,
    191, 214, 237–238

About the Author

Polly J. Price is Professor of Law at Emory University School of Law in Atlanta, Georgia. An honors graduate of Harvard Law School, Professor Price also received a B.A. with highest honors and an M.A. in American History from Emory University. Following a clerkship for Judge Richard S. Arnold of the Eighth Circuit Court of Appeals, she practiced law for several years at King & Spalding in Atlanta and Washington, D.C., before joining the Emory Law School faculty in 1995. Professor Price's publications include articles in the *American Journal of Legal History*, the *Virginia Law Review*, and the *Yale Journal of Law and the Humanities*. At Emory, she has taught American legal history, legal methods, pretrial litigation, and torts. She also taught courses in American constitutional history and products liability at the law faculty of the Technical University in Dresden, Germany, and she has twice lectured at the Free University of Berlin. In 2001, Professor Price was the U.S. representative in Pretoria, South Africa, at the Equality Law Conference for South African judges and magistrates, under the auspices of a speaker's grant from the U.S. State Department's Rule of Law Project.

DISCARD

MS GULF COAST COMMUNITY COLLEGE
JEFFERSON DAVIS CAMPUS LIBRARY